**DO NOT REMOVE
CARDS FROM POCKET**

# WORLDLY WISE INVESTOR

# WORLDLY
# WISE
# INVESTOR

## INTERNATIONAL OPPORTUNITIES IN TODAY'S MARKETS

David
Smyth

Franklin Watts   1988
New York   Toronto

Library of Congress Cataloging-in-Publication Data

Smyth, David, 1929–
Worldly wise investor.

1. Investments, Foreign—Handbooks, manuals, etc.
2. Stock-exchange—Handbooks, manuals, etc.   I. Title.
HG4538.S5134   1988        332.6'78        87-35735
ISBN 0-531-15532-3

# CONTENTS

*in value against other currencies—it declined 60%*
*against the Japanese yen in 1985–1987—other*
*Americans may get poorer but your companies' foreign*
*sales and earnings will probably rise in value and push*
*up your stocks' prices.*

## · CHAPTER 3 ·

## The World Series Team:
## American Stocks Quoted
## on Foreign Stock Exchanges

· 21 ·

*A small but growing number of American corporations*
*have their shares quoted on foreign stock exchanges as*
*well as in the United States. Foreign ownership is still*
*relatively small and has little impact on their stock prices*
*as yet. But as foreign ownership in these companies*
*expands, it may have a growing influence, pushing their*
*prices up whenever Wall Street lags behind other world*
*stock markets and American stocks begin to look like*
*bargains to investors overseas. A trend that may be*
*worth watching for the future—when these foreign-*
*traded U.S. stocks start resembling some European and*
*Canadian stocks, where the tail wags the dog—occurs*
*when trading activity is mainly outside their home*
*country.*

## · CHAPTER 4 ·

## The Global-League Team:
## American Mutual Funds
## that Invest Abroad

· 33 ·

*Before trying to pick your own individual foreign stocks*
*or plunging into overseas stock markets on your own,*

*try putting some money into a U.S. mutual fund that invests in foreign stocks or bonds. Some of these are global funds that invest in the United States as well as abroad; you could use one of them to combine all your American and foreign investments into one package if you like. Some are international funds that invest in non-U.S. securities only; such a fund could combine all your foreign investments into one parcel. Other mutual funds specialize in specific regions, such as the Pacific Basin or Europe, or in single countries, such as Canada.*

## · CHAPTER 5 ·
### U.S. Closed-End
### Funds Open Up
### Big Opportunities

· 55 ·

*Perhaps an even better alternative than mutual funds is to buy the stocks of U.S.-based closed-end funds that specialize in foreign securities. You can sometimes buy them at a discount and sell them later at a premium, a feature that offers greater profit opportunities than a mutual fund does. These funds, listed on the New York Stock Exchange, American Stock Exchange, or over the counter, may have global, international, or regional portfolios. There are many single-country funds among them too, which specialize in Korea, Taiwan, Germany, Malaysia, France, Britain, Switzerland, Italy, Mexico, and other nations.*

## · CHAPTER 6 ·

### The ADR Solution:
### Foreign Stocks
### You Can Buy in
### the United States

· 73 ·

*By studying the quarterly reports of your U.S.-based
mutual fund or closed-end fund you may pick up some
good ideas on what foreign stocks to buy on your own.
And you may be able to purchase some of these stocks
right in the United States through your regular
American broker. Hundreds of foreign companies have
their stocks listed in the United States through American
Depository Receipts. You can buy and sell ADRs with
no more trouble than when you buy or sell American
stocks.*

## · CHAPTER 7 ·

### Foreign Stocks,
### American Broker

· 107 ·

*When you feel ready to make the actual jump into
overseas stock exchanges, you may be able to count on
a familiar helping hand—your regular American broker.
A number of big U.S. brokerage firms are actually
members of the London or Tokyo stock exchanges, and
have representatives in other countries.*

## · CHAPTER 10 ·

### Switzerland for
### the Optimist

· 169 ·

*If you are an optimist rather than a pessimist, your Swiss bank can help you set up a worldwide investment program, buying stocks, bonds, and precious metals for you on Swiss exchanges and in other markets around the world.*

## · CHAPTER 11 ·

### London

· 185 ·

*London, usually ranked third behind New York and Tokyo, may well be the world's number-one financial center. The London stock exchange is much more internationally oriented than Wall Street. In combination with British tax havens in the Channel Islands and the Isle of Man, the British capital offers an alternative base for your worldwide foreign investments.*

## · CHAPTER 12 ·

### Australia and
### New Zealand

· 221 ·

*Australia, a country as big as the United States with a population less than California's, has the eighth-largest national economy in the world. Its stock market ranks among the world's top ten and offers big opportunities in Australia's economic development. New Zealand, Australia's little brother down under, runs a smaller— and riskier—market noted for its insider trading.*

## · CHAPTER 13 ·

## Hong Kong, Singapore, and Malaysia

### · 241 ·

*Hong Kong, one of the world's best examples of what unfettered free enterprise can achieve in a rocky, overpopulated little territory without any natural resources at all, has built itself up into one of the world's great financial centers. Unfortunately it will come under Communist China's jurisdiction in 1997. Its ministate rival, Singapore, will continue to be independent, but Singapore's stock market is closely entwined with the problems of neighboring Malaysia.*

## · CHAPTER 14 ·

## Japan

### · 261 ·

*All the markets discussed so far are in English-speaking countries, or countries well prepared to deal with English-speaking investors. Japan is the first of many foreign-language markets we shall examine where the language problem can be a serious obstacle. The Tokyo Stock Exchange is also the world's number-one stock market. Japanese stock market indexes rose more than twentyfold in the last twenty years compared with a threefold rise in U.S. stock markets. Price-earnings ratios also rose to more than three times the U.S. level. The world's greatest stock market boom? or another South Sea Bubble?*

*might become attractive in the future. They include economically advanced nations like Israel, South Africa, Korea, and Taiwan. This group also comprises economically weaker nations like Argentina, Brazil, Chile, Mexico, the Philippines, and others, whose potential allure is probably even further out into the future.*

## · CHAPTER 21 ·

## Summing Up

### · 363 ·

*Chapter 20 completed our world tour, and twenty seems to be a nice round number to aim at in maximizing your profit opportunities around the globe as well as minimizing your global investment risk. Investments in twenty different mutual funds or closed-end funds mentioned in this book would just about blanket all the foreign stock exchanges that have so consistently outperformed the U.S. stock market in the past decade. Twenty diversified investments is theoretically the most you will ever require to reduce your investment risk to a minimum. And in practical terms, twenty is probably the largest number of investments you will want to handle. The rest is icing on the cake—the opportunity to venture out on your own and pick a stock like Philippine Long Distance Telephone that gained 580% in one year.*

## · EPILOGUE ·
### Lordships of the Manor, Czarist Bonds, and Castles in Spain

· 375 ·

*The investment world has its far-out fringes, and here are a few of them that offer some fun and games. Did you ever hear of the 250,000-pound British government lottery where you never lose your money? Did you know that you can—quite legitimately—buy yourself a lordship of the manor for a rather modest sum? Have you ever thought of speculating in czarist bonds? Do you know that castles in Spain—and in Ireland—are sometimes quite moderately priced? Do you know where to place your bet on the next president of the United States?*

# DISCLAIMER

This book covers about 50,000 possible investments in dozens of stock markets around the globe. It would be absurd to pretend that we have thoroughly investigated every one of these securities. Detailed research on such a scale is a manifest impossibility. The various stock markets, furthermore, are subject to the laws and regulations of dozens of countries. Many of these laws and regulations may change between the time this book is written and the time you read it. Some governments will be replaced, and government policies will be altered. Economic circumstances will change too. The markets, as J. P. Morgan warned long ago, will fluctuate.

We have done our best to be accurate and up-to-date, but please keep all of the above in mind, and seek out the latest available information (from the sources suggested in this book, among others) before you actually do any investing.

You might bear in mind, too, that the United States government, reputedly the most creditworthy institution in the world, goes through a little political ritual every year in which the richest and most powerful capitalist nation in the world comes within hours of defaulting before Congress decides at the last minute to raise the federal statutory debt limit once again so that Uncle Sam's borrowing machinery can keep on going. It is for this reason that we hesitate to endorse the trustworthiness of U.S. government securities. One of these days Congress may go over the time limit.

Nor do we endorse the reliability of British Gilts or any of the other 50,000 securities sold around the world. As the treasury of imperial Rome used to say: *caveat emptor*. We may tell you in this book what securities are available on the world's stock markets, but the decision to buy or sell any of them is yours alone to make.

# WORLDLY WISE INVESTOR

# CHAPTER
# 1

## WHY INVEST
## ABROAD?

Why invest abroad?

There is one outstandingly valid reason, and that is to make more money than you would by investing at home in the United States.

The question is whether it is possible to do this.

The answer quite simply is yes. Furthermore, it is not only possible, it also appears to have been highly probable every year in the past decade or so if you survey the performances of the world's major stock markets since 1977. Wall Street is notable for its undistinguished record among them in this period.

Consider a few revealing figures. From 1977 to 1987, the number-one top-performing market for each year was: 1977, Britain (up 58%); 1978, France (up 73%); 1979, Norway (up 183%); 1980, Italy (up 81%); 1981, Sweden (up 38%); 1982, Sweden again (up 24%); 1983, Norway once more (up 82%); 1984, Hong Kong (up 47%); 1985, Austria (up 177%); 1986, Spain (up 113%); 1987, Japan (up 41%).

The yearly score is kept by Morgan Stanley Capital International of Geneva, Switzerland, which provides statistical and advisory services to major financial institutions around the world.

In 1987, the year of the worldwide stock market crash, when the Dow Jones industrial average plunged 508 points on Black Monday, October 19, and touched off a worldwide financial panic, Wall Street once again underperformed the rest of the world. This is illustrated by another respected measure of worldwide stock market performance, the *London Financial Times* actuaries index of 580 American stocks, which had sunk to 100.53 by the end of 1987, about 37% below its high for the year, and about 0.5% beneath its year-earlier level of November 1986. Meanwhile the *Financial Times* actuaries index for the rest of the world (covering 1,822 stocks in 22 markets outside the United States) stood at 24.22 on December 31, 1987, about 24% above its reading of 100.00 in December 1986.

All these indexes and percentages are figured in terms of U.S. dollars, so that they are directly comparable with the results you would have gotten from the U.S. stock market, which unfortunately has not figured in the top spot for more than a decade.

Well, how about the number-two spot then? Here are the second-best performances in the world stock market league over part of the same period according to Morgan Stanley: 1977, Switzerland (up 28%); 1978, Japan (up 53%); 1979, Hong Kong (up 84%); 1980, Hong Kong again (up 73%); 1981, Denmark (up 25%). And, finally, in 1982 the United States is number two with a 22% gain.

You could continue this survey of the past decade all the way down through the third-best-performing stock markets of the world, the fourth-best, and the fifth-best. You will find in third to fifth places the stock markets of Germany, Italy, Canada, Singapore, Holland, Australia, Belgium, and Spain in addition to those mentioned above. Some of them appear several times. But the United States does not show up even once after that solitary number-two spot in 1982.

Visualize what we have just said as a scoreboard with fifty squares on it—ten down for the number of years and five across for each year's five top markets. The United States stock market shows up once in those fifty squares.

Now think back over the past decade. If you had all your stock market investments in the United States throughout these ten years, you were consistently backing an also-ran. A competitor that never made it to first place, that hit second place in one year out of ten, and then never showed in the top five again. You were in the money once in fifty chances on that scoreboard. Would you bet on a horse with a track record like that?

Perhaps you don't bet on stocks at all but try to play it safe with bonds. In that case you might note that foreign bond markets outperformed U.S. bonds in nine of the last eleven years, according to studies made by Phillips and Drew of London and Salomon Brothers of New York. These studies show that you would have achieved a higher return from U.S. bonds only in 1982 and 1984.

Another study, by Bear, Stearns & Co., Inc., compared the average returns on the government bonds of the United States and twelve other countries in the 1975–1985 period. The United States came in seventh. Converted into dollar terms so as to make the results directly comparable, these were the average annual returns from government bonds from January 1975 to September 1985: Japan 12.9%, Denmark 12.1%, United Kingdom 10.5%, Germany 9.6%, Switzerland 9.5%, Netherlands 9.1%, United States 8.6%, Ireland 8.1%, Canada 6.9%, France 6.2%, Belgium 5.5%, Italy 3.2%, Australia 2.5%.

The stock market results are based, of course, on market averages. You might well have done better than the averages indicate if you had picked some hot individual stocks in the United States that zoomed far above the Dow Jones 30 Industrials Average or the New York Stock Exchange Index. If you invested in a U.S. mutual fund or in foreign mutual funds, so as to get a cross section of each market, the chances are that you would have done much better in some of the markets abroad.

How much better it is impossible to say. It would be a mouth-watering prospect to buy a mutual fund in the number-one market in the world every year and compound one's gains at the yearly rates of 58%, 73%, 183%, 81%, 38%, 24%, 82%, 47%, 177%, 113% and 41% over ten years. Mouth-watering, but, alas, an impossible dream. For foreign markets have their down years too, and you are sure to hit them also, just as you have ridden out bear markets on Wall Street since you began investing.

Nevertheless, this brings us to our next point. There is a

second-best reason for investing abroad. It is a defensive one rather than an aggressive quest for maximum profits, and it is based on the diversification of risk.

The basic principle is easily grasped by the merest novice in investing. If you put all your money into one stock, say a steel company called LTV, and your company files for bankruptcy as LTV did in 1986, then you have a 100% loss. If you spread your money over two steel companies, say Bethlehem Steel and LTV, the bankruptcy of LTV will hand you only a 50% loss. Own three steel companies and your loss on LTV is only 33% of your capital. And so on. Diversification over several companies reduces your risk. Diversification over several industries reduces it even further. If the whole American steel industry goes down the tubes, but LTV is the only steel company stock you own, while the rest of your investments are spread over utilities, airlines, banks, insurance companies, mining concerns, computer and high-technology companies, then the loss of the entire American steel industry need not necessarily mean the end of the world for you personally.

Now, extend this diversification process out one step further. The companies we mentioned would all be American if for the past decade you invested in American stocks exclusively. They are all thus subject in equal measure to the ups and downs of the U.S. stock market. A bear market in America most probably means a bear market for all the individual stocks you own.

But suppose that at least some of your stocks were in foreign markets—not necessarily the top-performing market. Let's say the fifth-best performing market each year, which is to say: 1977, Holland (up 16%); 1978, Belgium (up 33%); 1979, France (up 28.5%); 1980, Britain (up 41%); 1981, Spain (up 12%); 1982, Germany (up 12%); 1983, Holland (up 11%); 1985, France (up 86%); 1986, France again (up 76%); 1987, Denmark (up 15%).

These gains would tend to offset not only your possible losses in the U.S. stock market but your losses in other foreign stock markets as well. By investing internationally, in other words, you gain an extra dimension of safety—diversification over several nations as well as diversification into several industries within the United States.

This extra international dimension can cut your risk of loss in half, according to a study by Bruno H. Solnick of Stanford University. Solnick's study, published in the July-August 1974 edition of the *Financial Analysts Journal*, found that an international portfolio of twenty or more stocks carried about a 15% risk of loss compared with a 30% risk for an exclusively American portfolio of twenty or more stocks.

Incidentally, Solnick's study also illustrates another highly interesting and useful fact. The level of risk falls precipitously as you diversify out from one stock to ten different stocks. Between ten and twenty stocks the risk curve bottoms out, and beyond twenty it remains practically unchanged, no matter how many more stocks you add to your holdings.

This rapid falloff in risk reduction is systematically explored in another study by J.L. Evans and S.H. Archer in the December 1968 edition of the *Journal of Finance*. They too found that very little risk reduction is obtained after the portfolio contains about fifteen to twenty common stocks.

So around twenty different stocks is about the outside limit of all the diversification you will ever need. You could buy fifty stocks or 100 or 1,000, but the additional number would not add significantly to the safety you have gained with only twenty.

To sum up: by spreading your investments around the globe you not only increase your chances of big profits in one market or another, you also insure yourself against loss in your overall portfolio. And you don't need more than about twenty separate investments to achieve these results.

Let your friends weep into their beer at the local bar when Wall Street plunges. With part of your stake in Sydney or Tokyo or Frankfurt, you can afford to keep your cool as you console them.

The question is, why haven't you thought of these possibilities before? Probably for the same reason that most other Americans haven't thought of them. The United States is the world's number-one capitalist nation, it offers the best opportunities in the world, we live here, we understand how it works, and we believe in it. There may be some other capitalist nations out there, but they are full of foreigners, they have strange customs, the language is often incomprehensible, and for these and other reasons they are not worth bothering about when it comes to investments. This kind of attitude appears to be almost universal among individual American investors, from the farmer in Iowa to sophisticated big-city New Yorkers.

William F. Waters, senior vice-president and director of Merrill Lynch International Inc., was one of the American financial executives the author interviewed while writing this book. Merrill Lynch is the biggest American brokerage firm and has offices in forty foreign cities around the globe. Mr. Waters stressed that almost the entire thrust of his department was toward investments by foreigners in the United States.

Meanwhile the foreign-based purveyors of investment services have practically nonexistent sales operations in the U.S. market. Inquiries directed by the author to dozens of foreign brokers, banks, and mutual funds revealed widespread reluctance to get involved with the U.S. Securities and Exchange Commission. This watchdog agency insists that all foreign securities offered for sale to Americans be registered with the SEC, and many of them don't want to get into the resulting bureaucratic hassles that arise because of differences between U.S. and some other nations' securities laws. What with one thing and another, you will not find many salesmen beating down your door trying to sell you foreign securities.

What if you yourself take the initiative and ask your American broker about buying foreign stocks? The capability to serve you is there, and so are the research facilities. Interviewed in his Wall Street area office, Mr. Waters said, "The Merrill Lynch financial consultant you deal with would get in touch with our research department, which would give him its recommendations. We have 140 research professionals in seven cities around the world. But I suggest you get it straight from the horse's mouth.

Try dropping in on one of our branches and see what kind of service our people offer you."

In fact, subsequent talks with account executives who deal with the general public in New York at several brokerage firms besides Merrill Lynch revealed a general attitude of disinterest. Not because of any incompetence on the part of the brokers— these are professionals who are obviously making it in the very hub of U.S. capitalism—but rather because of the indifference of their customers. There is evidently no great yearning for foreign securities among most American individual investors.

Malcolm J. Babbin, a veteran Merrill Lynch account executive (or financial consultant, as Merrill Lynch calls them now) who has been serving a sophisticated and well-heeled clientele in midtown Manhattan for more than ten years, said, "We offer the service, but there isn't all that much demand. I have about ten customers, out of several hundred, who are occasionally interested in foreign stocks. But they invest only sporadically. Their interest is aroused when they see something in the paper about a foreign stock. Generally it's a British company, or Swiss, sometimes South African or Australian. In 99% of these cases it's an ADR (American Depository Receipt), which we handle just as if it were an American stock.

"In the few cases where there is no ADR stock available," Babbin added, "there is no great problem. We just contact our rep in London or Sydney or wherever and make the purchase there. It takes a little longer of course, but there are no insurmountable difficulties for the investor."

If there is one place in the United States where you can expect to find international financial sophistication it is New York, the author remarked. "Yes," Babbin said, "you can imagine the kind of interest there would be if I had my clientele in the Midwest."

Nevertheless, while individual investors resolutely ignore the opportunities to be found abroad, the professional investment advisers at some big American financial institutions have stolen a march on them and jumped into foreign markets in a big way. The pension plans of American corporations, for example, boosted their overseas investments from $5.2 billion in 1981 to a total of about $50 billion in 1987, and Drexel Burnham Lambert estimates they will have $140 billion invested overseas by 1990.

If your pension plan was one that invested overseas, rejoice. Capital International reckons that American investors abroad achieved an average return of 62% in 1986. About a third of this was derived simply from changes in foreign-currency exchange rates.

For the fact is that between 1985 and 1987 you did not really need to invest in anything at all in order to make money in major foreign countries. All you had to do was buy foreign banknotes and stick them under your mattress. You could, for example, have bought Japanese yen at about 240 yen to the dollar in 1985 and sold them for a 60% gain at 150 to the dollar in 1987. All you had to bet on was the decline of the American dollar—a decline that was not all that hard to predict since it was deliberately engineered by the governments of the five major industrial powers, including the United States, at a meeting at New York's Plaza Hotel in September 1985.

And this brings us to our third point: the ups and downs of the U.S. dollar. If you are scared stiff of the gyrations of the stock markets—whether in the United States or abroad—and don't even dare risk your money on American or foreign bonds, then you are limited to a bank account or money fund. But if you restrict yourself to U.S. dollar bank accounts or money market funds only, you are putting all your eggs at risk in one basket: the fragile, battered American currency. As you will discover further on in this book, it is a simple matter (and does not require any huge amounts of money) to open a bank account in Swiss francs, German marks, Japanese yen, British pounds, French francs, and other major currencies. With only $2,500 you can also buy into a money market fund specializing in any of these currencies from an outfit such as Pasadena, California–based International Cash Portfolios.

Investing exclusively in worldwide bank and money market accounts may be the ultimate in safety, since it insulates you from the ups and downs of the American dollar and avoids the fluctuations of the world's stock and bond markets. Such a strategy can provide you with safety, and perhaps profits, even in the face of global financial turmoil. To take one extreme example, consider the worldwide crash of October 1987. In normal times (which covers all of the past decade except possibly the first half of 1982, when most world stock markets turned lower), each country's stock market chugs along routinely, responding to local conditions in each nation's economy. It is difficult to imagine any greater or more violent departure from this state of normality than what happened in the week between Monday, October 19, to Friday, October 23, 1987. This was the week that the Dow Jones average of thirty industrial stocks plunged 508 points on Monday—a sickening 22.6% in a single day. It was the week that IBM, the bluest of blue chips, sank from $135 to $100 at one point. It was the week that Fidelity Magellan, the superstar of the American mutual fund industry, dropped $9.11 to $42.82.

The panic that broke out on Wall Street spread to every stock exchange in the world, and worsened over the following few weeks. But American investors were hit with a double-whammy— the plunge on Wall Street, and the nose dive of the American dollar. If you had sidestepped these two blows by having your money in a foreign currency bank account, this is how you would have made out. Your 1,000-pound British savings account would have risen in dollar terms from $1,665 on October 19 to $1,763 a month later. Your 1,000 Swiss-franc account would have climbed from $661 to $732, your 1,000 German-mark account from $556 to $600. A nice profit for only a month—with financial panic raging all around you, with no more risk than is involved in any U.S. bank account, and with your regular old $1,000 bank savings account stuck at the same $1,000 it was worth a month before.

The background to all this is that the financial world outside the United States is now considerably more important than it used to be. American securities markets, which in 1966 represented about 70% of the value of the entire world's financial markets, are now down to considerably less than half the world total. Foreign markets are growing year by year in Europe, the Far East, and particularly in Japan.

Bloated with years of huge trade surpluses, Japan is now the world's number-one creditor nation, with billions of dollars in foreign assets. It has also displaced the United States as the most creditworthy country, according to a survey of international bankers published twice yearly by *Institutional Investor* magazine. The United States, which had been the bankers' number-one favorite for years, was down to number four in the March 1987 survey, outranked also by West Germany and Switzerland, two other countries where you will find big investment opportunities.

Eight of the ten biggest commercial banks in the world are now Japanese. Citicorp of New York, until 1986 the top banana, is now number five, and is the only American bank among the top ten. Bank of America, for decades the world's biggest bank, doesn't even show in the top twenty.

Merrill Lynch, for many years the world's biggest brokerage firm, now lags behind Nomura of Tokyo by about $1 billion in assets, with Nomura's $3.1 billion to Merrill Lynch's $2.1 billion.

Lastly—and this is the bottom line for you as an individual investor—the Dow Jones Average of 30 Industrials has risen about threefold in twenty years, from 825 in 1968 to 2,700 in 1987, while the Tokyo Stock Exchange Index, which gives a similar measure of Japanese stock prices, rose twenty-two-fold in the same two decades, from 100 in January 1968 to 2,200 in mid-1987.

The point of all the above is not to prove that the United States, its economy, dollar, and stock markets are all in a terminal decline. They obviously are not. The American economy is still on the cutting edge of technical innovation, it is providing more new jobs than any other economy on earth, it still offers the highest living standards in the world. The American securities market is also the freest and most robust of any capitalist nation, and it offers American and foreign investors enormous opportunities.

But the figures show that there is also a world of largely unexploited opportunities out there beyond our borders, and this book will explore ways of turning those opportunities to your profit.

# CHAPTER
## 2

# THE ALL-AMERICAN TEAM: AMERICAN COMPANIES WITH OPERATIONS ABROAD

"A journey of 3,000 miles begins with a single step," said the Chinese sage as he stepped aboard the supersonic Concorde airliner that whisked him from New York to London in three and a half hours, "but nowadays one doesn't have to walk all that much anymore."

One does have to know where one is going, however, and how, and why. And the basic principle for the traveler abroad as well as the investor in foreign countries remains the same in modern New York as it was in ancient China: start at the beginning. So in this book we'll commence with the simplest, easiest, and most obvious steps, and proceed from there on in orderly progression until reaching the more complicated and exotic stages of our journey into foreign markets.

The first cautious step out into the world of international investing is absurdly simple and unadventurous. It does not involve you directly with any foreign countries, foreign stock markets, foreign stockbrokers, or foreign companies at all. All you have to do is buy the stock of big, well-known, well-regarded American corporations, such as Exxon, Coca-Cola, Gillette, or American Family, that have extensive operations abroad.

The most favorable time to do this is when the U.S. stock market is rising and the dollar is falling against other currencies abroad. You may be sure that both events will be extensively reported in the press, as they were from 1985 through 1987, a period in which Wall Street rose to record levels while the American dollar plunged in foreign exchange trading.

The rationale for buying these American international stocks at such a time is this: an American company that has more than half its sales abroad, or that makes over 50% of its profits in foreign lands, or both, stands to profit from a falling dollar. Its products will become cheaper and more competitive abroad, and its profits from overseas, when converted into dollars, will be worth more than before.

If the U.S. stock market as a whole is rising at the same time, as it was in the 1985–1987 period, these corporations have a further advantage. Their increasing foreign earnings give solid justification for the rising price of their stocks. While the bull market pushes the price-earnings ratios of other American stocks toward the stratosphere, the multinationals may still look reasonably priced as their rising dollar profits keep pace with their rising stock prices.

Buying these stocks is a leisurely strategy that does not require pinpoint timing or any undue haste. The dollar may be falling daily against the German mark or the Japanese yen, but a multinational corporation reports its earnings quarterly, and meanwhile all those foreign profits are piling up in the company treasury, probably to be converted into dollars that are even further depreciated against marks, yen, or other currencies three months ahead.

Let us see how this strategy works out in practice. Here is a list of companies that in recent years have made more than 50% of their sales, or 50% of their profits, or both, outside the United States. In parentheses are each company's earnings per share for 1985, before the dollar plunge got under way, and for 1986, when the dollar decline was in full swing:

Alcoa (deficit $0.23, $3.08)
American Brands ($3.67, $3.18)
American Cyanamid ($2.68, $4.36)
American Family ($0.67, $0.98)
American International ($2.45, $4.04)
American Standard ($0.56, $5.28)
AMP ($1.00, $1.52)
Castle & Cooke ($0.59, $0.56)

CBI Industries (deficit $2.18, $0.73)
Coca-Cola ($1.84, $2.42)
Colgate Palmolive ($1.39, $2.52)
CPC International ($1.46, $2.30)
Dow Chemical ($0.31, $3.87)
Emhart ($2.95, deficit $0.35)
Exxon ($6.46, $7.42)
Firestone (deficit $0.14, $0.49)
Gillette ($2.59, $0.25)
Intel ($0.01, deficit $1.57)
ITT ($1.89, $3.53)
Lafarge ($0.31, $0.58)
Lubrizol ($1.49, $1.97)
Mobil ($2.45, $3.45)
Monsanto (deficit $1.67, $5.55)
Pan Am ($0.42, deficit $3.42)
Trans World Airlines (deficit $6.55, deficit $3.87)

Nineteen of these twenty-five companies showed improvement in their earnings pictures—some of them fairly spectacular improvement—at a time when the dollar was plunging. Only six showed earnings declines.

As the crucial point under discussion is the foreign exchange value of the dollar, you must have some way of keeping abreast of developments in this area. The Associated Press provides a daily list of quotations of more than forty currencies that is published in the *New York Times*, the *Washington Post*, and many other newspapers around the country. At the bottom of this list you will find (if your local newspaper hasn't cut it out to save space) the U.S. Federal Reserve Board's daily index of the value of the dollar against a basket of ten major currencies. It also tells you where the index stood a year ago. The base for this index is March 1973 = 100, and it thus gives you a useful benchmark of the dollar's overall performance over the past few years. Many newspapers also run the AP's daily Dollar-Gold article on the day's gold and foreign exchange trading in their business section. You will find further comments on foreign exchange developments in the *Wall Street Journal*'s Currency Markets feature, *Barron*'s magazine's weekly International Trader column, and occasional articles in other business magazines.

The list of corporations above may vary slightly in future years, of course, as company strategies and activities change from year to year. The percentages of sales and profits derived from foreign operations will also fluctuate from one year to another. But the list is not likely to change all that much from one year to the next. A company does not improvise worldwide operations in just twelve months. To keep up with developments, however, you will have to read the latest reports on these corporations in the *Wall Street Journal*, *Forbes*, *Business Week*, and *Fortune* magazines so as to stay abreast of individual company activities.

You should also get in this way a clear idea of each company's basic operations abroad. Some are simply exporting American products to foreign customers. Others are manufacturing in foreign countries, and some of these are exporting to third countries, or even to the United States. A declining dollar may have a varying impact on them, depending on what they are doing.

Certain industries may be going through a private little bear market of their own at any given time. This was the case of the oil industry in the mid-1980s, when the price of oil plunged below $10 a barrel at one point. This affected oil industry companies such as Halliburton, Murphy Oil, NL Industries, Occidental Petroleum, Schlumberger, and Texas Eastern. All these companies make more than 50% of their sales or 50% of their profits outside the United States, but they all showed sharp earnings declines between 1985 and 1986 despite everything the preceding paragraphs said about the internationally oriented American companies and the plunging dollar. For them the damage done by the plunging oil price outweighed the benefits of the slumping dollar.

Each company, and the industry in which it operates, has to be considered individually. In fact, our list should probably be extended to include the country's biggest exporters, even though they do not meet our criterion of having more than half of their sales or profits coming in from abroad.

General Motors, the number-one U.S. exporter, for example, sells more than $8 billion worth of autos, parts, and locomotives abroad, but that is only 8% of its total sales. Boeing, number two, sells more than $7 billion worth of airplanes to foreign airlines, but that huge sum is still only about 45% of the company's total sales. Ford Motor Co., number three, has foreign sales of $7 billion—less than 12% of total sales. General Electric, number four, sells more than $4 billion worth of American machinery and other goods abroad, but that is only one-eighth of its total sales. IBM, du Pont, Chrysler, and McDonnell Douglas, numbers five to eight, each sell about $3 billion worth of goods overseas, but that is only a fifth to a twentieth of each company's sales.

United Technologies, of Hartford, Connecticut, which is number nine, derives about one-seventh of its sales revenue from abroad, and one of its units is heavily involved in supplying the world with Otis elevators and escalators. Otis does about two-thirds of its business outside the United States, and according to company spokesman Rick Whitmyre, "Each time the dollar drops 10% Otis increases revenue and profit by about 67%."

The other companies making up the roster of the top twenty-five American exporters are Eastman Kodak, Caterpillar Tractor, Hewlett-Packard, Allied Signal, Digital Equipment, Philip Morris, Occidental Petroleum, Union Carbide, Westinghouse Electric, Motorola, Raytheon, Archer Daniels Midland, General Dynamics, Weyerhaeuser, Dow Chemical, and Monsanto.

Caterpillar Tractor has been one of the most vigorous lobbyists in Washington for a lower dollar, and indeed in September 1985 the U.S. government did in fact join with four other industrial powers in a plan to drive the greenback down against other major currencies so as to reduce the chronically huge U.S. foreign trade deficit. The deficit climbed to more than $150 billion in 1986 and 1987, and is one of the U.S. government's major domestic and international problems. You can expect Washington to favor these major American exporting corporations with legislative breaks as long as that huge deficit persists, so you might as well include them in your All-American team for investing in the world economy.

We now have about sixty companies to choose from that are likely to benefit from a declining dollar and a rising U.S. stock market. Some of them (including Alcoa, American Cyanamid,

Coca-Cola, Colgate Palmolive, Control Data, Dow Chemical, Exxon, Gillette, Halliburton, ITT, Mobil, Monsanto, Occidental Petroleum, and Schlumberger) offer a further international feature. Their shares are traded on foreign stock exchanges as well as in the United States, which means that foreign investors exercise a growing influence on their stock market fortunes.

Let us now move on to examine these world-class stocks and pick our World Series team.

# CHAPTER
# 3

## THE WORLD SERIES TEAM: AMERICAN STOCKS QUOTED ON FOREIGN STOCK EXCHANGES

Having taken the first step of our journey, perhaps we should follow our Chinese sage a little further and peer as it were out of a Concorde window from the stratosphere to get an overview of what is happening on the earth far below.

What we see in the financial world is a new global market that is growing and taking shape before our eyes, a globe-girdling chain of financial centers on which the sun never sets and where trading continues almost without interruption twenty-four hours a day. Linked together by the latest computer and earth satellite technology, this global network of markets offers possibilities and opportunities that were largely undreamed of until the 1980s.

The world's financial centers from New York to London to Singapore and Sydney and Tokyo are joining together link by link in what may soon be a single global financial market functioning on traders' electronic screens twenty-four hours a day— even when every individual stock exchange in the world is closed.

The markets themselves are weaving themselves together in an ever-tighter web. In 1987 the Chicago Board of Trade and the London International Futures Exchange agreed to trade each other's financial contracts. The Board of Trade was already staying open late into the evening so as to mesh with Asian trading hours. The London Exchange has a similar mutual trading agreement with the Sydney Futures Exchange in Australia. The Sydney Exchange has a linkup with the New York Commodity Exchange to combine their gold and silver trading operations. The Chicago Mercantile Exchange and the Singapore International

Monetary Exchange joined forces to trade in financial securities around the clock in 1985. The European Options Exchange in Amsterdam first listed a 10-ounce gold option in 1981, a standard contract that can now be bought and sold in Montreal, Vancouver, and Sydney, which among them cover so many time zones that the gold option is traded on one market or another for eighteen and a half hours out of every twenty-four.

What this means too is that even if you live in New York or Mexico City, you can buy a gold option in Vancouver and sell it a few hours later in Sydney as though you were dealing in one and the same market. Other global market linkages were in the works as this was written. This global integration of finance, says the normally staid Morgan Guaranty Trust Company of New York in its monthly publication *World Financial Markets*, "is a force for revolutionary change."

In a fast-moving world investors around the globe are gradually acquiring the capability to respond at any hour of the twenty-four to developments—such as a war in the Middle East or a change of government in France or Japan—that can have a dramatic impact on their investments. As the sun sweeps around the planet on ordinary business days it wakens into action in hourly succession the Canadian penny mining stock speculator in Vancouver, then the shipping executive in Yokohama, the textile factory owner in Hong Kong, the Australian wool exporter in Melbourne, the stockbroker in Singapore, the government investment fund director in Kuwait, the Italian auto manufacturer in Turin, the Dutch retiree in sunny Spain, the American expatriate executive in Brussels, the pension fund manager in London, the Scottish investment trust manager in Edinburgh, the hotshot mutual fund trader in New York, the little old lady in Dubuque, Iowa, the grain elevator owner in Minnesota, and so back to the Canadian penny stock speculator in Vancouver and yet another day of global trading in Pepsico, Hitachi, British Petroleum, Deutsche Bank, Olivetti, and hundreds of other international stocks that have burst through their own national boundaries onto the world stage.

These are what you might call world-class stocks. They no

longer trade in their home countries only. They include such companies as General Motors, whose shares are bought and sold daily in New York, Montreal, Toronto, Frankfurt, Dusseldorf, Brussels, London, Tokyo, and Paris; or Procter & Gamble: New York, Amsterdam, Paris, Basel, Geneva, Lausanne, Zurich, Frankfurt, Antwerp, Brussels, and Tokyo; or the British industrial giant Imperial Chemical Industries: London, New York, Vienna, Antwerp, Brussels, Paris, Luxembourg, Amsterdam, Oslo, Basel, Geneva, Lausanne, Zurich, and Frankfurt. The number of these world-class stocks is growing by more than one hundred a year. *Euromoney* magazine counted 236 of them in 1984, 329 in 1985, and 473 in 1986. In 1988 there are probably more than 700. However these stocks that are traded on half a dozen different exchanges are perhaps only the forerunners of a new kind of stock, the Euroequity, which is being created for the specific purpose of trading internationally without being bound to any particular stock exchange.

The fact is that stock exchanges all around the globe are facing the same problem, imminent obsolescence. They no longer have a monopoly on their own listed stocks, and it is no longer necessary to use a stock market at all. They therefore run the risk not only of losing business to some other exchange abroad, but they may even be put out of business altogether as the computer and communications revolution continues its inexorable technological advance. In some cases it already is just as efficient, or perhaps even more so, to buy a Canadian stock on the American Stock Exchange in New York as it is to buy it on the Toronto Stock Exchange if it is dually listed—and eventually they will all be dually listed. No less than 250 stocks listed on the New York Stock Exchange are also listed on other world stock exchanges.

The loss of business to other exchanges is not the only or even the greatest danger the traditional exchanges face. Thanks to modern computer technology it is not necessary to use any traditional stock exchange at all. The National Association of Securities Dealers and Automated Quotations is the oldest and biggest of these alternative, amorphous markets that have no specific location anywhere but operate as a network of dealers across the country. NASDAQ is now the third-biggest market in the world behind Tokyo and the NYSE, with more than 20 billion shares traded yearly. More and more trading is also being done in dealers' offices. The dozen or so biggest, world-class securities firms—the so-called first-tier firms—act as principals, buying and selling large blocks of stock through trading desks set up to handle transactions in international stocks. British merchant banks such as Robert Fleming and the European Banking Corporation in London are among the dealers making markets outside the traditional stock exchanges. In Japan, the four big securities dealers—Nomura, Nikko, Daiwa, and Yamaichi—are also acting on their own behalf buying and selling big blocks of stock to huge international financial institutions.

All this off-exchange trading activity is facilitated by the worldwide suppliers of electronic financial information, such as Quotron, Reuters, and Instinet. And these information suppliers in turn are beginning to link up with each other to serve a super stock market that really has no overwhelming need of the NYSE and other traditional exchanges. For global equities, the 700 or so stocks that can be bought and sold anywhere, the usual trading method is by telephone from one first-tier securities house to another. These stocks have a capitalization that is more than a quarter of the capital on all the world's stock exchanges.

All of this is really no more than an extension to common stocks of a dealer-to-dealer system that took shape twenty years ago with the creation of the Eurobond market. Eurobond dealing grew into a multibillion-dollar giant in just two decades, and the Euroequity market is now growing at an equally furious pace. It already accounts for about 10% of the trading on all the world's stock exchanges, and by one estimate it is expected to grow to about $500 billion a year by 1990—about 15% of global stock trading.

Yoshihisa Tabuchi, president of Nomura Securities Co. Ltd., of Tokyo, the world's biggest stock brokerage firm, foresees a global financial market dominated by a dozen or so financial institutions by the beginning of the next century. Nomura itself already is obtaining 25% of its revenues outside Japan, and expects to make that 50% within five years. As Swiss Credit Bank said in a recent publication, "A global capital market is no longer a Utopian dream."

The stock in trade of the new global market is the Euroequity. Euroequities are stock issues underwritten by international banks, which sell them directly to big financial institutions around the world. Quoted on international electronic information systems, they are traded separately from a company's exchange-listed stock but are interchangeable with it. London is rapidly becoming the nerve center of the worldwide Euroequity market, but the Euroequities are usually quoted in dollars.

This is the new global stock market—probably the dominant market of the future—in which traders for huge pension funds and other investment trusts stare into their television screens at the latest prices flashed around the world at all hours of the day, regardless of which particular stock exchanges are open or closed. This new market has grown spectacularly since 1983 when Union Bank of Switzerland launched it on the world with a $26 million Euroequity issue for Bell Canada. In 1986 alone, $8 billion worth of new stock was poured into the Euroequity market. Still, its greatest growth probably still lies before it. "The popularity of Euroequities will double, then redouble, as more and more finance directors appreciate their usefulness," predicts Stanislas Yassukovich, managing director of Merrill Lynch Europe/Middle East Ltd.

Most of the Euroequities created so far are the stocks of European companies, with only a few American participants, but U.S. corporations are expected to flock into the Euroequity market in coming years. "The pressure to go international is getting irresistible," says Yassukovich.

So how do we fit ourselves as individual investors into the big financial picture we have just drawn? Into the Euroequity market probably not at all just yet. It is still mainly a preserve of the big financial institutions. If you want to buy Korea International Trust on this market, for example, it is traded only in the form of International Depository Receipts, each of which consists of

1,000 shares and costs about $20,000. In any case this panoramic view was only to give us a general sense of where we are going, a preliminary glimpse such as Moses got when he climbed Mount Nebo to survey the Promised Land from afar.

At this stage of our journey we had best keep our eye on the next few steps ahead of us. Consider, for example, one specific American stock and the possible impact of international trading upon it. Minnesota Mining and Manufacturing (known popularly as 3M, ticker symbol MMM on the New York Stock Exchange) is traded also in Zurich, Paris, Amsterdam, Frankfurt, and Tokyo. As this is written, MMM is selling at eighteen times earnings, a price that seems reasonable in New York, where the average blue chip stock is priced currently at twenty times earnings. In Tokyo, however, where the stock market has been booming for years and the average Japanese stock is selling for sixty times earnings, MMM may look like a great bargain by comparison. If Japanese investors start to bid the price up in Tokyo this will push the price of MMM stock up in New York also. Some of the Japanese investors' bullishness is thus injected into the New York market for MMM, and its stock is given support from abroad that may not be available to other American companies whose shares are traded exclusively in the United States.

As foreigners own only 7.5% of MMM stock, the influence of foreign ownership may not be all that large or decisive. But in some companies, foreign ownership has grown to such an extent that the tail wags the dog. Such appears to be the case, for instance, with Philips, the huge Dutch appliance and household goods company, which is 60% foreign-owned; or Novo Industri, a Danish medical technology company that is 75% in the hands of non-Danes; or Echo Bay Mines, a Canadian gold-mining company, 84% of which is owned by non-Canadians.

Even major companies of big countries like Germany and Britain have a surprisingly large percentage of foreign ownership. Reuters Holdings, for example, the big British financial and communications firm, is 30% foreign-owned. Dresdner Bank, one of Germany's big three, is 33% foreign-owned, and Hitachi of Japan, which is also quoted on the New York stock exchange, has 22% of its stock in the hands of non-Japanese investors.

There are whole national markets where foreign investors are frequently the decisive influence. Deutsche Bank complained in early 1987 that while Japan's stocks soared in blissful disregard of reasonable valuations, or the opinions of foreigners, or the competition of other national markets, "Germany's securities markets continue to be heavily impacted by actual or anticipated activity of foreigners from East or West." As *Business Week* noted April 17, 1987, "Japanese investors have plunged into equities in New York and London, helping push those markets to record highs. Now it looks as if Frankfurt is in for the same treatment. German stocks appear cheap compared with issues on the superheated Tokyo Stock Exchange. Japanese buying is credited with pumping up the Frankfurt exchange's trading volume to $440 million a day recently, double its usual level."

Among American corporations foreign stock ownership tends to be lower, but non-Americans own 5% of Coca-Cola and 25% of Tenneco, for example. Even so, the U.S. stock market is still closer to Tokyo's independence in calling its own tune than it is to Frankfurt's dependence on foreign investors. As the globalization of financial markets proceeds, one can anticipate that foreign ownership of American corporations will grow—the Securities Industry Association estimates that foreign trading already averages 11% to 12% of NYSE daily volume—and that trading in their shares in markets abroad will also grow until many American companies become an integral part of the global market.

Even now you find items such as these on the Dow Jones news wire: "While much of the recent activity in Gillette Co. has been attributed to takeover speculation, Shearson Lehman analyst Andrew Shore says the real reason may be buying by the Japanese in the expectation that Gillette will be listed on the Tokyo Stock Exchange." You also find comments such as these by George Michaelis in the March 1987 quarterly report of Source Capital Inc.: "It is quite possible that Japanese investors, with their growing pool of liquid capital, will export Japanese stock valuations to major markets around the world. On the other hand, an ultimate decline in Japan's lofty market valuations will certainly affect markets elsewhere."

At present, foreign trading in most American stocks may in many cases not yet be big enough to influence their prices in their home market. But taking the long-term view, as foreign influence grows they are likely in the years ahead to form a privileged caste—international aristocrats that are largely unperturbed by the more violent ups and downs of the local yokels.

If you want to make a long-term bet on the greater stability that a global market is likely to bring them, here is a list of some leading American companies whose shares are traded in stock markets around the world. Each of them has other merits and peculiarities, but from this point of view consider them as long-term defensive issues to cushion you against future bear markets on Wall Street rather than as aggressive profit-makers.

So far, you don't need to worry about the prices these stocks are selling at on the foreign markets. It is the primary U.S. market that calls the tune, and all the other markets then have to follow the band. The professional arbitrageurs who scavenge their pickings by buying a stock cheap in one market and selling it higher in another take daily care of evening out the intermarket differences.

What you should take into account, however, is the price of the U.S. dollar on foreign exchange markets. When the dollar is down against the pound, mark, or yen, these American stocks are going to look like attractive bargains to British, German, or Japanese investors and they will tend to bid them up. So the general rule is, buy the following stocks when the dollar is low, sell them when it is high.

| | |
|---|---|
| Abbot Laboratories | American Motor Corp. |
| Aluminum Co. of America | American Telephone & Tele- |
| AMAX | graph |
| American Cyanamid | AMOCO |
| American Express | Atlantic Richfield |

BankAmerica
Baxter Travenol
Boeing
Burroughs
Caterpillar Tractor
Chase Manhattan
Chevron
Chrysler
Citicorp
Coca-Cola Co.
Colgate Palmolive
Consolidated Natural Gas
Control Data
Crown Zellerbach
Data General
Digital Equipment Corp.
Dow Chemical
du Pont
Eastern Air Lines
Eastman Kodak
Exxon
Fluor Corp.
Ford Motor
General Electric
General Mills
General Motors
Gillette Co.
Goodyear Tire & Rubber
Gulf & Western
Halliburton Co.
Hewlett Packard
Homestake Mining
Honeywell
IBM
ITT
Litton Industries
McDonald's Corp.

Merck & Co.
Merrill Lynch
Minnesota Mining &
    Manufacturing
Mobil Oil
Monsanto
National Distillers &
    Chemicals
NCR Corp.
Occidental Petroleum
Pennzoil
Pepsico
Pfizer
Phelps Dodge
Philip Morris
Phillips Petroleum
Procter & Gamble
Quaker Oats
R.J. Reynolds Industries
Rockwell International
Sara Lee Corp.
Sears Roebuck
Squibb Corp.
Tandy Corp.
Tenneco
Texaco
Texas Instruments
Union Carbide Corp.
Union Pacific
United Technologies
USX
Warner Communications
Warner Lambert
Westinghouse
Woolworth (F.W.) Co.
Xerox

We should stress that this is a long-term bet on the future. There is no evidence that the above stocks are performing any better right now than the general American stock market. A computer analysis made by Wright Investor's Service of Bridge-port, Connecticut, at the request of the author in May 1987 showed, if anything, a slight tendency to underperform. Over the 1981–1986 period this group of stocks showed an average annual total return of 17.46% compared with 19.36% for the Standard & Poor's 500 Stock Index.

Our lineup of more than seventy companies for our World Series team thus does not look particularly promising at this time. You could have said much the same of the American stock market over the past decade. But it is not only in the Bible that seven lean years alternate with seven fat years.

And in any case, why choose only American companies for a World Series team? you might ask. Well, that's the way it works in baseball. The Yomiuri Giants of Tokyo may be a fine squad, but they have yet to get the chance to play at Yankee Stadium. We just aren't ready for the Japanese yet in this chapter. But we'll take our first look at the foreign contestants in the next chapter as we enter the real global investment league.

# CHAPTER
## 4

## THE GLOBAL-LEAGUE TEAM: AMERICAN MUTUAL FUNDS THAT INVEST ABROAD

The Tao requires us to shift mental gears. Imagine that our Chinese sage is now on a world bicycle tour. In Chapters 2 and 3 he started climbing the Rockies in Arizona. Now he is at the Continental Divide and ready to coast downhill through California to the Pacific.

The analogy we are making here is with the ups and downs of the U.S. dollar. The investments discussed earlier were stocks generally advantageous to buy when the dollar is down in the dumps against other currencies and you reckon to make money as the greenback starts climbing back up again. They are the stocks of American companies that are denominated in dollars, which will do well when their foreign profits are converted into dollars or when their stocks look cheap to foreign investors.

We come now to the Great Divide.

Exactly the opposite happens with non-American stocks denominated in foreign currencies—British Petroleum, for example, which is quoted in pounds sterling in London, or Hitachi, which sells for yen in Tokyo. The time to buy these stocks is when your dollars are strong in foreign exchange markets and you get more marks, francs, pounds, or yen for each dollar. These stocks will rise even further in American monetary terms if the dollar then starts coasting downhill from the level at which you bought them.

We are not talking about shaving a penny here or 5 cents there on the exchange rate. Foreign currency fluctuations can be astonishingly large. The German mark, for instance, has traded at rates ranging from less than 2 marks per dollar to more than 4 marks in the past twenty years. The impact on German stock prices is obviously dramatic. One Daimler-Benz share worth 1,000 marks in Frankfurt could thus be bought for only $250 at 4 marks to the dollar, but would rise to $500 at 2 marks to the dollar. And if the Daimler-Benz stock price should rise 50% to 1,500 marks, its dollar value would triple to $750.

It is absolutely crucial therefore to buy foreign stocks when the dollar is strong against the foreign currency involved. If you buy when the dollar is weak, the entire logic of the situation is going to turn against you. You may end up buying Daimler-Benz at $500 (when the mark is worth 50 cents) and then find it worth only $250 (if the exchange rate drops to 25 cents per mark). So if you skipped the comments on how to keep up with foreign exchange rate developments in Chapter 2, please turn back now and read them. It is basic to all your plans for investing abroad.

Once you have decided the time is right to invest abroad with dollars that seem to be more than fully valued against other currencies, the next step is to decide where and how to invest them and in what securities. You will find that you are faced with a mind-boggling choice of something like 50,000 stocks and bonds traded on more than 100 stock exchanges in over three dozen countries around the globe.

Obviously, a universe of 50,000 stocks and bonds is a lot more than you can digest at one bite. Later chapters will break this intimidating total down into more manageable chunks. The foreign markets, furthermore, are full of pitfalls for the unwary and the inexperienced. London brokers, for example, bill you at intervals of two weeks called "accounts" and throw words at you like "contango days" that will thoroughly confuse neophyte American clients accustomed to dealing with Merrill Lynch in Peoria. Some Swiss and Swedish companies have two classes of stock: one for the natives and the other for foreigners—the latter selling at a premium. The Japanese won't let foreign investors vote their stock; you have to get a Japanese broker or nominee to do that for you. He will charge you a minimum $160 a year to do it—for each stock you own. In some foreign markets stocks aren't quoted in monetary terms; they are quoted as a percentage of their par value. We'll get to all these problems, and how to deal with them, in later chapters.

For the present, however, it seems prudent to let investment professionals deal with all these arcane matters, at least to begin with. Let them select the foreign markets, choose the stocks, and handle all the nitty-gritty details. Which means making use of an investment company—either open-end mutual funds, examined in this chapter, or closed-end funds, investigated in the next chapter.

There are thousands of mutual funds based in foreign countries, more than 1,000 of them in Britain alone, but we are not quite ready for them yet. We will start with the sixty or so mutual funds available right here in the United States, since they involve you in no more complications than you face in buying any ordinary American mutual fund.

The American-based mutual funds for investing abroad divide up into several categories: (1) global funds, which invest in all countries, including the United States, (2) international funds, which invest in all countries except the United States, (3) regional funds, which invest in certain areas, such as Europe or the Asia-Pacific region, (4) bond funds, which specialize in foreign fixed-interest securities, (5) gold and precious-metals funds, which buy foreign mining stocks or bullion, and (6) single country funds, which specialize in one particular country's stocks, such as Canada.

You would have had rich pickings among these funds in recent years. In 1986, no less than seventeen of the twenty-five top-performing United States-based mutual funds were global, international, or regional funds. They ranged from Merrill Lynch Pacific, which according to Lipper Analytical Services Inc. racked up a 95.21% gain for the year, down to Keystone International, which took twenty-fifth place with a 49.06% gain. Considering that the U.S. stock market did not show among the top five stock markets of 1986 (it ranked sixteenth despite rising to new record highs), it is not surprising that mutual funds that concentrated exclusively on American stocks did relatively poorly.

Meanwhile, thanks largely to a 98% gain by the Tokyo stock market in 1986, five of the six top-performing funds were regional funds specializing in the Pacific Basin.

## · GLOBAL FUNDS ·

If you have absolutely no time at all to spend on your investments, nor the inclination or desire to even think about them, the global fund is for you. It is the ultimate one-shot investment, wrapping up in one hassle-free package not only your foreign investments but your U.S. investments as well. The global fund decides for you what percentage of your money will be allocated to American stocks and to foreign stocks and selects which overseas markets to invest in and which particular stocks to buy. All you have to do is read the fund's quarterly reports, watch the fund's price in your daily newspaper, collect your dividends, and sell the fund if you are not happy with the results it is getting for you.
Global Funds include:

Alliance Global Fund
140 Broadway
New York, NY 10005

Dean Witter World Wide Investment Trust
1 World Trade Center
New York, NY 10048

Fidelity Overseas Fund
82 Devonshire Street
Boston, MA 02109

First Investors International Securities Fund
120 Wall Street
New York, NY 10005

GAM Global Fund
455 Park Avenue
New York, NY 10022

J. Hancock Global Trust
John Hancock Place
P.O. Box 111
Boston, MA 02117

Keystone International Fund
99 High Street
Boston, MA 02110

Merrill Lynch International Holdings
P.O. Box 9011
Princeton, NJ 08540

New Perspective Fund
333 South Hope Street
Los Angeles, CA 90071

Oppenheimer AIM Fund
2 Broadway
New York, NY 10004

Paine Webber ATLAS Fund
1285 Avenue of the Americas
New York, NY 10019

Pax World Fund
244 State Street
Portsmouth, NH 03801

Principal World Fund
6310 N. Scottsdale Road
Scottsdale, AZ 85253

Prudential Bache Global Fund
1 Seaport Plaza
New York, NY 10292

Putnam International Equities Fund
1 Post Office Square
Boston, MA 02109

Sci-Tech Holdings
P.O. Box 9011
Princeton, NJ 08540

Scudder Global Fund
175 Federal Street
Boston, MA 02110

Shearson Global Opportunities Fund
2 World Trade Center
New York, NY 10048

Templeton Global I
405 Central Avenue
P.O. Box 3942
St. Petersburg, FL 33731

Templeton Global II (same address as above)

Templeton Growth (same address as above)

Templeton World Fund (same address as above)

Thomson McKinnon Global Fund
1 New York Plaza
New York, NY 10004

United International Growth Fund
2400 Pershing Road
P.O. Box 1343
Kansas City, MO 64141

USAA Cornerstone Fund
9800 Fredericksburg Road
San Antonio, TX 78288

World of Technology Fund
P.O. Box 2040
Denver, CO 80201

## · INTERNATIONAL FUNDS ·

The international fund is one step up from the total abdication
of responsibility for your investments that buying a global fund
implies. The international fund invests in all countries except
the United States. This is the type of fund for you if you want
to retain control of your U.S. investments but feel that you need

some foreign stocks in your portfolio. The international fund provides these overseas stocks for you in one neat package. It is the ideal solution if you want to stay in charge of your U.S. holdings but don't have the time or inclination to check out the performance of foreign stock markets or to check up on the current merits of individual foreign stocks.

International funds include:

Alliance International Fund
140 Broadway
New York, NY 10005

Fidelity Overseas Fund
82 Devonshire Street
Boston, MA 02109

FT International Trust
421 Seventh Avenue
Pittsburgh, PA 15219

GAM International Inc.
455 Park Avenue
New York, NY 10022

GT International Growth Fund
601 Montgomery Street
San Francisco, CA 94111

IDS International Fund
1000 Roanoake Building
Minneapolis, MN 55474

Kemper International Fund
120 South Lasalle Street
Chicago, IL 60603

Prudential Bache Global Fund
1 Seaport Plaza
New York, NY 10292

Scudder International Fund
175 Federal Street
Boston, MA 02110

Shearson Lehman International
2 World Trade Center
New York, NY 10048

Sigma World Fund
Greenville Center
3801 Kennett Pike
Wilmington, DE 19807

Templeton Foreign Fund
405 Central Avenue
P.O. Box 3942
St. Petersburg, FL 33731

Transatlantic Fund
100 Wall Street
New York, NY 10005

T. Rowe Price International Stock Fund
100 East Pratt Street
Baltimore, MD 21202

U.S. Boston International Fund
6 New England Executive Park
Burlington, MA 01803

Vanguard Trustees Commingled International Portfolio
Vanguard Financial Center
P.O. Box 2600
Valley Forge, PA 19482

Vanguard World International Growth Fund (same address
    as above)

## · BOND FUNDS ·

You presumably have your U.S. investments divided between
stocks and bonds. You alter the proportion between equities and
interest-bearing investments according to the outlook you foresee
for the stock market and the returns available from bonds or
money market funds. You can do exactly the same thing on a

worldwide scale. Having selected your global or international stock fund from the list above, you can then complement it with a global or international bond fund. Some of the bond funds available (new ones seem to be coming on the market every day) are listed below:

## Global

Fidelity Global Bond Fund
82 Devonshire Street
Boston, MA 02109

International Cash Portfolios
2044 Armacost Avenue
Los Angeles, CA 90025

Massachusetts Financial International Trust Bond Portfolio
200 Berkeley Street
Boston, MA 02116

Merrill Lynch Retirement Global Fund
P.O. Box 9011
Princeton, NJ 08540

Van Kampen Merritt High Yield Fund
1001 Warrenville Road
Lisle, IL 60532

## International

Prudential Bache International Bond Fund
1 Seaport Plaza
New York, NY 10292

Transatlantic Income Fund
100 Wall Street
New York, NY 10005

T. Rowe Price International Bond Fund
100 East Pratt Street
Baltimore, MD 21202

The global and international bond funds do yeoman service during financial panics such as October 1987, when the American dollar and the United States and foreign stock markets were all plunging. From August 20, 1987, when the Dow Jones average peaked at an all-time high of 2,722.42, to October 29, when it closed nearly 800 points lower at 1,938.33, less than one in every ten American mutual funds managed to avoid posting losses. All eight funds listed above were among the country's twenty-five top-performing mutual funds in this period, scoring price gains of 4% to 7.85%, according to a Lipper Analytical Services survey.

It is up to you, of course, to decide how much of your money you want in a global or international stock fund and how much in a bond fund, but the basic rule for both types is the same: buy the foreign fund when the dollar is strong against the foreign currencies involved; sell when it is weak. Check the Federal Reserve Board's monetary index as published daily in the AP table of foreign exchange rates in order to get an overall idea of the dollar's current standing against other major currencies. This strategy will enable you to profit from fluctuations in the foreign exchange rate as your fund rises or falls in dollar terms, a factor that can be just as important as the fluctuations in foreign stock market prices.

The next consideration when selecting a bond fund is the yield. Interest rates vary widely from one country to another at any particular time. In early 1987, for instance, long-term government bonds were yielding 7.7% in the United States, 9.25% in Canada, 6.3% in Germany, 13.5% in Ireland, 4.1% in Switzerland, and an outstanding 16% in New Zealand.

If you were choosing individual bonds yourself, you would have to balance that tempting 16% yield on New Zealand bonds against the chances of the New Zealand dollar depreciating sharply against the United States dollar (a matter we will get into further on in the book). As the international bond fund is going to select the bonds for you, however, all that remains for you to do at this point is to compare the yield available on the international bond fund with the yield on comparable U.S. bond funds. If the dollar is riding high and in addition the yield on the international bond fund is better than the yield on U.S. bond funds, then buy the international fund. You are then likely to win (1) on the higher current interest rate and (2) on a possible future decline of the dollar.

Incidentally, you may perhaps have a mental image of the bond market, whether in the United States or abroad, as a genteel clubroom for old fuddy-duddies. But nowadays it is more like an offtrack betting parlor, and the payoffs can be startling. In 1985, for example, the U.S. inflation rate finally started coming down to reasonable levels from the double digits of previous years; interest rates came down too, and as a corollary to this, U.S. bond prices went up through the roof. If you add the increase in the bond price to the interest yield, you ended the year 1985 as a fuddy-duddy old investor in American bonds with a total return of 28.5% for the year. But even this paled in comparison with the go-go returns from foreign bonds in 1985. When you factor in the sinking value of the dollar on foreign exchange markets, the dollar return for the American investor in foreign bonds in that same year was 37.3% on Japanese bonds, 40.6% on British bonds, 52.8% on French bonds, and 34.3% on even the normally staid and stodgy Swiss bonds. Do not expect too many such years, however.

And while you are making up your mind about your foreign investments you might consider International Cash Portfolios in the list above as a first tentative step abroad. This is a money market fund in which you can switch among a U.S. cash portfolio (money market instruments denominated exclusively in the U.S. dollar), a Eurocash portfolio (invested in money market instruments denominated primarily in currencies other than the U.S. dollar), and six other portfolios specializing in individual foreign currencies (yen, pound, mark, Swiss franc, Canadian and Australian dollars). You can use this fund to hedge your bets on the level of the U.S. dollar and American interest rates against the level of foreign currencies and interest rates without worrying about additional complications such as foreign stock and bond price fluctuations.

## · REGIONAL FUNDS ·

Buying a regional fund means you have to make your first really positive decision rather than playing a purely passive role in international investing. You have to make up your mind that Europe or Scandinavia or the Pacific Basin or the Third World is the place to make money in the years ahead (we have some suggestions on the prospects for these areas in future chapters), and then find a fund that covers that particular area. In recent years the overwhelming favorite has been the Pacific Basin, followed by Europe:

EuroPacific Growth Fund
333 South Hope Street
Los Angeles, CA 90071

Fidelity Europe Fund
82 Devonshire Street
Boston, MA 02109

Fidelity Pacific Basin Fund
(same address as above)

Financial Strategic Portfolios—European Portfolio
P.O. Box 2040
Denver, CO 80201

Financial Strategic Portfolios—Pacific Portfolio
(same address as above)

GT Europe Growth Fund
601 Montgomery Street
San Francisco, CA 94111

GT Pacific Growth Fund
(same address as above)

Merrill Lynch Pacific Fund
P.O. Box 9011
Princeton, NJ 08540

Nomura Pacific Basin Fund

180 Maiden Lane
New York, NY 10038

In addition to the above mutual funds there are also closed-end regional funds specializing in Scandinavia and Third World nations which will be dealt with in the next chapter.

## · SINGLE-COUNTRY FUNDS ·

With the single-country fund you narrow your choice down to one particular nation where you think the action is going to be in coming years. For some reason, probably because mutual funds find it difficult to maintain high sales for single-country funds year after year, the majority of single-country funds are of the closed-end type. They enable you to make one-package invest-ments in Switzerland, Australia, South Africa, Mexico, Taiwan, Britain, Korea, Italy, Germany, Israel, and France. However, closed-ends have some notable peculiarities that demand closer study in the next chapter.

Single-country mutual funds include:

Canadian Fund
40 Rector Street
New York, NY 10006

GT Japan Growth Fund
601 Montgomery Street
San Francisco, CA 94111

Japan Fund
175 Federal Street
Boston, MA 02110

## · GOLD AND PRECIOUS-METALS FUNDS ·

Precious-metals funds, and particularly gold funds, are the refuge of people who are scared of inflation, distrust paper money, and generally take a gloomy view of the world's economic future. These funds are trickier than they seem at first sight. They invest in the stocks of companies involved in precious metals, mainly gold, but also silver and platinum. Some of them also invest in gold and silver bullion. Make sure you know what a particular fund is doing before you buy it, because a differing emphasis on mining stocks or bullion in its portfolio can be of vital importance.

South Africa is the world's major gold producer, and the biggest gold-mining companies on the market are South African. This is a country where racial strife between blacks and whites has been hitting the world's headlines for years and is likely to worsen. If this racial and social turmoil should ever shut down the South African gold and platinum mines, two divergent results may follow. The mutual fund holding South African mining stocks may suffer, while the fund holding gold bullion is likely to profit, since the price of gold will probably soar as South African production shuts down and cuts off about 70% of the global supply of newly mined gold.

Also likely to profit from such a scenario are gold-mining companies located outside South Africa (mainly in the United States, Canada, and Australia). Some of the funds listed below have foreseen this eventuality and include non–South African mining stocks in their portfolios:

Chubb America Fund Gold Stock Portfolio
832 Georgia Avenue
Chattanooga, TN 37402

Colonial Advanced Strategies Gold Trust
1 Financial Center
Boston, MA 02111

Fidelity Select American Gold
82 Devonshire Street
Boston, MA 02109

Fidelity Select Precious Metals
(same address as above)

Financial Strategic Portfolios—Gold Portfolio
P.O. Box 2040
Denver, CO 80201

Franklin Gold Fund
155 Bovet Road
San Mateo, CA 94402

Franklin Institutional Fiduciary Trust
Precious Metals
(same address as above)

Golconda Investors Ltd.
11 Hanover Square
New York, NY 10005

IDS Precious Metals Fund
1000 Roanoake Building
Minneapolis, MN 55474

International Investors
122 East 42 Street
New York, NY 10168

Keystone Precious Metals Holdings
99 High Street
Boston, MA 02110

Lexington Gold Fund
Park 80 West, Plaza Two
P.O. Box 1515
Saddle Brook, NJ 07662

Oppenheimer Gold & Special Minerals Fund
2 Broadway
New York, NY 10004

United Services Gold Shares Fund
P.O. Box 29467
San Antonio, TX 78229

United Services Prospector Fund
(same address as above)

USAA Investment Trust Gold Fund
9800 Fredericksburg Road
San Antonio, TX 78288

Van Eck Gold-Resources Fund
122 East 42 Street
New York, NY 10168

Vanguard Specialized Portfolios—Gold and Precious Metals
   Portfolio
P.O. Box 2600
Valley Forge, PA 19842

## · CHOOSING A FUND ·

We come now to a sad fact. Some, perhaps many, of the funds of all types listed above will achieve for you investment results that are considerably less spectacular than you would expect from the stellar performances of foreign stock markets as described in Chapter 1. The reasons for this are hard to pin down precisely, but the phenomenon itself is undeniable. The international funds as a group gained 53.5% in 1986, according to Lipper Analytical Services, which keeps quarterly statistical data on about 1,100 United States–based mutual funds. However, the EAFE (combined Europe, Australia, and Far East) stock market index gained 69.3%, while the Pacific Basin stock index jumped 93.4% that year.

On the average, therefore, the international funds underperformed by a considerable margin the average results of the stock markets they were operating in. If mutual funds that invest in U.S. stocks exclusively are anything to go by, that underperformance is not just a flash in the pan. It is likely to be a permanent condition. For the melancholy truth is that the average U.S. mutual fund, too, habitually underperforms the U.S. stock market year after year.

According to Lipper's statistics, the median U.S. mutual fund (median means that half did better and half did worse) was outperformed in 1986 by every major market index, including the Dow Jones 30 Industrials, Standard & Poor's 500, the New York Stock Exchange Index, and the Wilshire 5,000 Stock Index. The median mutual fund was also unable to match the Standard & Poor's 500 over the previous three months, over the previous five years, the previous ten years, and the previous fifteen years, all the way back to December 31, 1971.

In some of the funds, incompetent stock pickers may have been largely to blame for these disappointing results. But in all funds, national and international alike, there is also one common factor: the fund's operating expenses. The higher these expenses are, the more they will drag down the fund's investment results. So the first thing to check when your chosen fund's prospectus arrives in the mail is the fund's expense statement. You will find the telltale figures in a standard table included in each prospectus at the line reporting Expense Ratio to Average Net Assets over the past five or ten years. The average fund has an expense ratio of about 1.1%. If your prospective fund has a ratio much above that, don't buy it.

While you are looking at this table, check also the Portfolio Turnover, another standard item in all prospectuses. This figure tells you how much buying and selling of stocks the fund is doing. It is expressed as a percentage. A 100% ratio means the fund is turning over its entire portfolio once a year. A 50% ratio means it is selling and replacing all its stocks every two years. If the ratio is much over 80%, don't buy the fund either—the fund manager is just churning the portfolio, possibly to maximize commissions, which will be added to the fund's expenses and charged to you the fundholder.

Some of the funds listed above are load funds, others no-loads (the no-loads are the ones with only one price quoted plus the notation NL in your daily newspaper). If you don't mind paying an 8.9% sales commission, that is of course up to you, but you are then going to start out with only 91.1% of your money working for you, and it is going to be very difficult to catch up with a comparable no-load that puts 100% of your money to work. Watch the no-loads too, however. Some of them are actually backloaded and hit you with a commission when you sell. Others have 12b1 plans, which enable them to charge all their advertising and promotional expenses to you and their other fundholders.

All the above factors are to be considered in choosing a fund, but what it finally boils down to on the bottom line is performance. How does your fund stack up against the market averages?

One way to find out is to check the indexes provided by Morgan Stanley Capital International Perspective. You will find them in *Barron's* magazine. Turn to a weekly feature titled The International Trader and look up the table headed Global Stock Markets. The table gives the weekly index figures for twenty-one stock markets. The first index on the list (The World) makes a good benchmark for the global funds. It gives the latest reading and also the index's fifty-two-week range, expressed in two ways—in foreign currencies and in U.S. dollars. Compare these figures with the historical price data given in your prospective fund's literature. If it looks as though the fund has not been keeping up with the world market average, don't buy it. The next index in the *Barron's* table (EAFE, for Europe, Australia, Far East) makes a good standard of comparison for the international funds that exclude American stocks. And the last index in the table (USA) is a useful reference point to judge whether it is advisable to be in foreign markets at all at this particular time, or whether the American market looks more enticing.

You can do a similar performance-checking job with a table in the *Financial Times* of London headed FT-Actuaries World Indices. This table provides daily stock market index figures for the stock exchanges of twenty-three countries and eight regions, among which the most useful for our present purposes are Europe, Pacific Basin, Euro-Pacific, The World, and The World Except the United States. The *Financial Times* provides the year-ago figure for each index, which makes it easier to compare with the present and year-ago price of the fund you are considering.

The *Financial Times* also expresses these indexes three ways—in terms of local currencies, of U.S. dollars, and of pounds sterling—and it provides the year's high and low figures in dollar terms.

The *Financial Times*, which incidentally is a daily gold mine of information on foreign investing, may be purchased at some newsstands on the same day of issue in Atlanta, Boston, Chicago, Cleveland, Detroit, Houston, Los Angeles, Miami, Minneapolis, New York, Philadelphia, Pittsburgh, Rochester, Seattle, Washington, West Palm Beach, Montreal, Ottawa, Quebec, Toronto, Vancouver, Bermuda, and San Juan, Puerto Rico. A yearly subscription costs $365.

The Associated Press compiles a daily table of stock market indexes of a dozen foreign stock exchanges that is published by the *New York Times* and a number of other American newspapers. The *Investor's Daily* also publishes in each issue rather rudimentary graphs of twelve foreign stock market indexes showing the performance of prices over the past fifty-two weeks.

## · INDEX FUNDS ·

If you are unable to find any funds that are outperforming the market, there is still one solution left, the index fund.

This type of fund was invented largely in response to the complaints of big institutional investors who got tired of putting their money into mutual funds run by managers who charged fat fees, collected juicy salaries, and then could not match the results a chimpanzee might have achieved by throwing darts at the stock tables of spread-out newspapers to make his stock selections. U.S. index funds just give up on trying to outsmart the market. They merely try to match the market averages by replicating the component stocks of the Standard & Poor's 500 average, for example. They have no investment adviser's fees, minimal portfolio turnover, and so save on brokerage fees.

The concept has spread to the international scene, although targeted initially at the big institutional investors. International index funds now include the Travelers International Index Fund, which tracks the FT-Actuaries Europe–Pacific Basin index by holding about 800 of the 1,622 component stocks of this index. The entry fee is still a little high for the individual investor, however. The minimum initial investment is $1 million. Nevertheless, the concept is a useful one, and no doubt by the time you read this book there will be other index funds available on a more modest scale for the individual investor.

In fact mutual funds of all types are constantly springing up like mushrooms, and you can get the latest directory of all funds by writing to the Investment Company Institute (1600 M Street NW, Washington, DC 20036) for the latest edition of its *Guide to Mutual Funds*.

# CHAPTER
# 5

## U.S. CLOSED-END FUNDS OPEN UP BIG OPPORTUNITIES

Closed-end funds are the wallflowers of the investment company industry. They make minimal efforts to advertise themselves. Brokers shun them. Investors ignore them. Mutual funds outnumber them twenty to one. In fact, American investors have such a passionate love affair going with mutual funds that funds of this type actually outnumber the 1,500 or so stocks listed on the New York Stock Exchange.

Closed-end funds, meanwhile, total less than 100 against the more than 2,000 mutual funds, and their combined assets of $18 billion are dwarfed by the mutual funds' $500 billion. Nevertheless, like the mousy little girl at the party, they may turn out to be more rewarding company when you get to know them better than the extravagantly popular queen of the ball.

United States–based closed-end funds presently in existence enable you to make convenient one-package investments in the stock markets of Australia, Britain, Canada, France, Germany, Israel, Italy, Korea, Malaysia, Mexico, Scandinavia, South Africa, Switzerland, and Taiwan. There is also a fund through which you can invest in Third World nations as a group, and there are several more closed-ends with worldwide portfolios of stocks and bonds. There may be other new funds on the market by the time you read this book, providing you entry into more foreign lands.

Now, to come straight to the jugular: closed-end funds offer you a double advantage over mutual funds. First, you can sometimes buy them at a large discount. Second, you can at times sell them at a considerable premium.

The ensuing difference in investment results can be impressive. Imagine, for instance, that a new mutual fund comes on the market at $12 a share and you buy it at that price. The fund does well and twelve months later its net asset value is up to $22.38 a share. However, its market price is up even further, to $33.38 a share, so that if you sell at that price you will nearly triple your money instead of nearly doubling it. Impossible for a mutual fund, of course. But not for a closed-end like Korea Fund, which achieved exactly those figures from mid-1984 to mid-1985.

Or imagine that an old, established mutual fund is selling at $37 a share in January 1987, a 54% discount from its net asset value of $80.46. Three months later the discount has shrunk to only 26.6% of net asset value and the fund's market price has nearly doubled to $60.25. Another impossibility, you say. Certainly, when you deal in mutual funds, because they don't have discounts. But these figures state exactly what happened in early 1987 with ASA Ltd., a closed-end fund specializing in South African shares.

As this is written, here is a sampling of some current closed-end fund prices. First Australia Fund is selling at a 19.3% discount from its net asset value, France Fund at a 20.6% discount, Italy Fund at a 12.6% discount, and Mexico Fund at a 30.8% discount.

Pause for a moment to consider what this means. The above funds offer you a cross-section of four foreign stock markets, all of which have outperformed the United States stock market in the past ten years. And you are able to buy into them at discounts of up to 30%.

Now let's take a look at the other extreme, the funds selling at a premium. At the time of writing, Korea Fund is selling at $70 a share, a whopping premium of 113.8% over its net asset value of $32.74 a share. Taiwan Fund is trading at $32.50 a share, an even more monstrous 152.1% premium over its net asset value of $12.89 a share. These are obviously two funds whose investors are currently in a state of euphoric optimism that appears to be approaching delirium. Since it seems unlikely that any new investors are going to bid these funds up to even more inflated premiums over their real intrinsic worth, Korea Fund and Taiwan Fund are probably in for a fall in the not too distant future.

You can thus see quite clearly that the premium-discount feature of the closed-end fund is really a two-edged sword. If you don't handle it properly you are likely to do yourself considerable financial injury. The basic rule is: buy when a closed-end fund is at a large discount, sell when it is at a big premium.

You may wonder how it is that such discounts and premiums come about. The explanation lies in the different structures of the mutual fund and the closed-end fund. When you buy a mutual fund, you deal only with the fund manager, who undertakes to sell you the shares or to buy them back from you at one particular price: the fund's net asset value, which is the value each share would have if all the fund's assets were liquidated and distributed equitably among the fund's investors. A closed-end fund, in contrast, is just like any other stock quoted on the stock market—say IBM or AT&T—which you and other investors bid up or down depending on how you view the company's prospects. The closed-end fund's management usually does no buying or selling of the fund's shares itself. So, if investors think Italy Fund is going to do exceptionally well they may bid its stock market price up above its net asset value. If they suspect it will do very poorly they may let it sink below its net asset value before they consider it worth buying.

The swings from investor optimism to pessimism and vice versa can be swift and dramatic. Italy Fund was selling at a 45% premium in March 1986 but had sunk to a 30% discount by November of that same year.

You may also wonder why such wild, swift mood swings take place at all. Obviously the Italian economy is not going to disappear overnight, nor is it going to double by next week. In part this phenomenon may simply be confirmation that most investors let themselves be carried away by fear and greed into extremes of pessimism and optimism. And in part it may also be that most investors don't do their homework; strange as it may seem, perhaps they don't bother to find out whether the fund they are buying or selling is trading at a premium or a discount.

All the closed-end funds listed below are traded just like any other stock on the New York Stock Exchange, the American Stock Exchange, or the over-the-counter market. The fund managements take care of all the foreign angles, such as paying taxes and collecting dividends abroad and converting all foreign income into dollars. The funds are priced in dollars and they pay dividends in dollars.

But before you buy any of them, remember that this one vital piece of information—the discount or premium—is missing from the market price you are looking up in the newspaper's stock tables. We will explain how to check on the premium or discount further on.

*United States–Traded Closed-End Funds That Specialize in Foreign Stocks*

Anglo American Gold Investment Company, OTC\*
44 Main Street
Johannesburg 2001
South Africa

Anglo American South African, OTC
(Same address as above)

ASA Ltd., NYSE,
P.O. Box 39
Chatham, NJ 07928

Asia-Pacific Fund, NYSE
1 Seaport Plaza
New York, NY 10292

\*   NYSE, New York Stock Exchange
    ASE, American Stock Exchange
    OTC, over the counter

Central Fund of Canada, ASE
P.O. Box 7320
Ancaster, Ontario L9G 3N6
Canada

First Australia Fund, ASE
1 Seaport Plaza
New York, NY 10292

First Australia Prime Income Fund, ASE
1 Seaport Plaza
New York, NY 10292

France Fund, NYSE
535 Madison Avenue
New York, NY 10022

Germany Fund, NYSE
40 Wall Street
New York, NY 10005

Global Growth Fund, NYSE
1 Seaport Plaza
New York, NY 10292

Global Yield Fund, NYSE
1 Seaport Plaza
New York, NY 10292

Helvetia Fund, NYSE
10 Hanover Square
New York, NY 10005

Israel Investors Corp., OTC
10 Rockefeller Plaza
New York, NY 10020

Italy Fund, NYSE
2 World Trade Center
New York, NY 10048

Kleinwort-Benson Australia Income, NYSE
200 Park Avenue
New York, NY 10166

Korea Fund, NYSE
345 Park Avenue
New York, NY 10154

Malaysia Fund, NYSE
P.O. Box 9011
Princeton, NJ 08540

Mexico Fund, NYSE
477 Madison Avenue
New York, NY 10022

Scandinavian Fund, ASE
136 Nassau Road
Huntington, NY 11743

Taiwan Fund, ASE
111 Devonshire Street
Boston, MA 02109

Templeton Emerging Markets Fund, ASE
700 Central Avenue
St. Petersburg, FL 33701

United Kingdom Fund, NYSE
55 Water Street
New York, NY 10041

Worldwide Value Fund, NYSE
7 East Redwood Street
Baltimore, MD 21202

## · HOW TO GO ABOUT IT ·

Now for the practical details: which funds to buy or sell and when to do it. The missing information on premiums and discounts that you need before you can make any decision is to be found in a weekly table that is published under the heading Publicly Traded Funds, or Closed-End Funds, in *Barron's* weekly magazine, the Saturday edition of the *New York Times*, and in Monday's *Wall Street Journal*, as well as other newspapers.

A number of the funds listed above are not published in this table, so unless you are able to find some alternative source for the current premium or discount figure you have no really intelligent way of trading the funds that are not in the table.

The table looks like this (we have excluded the funds that do not concern us here, as they are purely American investments):

## · CLOSED-END STOCK FUNDS ·

| Diversified Common Stock Funds | | | |
|---|---|---|---|
| | NET ASSET VALUE | STOCK PRICE | % DIFF. |
| Global Gr Cap. | 10.63 | 9⅜ | − 11.8 |
| Global Gr. Inc. | 9.36 | 10¾ | + 14.9 |
| GSO Trust | 9.85 | 9½ | − 3.6 |
| Worldw Value | 21.80 | 18¼ | − 16.3 |
| Specialized Equity and Convertible Funds | | | |
| ASA Ltd | 85.70 | 55⅞ | − 34.8 |
| Asia-Pacific | 9.69 | 10¼ | + 5.8 |
| Cen Fd Canada | 6.37 | 6⅝ | + 4.0 |
| 1st Australia | 14.00 | 11⅝ | − 16.9 |
| France Fund | 14.69 | 11⅝ | − 20.9 |
| Germany Fund | 10.82 | 11 | + 1.6 |
| Helvetia Fund | 13.82 | 13½ | − 2.3 |
| Italy Fund | 12.73 | 12¼ | − 3.8 |
| Korea Fund | 31.37 | 60¼ | + 92.1 |
| Malaysia Fund | 11.09 | 12⅞ | + 16.1 |
| Mexico Fund | 11.34 | 8 | − 29.5 |
| Scandinavia | 11.07 | 9 | − 18.7 |
| Taiwan | 17.00 | 31¾ | + 86.8 |
| Tmpl Emerg Mkt | 9.64 | 9½ | − 1.5 |
| United Kingdom Fd. | 11.44 | 12 | + 4.9 |

Now let's take a closer look at some of these funds. The details that follow are taken from each fund's prospectus or its latest report.

Global Growth and Income Fund, assets about $90 million, is a dual purpose fund with two kinds of stock: capital shares that receive all the capital gains, and income shares that get all the income. The income shares will be redeemed in 1997, when the fund must decide whether to liquidate, convert into a mutual fund, or continue in its present form. Global Growth invests at least 75% of its assets in dividend-paying common stocks, with at least 50% of its assets in the United States.

Worldwide Value Fund, assets about $50 million, is a global fund with a balanced portfolio 60% in stocks and 40% in bonds. It had nearly a quarter of its assets in the United States in 1987, the remainder in Belgium, France, Germany, Italy, the Netherlands, Spain, and the United Kingdom.

ASA Ltd., assets about $550 million, is a South African company and one of the oldest of the foreign funds listed on the New York Stock Exchange. It has about 80% of its assets invested in gold-mining companies, the remainder in other South African industrial stocks. An efficiently run fund, it has a very low ratio of expenses to net assets at around 0.25%. The fund's price fluctuations mainly reflect investors' manic-depressive mood swings about the price of gold on the one hand and racial strife in South Africa on the other. Ten years ago, when the price of gold was soaring, ASA sold at a 14% premium. In 1986, with South African racial riots hitting the world's headlines nearly every day, the fund sank to a 54% discount.

Central Fund of Canada, assets about $60 million, is another gold play you might use to keep your pulse steady while ASA plunges and soars. This fund has 95% of its assets in gold and silver bullion, the remainder in precious metals mining stocks. It is in fact a big heap of gold and silver bars that will probably rise sharply in value if the South African gold mines are ever shut down by social and political upheavals. When this fund is selling at a discount, moreover, you might figure that it is an excellent way of purchasing gold and silver at 10% or 15% off the going world price.

First Australia Fund, assets about $60 million, launched in December 1985, does not yet have a very long track record, but is an attractive way of investing in the Australian economy when you can get it at a sizable discount. The fund invests in a broad spectrum of Australian industries, including metals and minerals, construction, electronics, food, transport, tourism, the media, and financial institutions.

France Fund, assets about $80 million, another newcomer, launched on the New York Stock Exchange in June 1986, rose to an 8% premium in the first few weeks but was down to a 20% discount within a few months. The fund started out with a rather high expense ratio at 1.85% but outperformed the Paris stock market in its first year of operation. Its main investments are in financial services, distribution services, food, electrical and electronics companies.

Germany Fund, assets about $70 million, launched in 1986, has a wide spread of German stocks, mainly in insurance, retail, electrical, chemical, and automotive companies.

Italy Fund, assets about $85 million, launched February 1986, provides a good cross-section of the Milan stock market, with major emphasis on holding companies, insurance, communications, banking, and consumer services. Its main objective is capital appreciation.

Korea Fund, assets about $150 million, seeks long-term appreciation of capital. Thanks to the astonishingly large premium it commanded shortly after its inception in 1984, many early investors enjoyed a lot of short-term capital appreciation as well. The huge premium was due mainly to the fact that Korea Fund was the only investment vehicle available to Americans eager to place their money in a dynamically growing economy which they saw as the new Japan of the 1980s and 1990s. The Korean stock exchange itself has been largely off-limits to foreign investors, although the Korean government has been loosening the rules. Meanwhile, similar Korean investment funds available in London are challenging Korea Fund's monopoly status. South Korea also faces the ever-present threat of North Korea, an aggressive and militaristic neighbor, whose huge and well-armed forces are poised a mere 25 miles from the Seoul Stock Exchange. A menacing move by North Korea could easily knock the Seoul

Exchange for a loop and reduce Korea Fund's fat premium to a big discount in short order.

Malaysia Fund, with an initial offering of $85 million worth of shares, also made its debut on the NYSE in mid-1987. Although Malaysia is not as well known to American investors as Korea and Taiwan, the fund rose initially to a 16% premium, boosted by the Malaysian Treasury's decision to waive the 40% withholding tax on dividends to nonresidents of Malaysia who invest in the fund. This is an outstanding example of our general principle that it is better to invest through a U.S.-based security rather than to go exploring in exotic stock markets abroad.

Mexico Fund, assets about $80 million, has a portfolio of about two dozen Mexican companies ranging from auto parts to chemicals, petrochemicals, construction, consumer goods, electronics, insurance, metallurgy, mining, paper, and retail trade. The country has had some well-publicized economic woes, including the developing world's second-largest foreign debt ($100 billion) and a 60% inflation rate. But the Mexico City Bolsa has soared despite all that, carrying the Mexico Fund's net asset value up with it. Once Mexican national problems look like they are coming under better control, the fund's discount may narrow to reflect the improved outlook.

Scandinavia Fund, assets about $60 million, was launched on the American Stock Exchange in June 1986. It invests in the stock markets of Sweden, Denmark, Norway, and Finland. Its biggest holdings at the time of writing are ASEA, Electrolux, Ericsson Telephone, Esselte, and Skonska. Following the usual pattern of newly launched funds it rose to an 8% premium and then sank as low as a 20% discount six months later.

Taiwan Fund, assets about $25 million, is one of the newest and most speculative entrants in the closed-end field. Launched at $12 a share in November 1986, its market price almost tripled to more than $32 four months later even though its net asset value rose to only $12.89 in that time. The big attraction here is the same as with Korea Fund, a monopoly position in the American investment market. United States investors have no other practical way of investing in Taiwan, whose stock market is largely closed to foreigners. As Taiwan has a huge trade surplus with the United States and is one of Asia's "Little Dragons," whose economic growth rivals the runaway development of Japan two decades ago, there are plenty of eager buyers of Taiwan Fund. Nevertheless, they may be unaware of major problems, including restrictions on repatriation of capital invested in Taiwan, and a Taipei stock market so speculative in character that few of the natives risk their money on it. And then there is the political outlook, which includes the rather large fact that Communist China lays claim to Taiwan, the last island remnant of Chiang Kai-shek's anticommunist Republic of China.

Templeton Emerging Markets Fund, with assets of about $100 million, was launched on the American Stock Exchange in March 1987 and rose to an 18.4% premium in barely a month. It is probably the most speculative of all the foreign closed-end funds. It plans to achieve long-term appreciation of capital by investing in the stocks of forty-two "emerging" countries, including such nations as Argentina, Brazil, Egypt, India, Pakistan, Papua-New Guinea, the Philippines, Trinidad, Turkey, and Zimbabwe. It may even invest in some communist countries, such as Communist China and Yugoslavia. As many of these underdeveloped countries are perennially short of cash and frequently restrict the outflow of foreign exchange, the fund may experience difficulties getting its money out to pay dividends. The fund might make an interesting speculation when it sinks to a discount comparable to ASA's 50%.

The United Kingdom Fund, launched in mid-1987 on the New York Stock Exchange with an initial offering of 6 million shares at $12.50, is one of the latest entrants in the foreign closed-end fund field. It seeks long-term capital appreciation through a diversified portfolio of British stocks.

## · CLOSED-END BOND FUNDS ·

You also have the choice of a few closed-end bond funds that specialize in foreign interest-bearing securities. The data on their premiums and discounts are to be found in a separate table published weekly by *Barron's* magazine and in the Wednesday editions of the *Wall Street Journal* and the *New York Times*.

The table looks like this (excluding the funds that do not concern us here):

| | NET ASSET VALUE | STOCK PRICE | % DIFF. |
|---|---|---|---|
| First Austr Pr | 9.14 | 8⅜ | −8.4 |
| Glob Yld Fnd | 10.25 | 9½ | −7.3 |
| KlnwtB Austr | 10.65 | 10 | −6.1 |

*Closed-End Bond Funds*

First Australia Prime Income Fund was launched on the American Stock Exchange in April 1986 at $10 a share, and raised an astounding $855 million from eager American investors. It then quickly rose to an 18.3% premium before sinking back to a lower net asset value—and a discount—a year later. The great attraction initially was the level of Australian interest rates, which, at 12.8% for Australian government five-year bonds, were about five percentage points above comparable United States government bonds. The fund has about three-quarters of its assets invested in Australian bonds and the other quarter in New Zealand bonds, where interest rates were equally high. The initial yield was attractive to Americans seeking the double-digit rates they had grown accustomed to in the United States in the previous few years but that were no longer available at home. Many of the less sophisticated buyers of the fund perhaps did not take into account the danger that the Australian and New Zealand dollars might subsequently decline against the American dollar.

Global Yield Fund, with assets of about $550 million, is an international fund seeking to achieve a higher yield in foreign debt markets than are available in the U.S. debt market. It is invested in a broadly based basket of major currencies rather than in a narrow spectrum like First Australia Prime.

Kleinwort Benson Australian Income Fund, assets about $100 million, was launched on the New York Stock Exchange in December 1986. It seeks high income through investment in Australian debt. This fund faces the same currency risks as First Australia Prime Income Fund. Income from both these funds is subject to Australian withholding tax.

## · CHOOSING A FUND ·

Which fund to buy? You might divide the decision-making process into three stages.

Step 1. Look up the latest weekly table of premiums and discounts in the financial press, and select the funds with the widest discounts. If you have any back numbers of the *Wall Street Journal* or *Barron's*, check back to see whether the discount has been even larger in the past than it is now; it may sink back to that level again. (In any case clip out the table and save it for future reference.) Price-earnings ratios of the closed-end funds are usually not given in the stock quotation tables. They might be misleading in view of the possible wide discrepancies between the fund's market price and its net asset value. But the number of shares traded daily is provided and it can give a good indication of investors' interest in each fund.

Step 2. You may come up with three or four funds with attractive-looking discounts. Now check the AP foreign exchange table to see how the dollar is doing against foreign currencies. If the Federal Reserve Board index is at a low point this may not be the time to buy any foreign funds. To narrow it down, if you are thinking of buying France Fund, for instance, make sure that the dollar is riding high at least against the French franc. Write for France Fund's latest quarterly report; you are almost certain to find in it some comments on the latest developments in the dollar-franc exchange rate. If the franc is unusually low against the dollar, so much the better. You will gain on the exchange rate when it comes back up again and France Fund is worth more in dollars.

Step 3. Check the foreign stock market index tables in *Barron's*, the *London Financial Times*, and your local newspaper if it carries the AP table. If the particular stock market you are going to buy into is at a low point, go ahead and buy the fund.

You now have three things going for you: if the fund's discount shrinks or even turns into a premium, if the dollar sinks against the foreign currency involved, and if the foreign stock market rises, you are going to be a winner on all three counts.

You might also try checking your fund's performance as compared with the stock market it operates in, but this is not as important with a closed-end fund as it is with a mutual fund, because the closed-end fund's management may do very well raising the fund's net asset value, only to have its investing expertise set at naught by that pesky market discount. Besides, many of the closed-end funds have been in existence too short a time to establish a reliable track record.

In any event, new funds just coming into the market for the first time are to be avoided for other reasons. They have not yet had time to sink to a discount and are thus not much of a bargain. The underwriters launching these new funds typically collect a commission of about 7% on the newly issued shares. You might as well buy a load fund at that rate.

Furthermore, the only time a new fund can be launched successfully is when there is an investor craze for its particular wares—Australian or Korean or Taiwanese stocks or whatever. The fund will very likely hit the crest of the boom as it comes out and then sink into mediocrity as the craze wanes.

Toward the end of its life, however, a closed-end fund selling at a big discount offers one further opportunity. Corporate raiders sometimes see a big chance to take over a fund that is trading at a discount say of 20% or 30% and make an instant 20% or 30% profit by liquidating the fund at net asset value, or converting it into a mutual fund, which automatically commands the full 100% of net asset value. The closed-end fund's stockholders, who also share in the profit, are usually only too glad to cooperate with the raider. For this reason, some funds have made it very difficult for such a takeover to succeed.

All the buying and selling operations mentioned in this chapter are of course regular stock exchange transactions and will be handled by your broker, who probably doesn't know much about closed-end funds, and if he is like most brokers probably doesn't care for them either. If you are going to buy a fund he would much rather sell you a load mutual fund at an 8.9% commission.

Among all the hundreds of brokerage firms in the United States there appears to be only one that specializes exclusively in closed-end funds: Thomas J. Herzfeld & Co., Inc. (7800 Red Road, South Miami, FL 33143; tel. 305-665-6500).

One last word. Even if you have no intention of investing in any of these closed-end funds, write for their latest reports anyway. Write also for the latest reports issued by the mutual funds mentioned in Chapter 4. You will find them all a gold mine of useful information when you set out to buy individual foreign stocks on your own, which is the subject of the next chapter.

# CHAPTER
# 6

# THE ADR SOLUTION: FOREIGN STOCKS YOU CAN BUY IN THE UNITED STATES

You may now feel ready to leave prepackaged investments like mutual funds and closed-end funds behind and to venture forth on your own to select and buy your own individual foreign stocks. In planning your strategy you might well remember the example of Mikhail Ilarionovich Kutuzov, the czarist general who defeated Napoleon by retreating all the way from the Russian border to Moscow, and then chasing the French emperor all the way back to Paris.

You will probably find it pays to lie in wait and let your quarry come to you rather than to advance recklessly seeking new worlds to conquer. In plain language: do whatever buying and selling of foreign securities you plan to do initially within the borders of the United States. You are then on your own turf, operating under the rules of a game that you already understand from your dealings on the U.S. stock market. And you are also under the protection of American authorities such as the U.S. Securities and Exchange Commission. Once you venture abroad to deal directly with foreign stockbrokers and foreign stock exchanges you will be exposed to an alien business culture and find yourself under the jurisdiction and regulation of foreign authorities, who may have startlingly different ways of seeing and doing things. In New Zealand, for example, insider trading has traditionally been quite an acceptable way of doing business.

You will find no lack of foreign stocks to choose from on American markets; about 800 foreign companies are available to you without ever leaving the United States. They include companies from such unexpected places as Bermuda, the British West Indies, Panama, the Netherlands Antilles, and Zambia.

However, we are not dealing here primarily with exotica. Many of these foreign companies you can buy in the United States are no lightweights. On the New York Stock Exchange you have companies that are major presences on the world scene, corporations like Bell Canada Enterprises, Alcan Aluminium Ltd., British Petroleum, British Telecommunications, Imperial Chemical Industries, Shell Transport & Trading, Hitachi, Honda, Matsushita Electric Industrial Co., Sony Corp., Royal Dutch Petroleum Co., and Unilever N.V. These giants are the peers of the biggest American corporations. On the American Stock Exchange you will find the British American Tobacco Company, Ford Motor Co. of Canada, Courtaulds, and Imperial Oil.

On the over-the-counter market, according to Standard & Poor's, the six companies with the highest market value (that is, the number of shares multiplied by the current share price) are foreign stocks: Glaxo Holdings, Beecham Group, and Fisons of Britain; Ito Yokado Ltd. and Fuji Photo Film of Japan; and Broken Hill Proprietary of Australia. In fact, more than thirty of the 100 biggest companies on the over-the-counter market are foreign corporations, including a dozen Canadians.

Overall, the total number of foreign stocks in the United States breaks down like this: about sixty listed on the New York Stock Exchange ("about" is used here because there may be new additions by the time you read this book), about fifty on the American Stock Exchange, and approximately 260 traded through the National Association of Securities Dealers Automated Quotations System (NASDAQ), which is to say the over-the-counter market. Quotations of these stocks are carried daily in the financial press. There are a further 350 or so foreign companies listed on the daily "Pink Sheets" which are less actively traded, have rather thin markets, and may not be quoted daily in the press. In addition, another 100 or so foreign stocks are duly registered but not actually issued.

You will find some real swingers in the ranks of this foreign legion. The top-performing stock on the American Stock Exchange in 1986 was Philippine Long Distance Telephone Co., which rose 580% in the year. The second-best performing stock on the New York Stock Exchange that same year was Banco Central of Spain, up 226%.

However, the bulk of the action in foreign stocks is in the over-the-counter market. About 2.4 billion shares worth $25 billion changed hands in 1986, accounting for about 8% of all NASDAQ trading for the year.

Now, as to why you should consider giving preference to U.S. markets rather than overseas stock exchanges for buying foreign stocks, here are three good reasons. First, when foreign companies make a public offering of their stocks in the United States, they become subject to U.S. federal securities laws, basically the Securities Act of 1933 and the Securities Exchange Act of 1934. These two laws regulate all publicly offered stocks in the United States, those of domestic and foreign corporations alike. Second, at the state level, all companies offering their securities to the public must also comply with state securities legislation—so-called blue-sky laws, which protect investors against securities fraud. And third, the foreign companies traded in the United States must also comply with the rules and regulations of the United States stock exchanges on which their shares are traded.

You thus have three layers of official protection against any financial flimflam and a threefold insistence on full and timely disclosure by the company you invest in of any facts that might affect your investment—a triple safety net that is simply not there in some markets abroad.

Generally speaking, a company based outside the United States is required to register with the U.S. Securities and Exchange Commission and to make reports and disclosure statements to this body when the company's securities are publicly offered to U.S. residents.

There are a few exceptional cases, however. Canadian securities markets are so similar to U.S. markets, for instance, that U.S. securities laws treat Canadian companies differently from other foreign companies. This means simply that many Canadian companies are subject to the same disclosure and reporting requirements as U.S. companies rather than the special rules that apply to other foreign corporations.

A few small foreign companies may slip in under the net altogether. If a small foreign company's shares are not going to be quoted on a U.S. stock exchange or NASDAQ, if it has assets of less than $3 million and less than 300 shareholders resident in the United States, it may be exempt from the SEC's reporting requirements. A telephone salesman might use this pitch for some hot little foreign stock. However, before you buy his wares you might reflect that there is no public market for these shares and you might well be stuck with them forever. If the pitch sounds attractive but you are in doubt about the company being touted, the SEC periodically publishes a list alerting the investing public to foreign restricted securities that have not been registered with the SEC but are being advertised or sold in the United States. If your broker doesn't have the list, you can write the SEC for it (450 Fifth Street, N.W., Washington, DC 20549).

To get back to legitimate enterprises, the first thing a foreign company entering the U.S. securities market has to do is file an F-1, F-2, F-3, or F-6 form with the SEC. These are all public documents and open for public inspection, if you want to take the trouble. F-1 includes the company's prospectus—which normally is the only part of the registration statement that goes to potential investors—plus additional financial information. F-2 and F-3 are for "world class" issuers that have a market value of at least $300 million, or that meet other conditions. F-6 is for companies that issue American Depository Receipts. These forms require specific information from the company about the securities being registered, the offering price, and the plan of distribution.

The foreign securities come in three different kinds: (1) the original shares, exactly the same as those traded in their home country, (2) "American depository shares" (ADS), specifically issued for U.S. trading, and (3) American Depository Receipts, or ADRs. The first kind are the stocks of companies incorporated in countries such as Canada, Israel, and the Philippines, where securities laws are similar to U.S. laws. "American shares" are a class of shares issued to conform with U.S. laws by companies from countries whose securities laws are different from U.S. legislation. But most of the foreign shares on the market are in the form of ADRs, a type of security invented sixty years ago to eliminate many of the problems American investors encountered when investing abroad up to that time.

An ADR is simply a receipt issued by an American bank certifying that a certain number of shares of a foreign company has been deposited in the foreign country with the bank's branch or some other custodian there. This device eliminates the need to ship documents abroad each time the shares are sold; the ADR receipt changes hands in the United States instead.

The ADR also makes it easier to collect dividends, which are collected by the overseas depository, converted into dollars, and transferred to the ADR holder in the United States. The United States bank distributes the ADR company's annual reports and other communications, handles voting rights, stock dividends, subscriptions, and other payments due to the American ADR holders.

These are services that foreign securities as issued in their home countries or "American shares" do not necessarily provide. You might sometimes have to wait a long time to collect the dividends on your Philippine Long Distance Telephone stock, for instance. Delays of up to nine months have been known to occur with this stock.

Until ADRs were invented in 1927, American investors had to deal with a transfer agent in a foreign land thousands of miles away whenever they bought or sold shares, and when they received dividends in a foreign currency. Dividends and share certificates took a long time to deliver when they came by seamail in those days.

Buying an ADR means: (1) you don't need to have shares held in custody abroad, thus avoiding one additional expense, (2) you don't send any documents abroad, (3) share prices are quoted in dollars, (4) you collect all distributions in dollars,

(5) trades are settled in five business days, as with any other U.S. stock market transaction, and (6) foreign tax payments are minimized as well as being taken care of for you.

Because of its simplicity and advantages, the ADR has established itself as the most common type of foreign security traded in the United States, and the one you are most likely to encounter. Thomas D. Sanford, vice-president of the institutional products group at Irving Trust's London branch, says, "The ADR is so well entrenched, convenient and practical for issuers, investors and market makers that its continued growth and role in the international capital markets are certain." Irving Trust is one of the big New York banks that issue and service ADRs. Others are Morgan Guaranty Trust, Citicorp, and Chemical Bank.

The SEC requires that ADRs fulfill certain conditions before they are offered to the American public. One condition is that ADRs must be issued in registered form, which means that the shareholder's name is registered on the company's books, the standard practice for all domestic U.S. shares. In some foreign countries all shares are issued in bearer form, which among other things makes things easier for thieves. Accounting rules and standards also vary widely between the United States and some foreign countries. The SEC demands that the company issuing the ADR should either present its financial statements in accordance with the accounting principles generally accepted in the United States or provide a full explanation of the accounting principles it uses.

These reporting and disclosure requirements are of course imposed not only on ADRs but on the shares and "American shares" of all non-U.S. companies with assets of more than $3 million and 500 or more shareholders, 300 or more of whom live in the United States.

Foreign companies must also file an updated form 20-F with the SEC every year, in the same way that domestic U.S. corporations file 10-K forms, reporting any and all information of material interest to shareholders. The 20-F requires, in addition to this, information on any foreign exchange controls and tax laws that might affect U.S. investors. Companies that want their

shares listed on U.S. exchanges have to meet further requirements from the exchanges.

The New York Stock Exchange demands that a foreign company meet these minimums before it is listed on the Big Board:
at least 5,000 owners of 100 shares or more worldwide, at least
2.5 million shares publicly held worldwide, a total market value
of $100 million, worldwide assets of $100 million, and pretax
cumulative income of $100 million over the past three years. So
you know that any foreign stock you may buy on the New York
Stock Exchange is a pretty big company with a liquid worldwide
market for its shares.

The American Stock Exchange has considerably lower minimum requirements: 2,000 owners of 100 shares or more worldwide, a worldwide market value of $20 million, a worldwide total
value of $20 million for publicly held shares, a net worth of $25
million, and $30 million of pretax income over the last three
years. On the American Stock Exchange you may thus be running into companies about one-fifth the size of New York Stock
Exchange–listed companies.

On the over-the-counter market you may possibly find much,
much smaller foreign companies listed, although there are some
giants there too. NASDAQ does not require a foreign company
to have any minimum number of shares initially, but if it does
not trade at least 500 shares daily for the first ninety days it is
delisted. The company must also have total assets of at least $2
million. So, compared with the New York and American stock
exchanges, NASDAQ lets some real pipsqueaks through that
don't have much capital behind them and may be pretty thinly
traded.

One further reason to be doubly careful on the over-the-counter
market, particularly with ADRs, is that they come in two varieties, sponsored and unsponsored. The unsponsored kind outnumber the others by about eight to one. The New York and
American stock exchanges allow only sponsored ADRs to be
listed. You will find all the unsponsored ADRs on the over-the-
counter market.

A sponsored ADR comes into existence when the foreign

company itself actively promotes the new security, sometimes because it wants to raise new capital in the United States, sometimes because it wants a wider international market for its shares. In any case, the fact is that the company is actively interested in its ADRs and will go out of its way to back them up by providing timely information on company developments, quarterly and annual reports, and other information—in English—and whatever else is likely to keep American shareholders happy.

Unsponsored ADRs may have no such backing. They are created when an American bank sees what it thinks might be a profitable market for the shares of, say, the Australasian Global Conglomerate of the Republic of Australasia, and decides to launch Australasian ADRs on its own initiative. The bank has to get the consent of the company to do this, but if Australasian Global itself has no great interest in the American capital market the company may not put itself out too much for its American shareholders in the way of financial reports and information. This need not necessarily be an obstacle to buying some unsponsored ADRs, though. Glaxo and BAT, two of the biggest and most active ADR issues, are both unsponsored. However, the bottom line is that with some companies, as the owner of their unsponsored ADRs you may feel like an underprivileged financial orphan, while a sponsored ADR is more likely to give you the feeling that somebody up there cares about you.

In any event, this is how the ADR system works. The ADR, sponsored or unsponsored, gets onto the American securities market and starts trading in the following way. The U.S. issuing bank completes all the registration formalities with the SEC and then informs U.S. brokers that it is ready to "extend a facility" in Australasian Global. This means in plain English that it undertakes to issue ADR certificates certifying that the actual securities are on deposit with a custodian, usually its own branch, back in Australasia. The brokers who like the looks of the deal, big international firms, then act as professional "arbitrageurs." They buy Australasian Global shares in the company's home country, deposit them with the custodian bank there, collect the equivalent in ADRs from the issuing bank's office in the United

States, and then try to sell the ADRs to American investors—at a markup, of course, to make it worth their while.

The new ADR's initial price is thus the going price in Australasia, plus the bank's fee plus the broker's markup. Once trading gets going in the United States, the only difference in price between the shares in Australasia and the ADRs in subsequent transactions is the broker's markup or markdown.

If Australasian Global proves to be a popular, active stock, other brokers may also get into the act as arbitrageurs. The brokers keep a close watch on the ADR price and sell it for a profit if it rises above the current price on the Australasian Stock Exchange, or buy it for a profit if it sinks below the price on the home market. This constant scalping for small gains by the professional arbitrageurs keeps the price of the ADR constantly in line with the price of the original shares back home in Australasia.

There is one practical problem, however, that sometimes comes up because of different mindsets in various world markets. In Tokyo, for example, it is considered quite normal for the bluest of blue chips to sell for, say, $2 or $3 a share. In the United States this kind of price arouses instant suspicion. American investors tend to respect a $50 stock more than a $20 stock, and a $100 stock more than a $50 stock. A stock selling at $1 or $2 is a "penny stock" to the American mind, and definitely causes a Japanese ADR to lose face in America. It is for this reason that one ADR sometimes represents more than one original foreign share. For example, one Hitachi ADR represents ten Hitachi shares on the Tokyo Stock Exchange, and one Mitsui ADR represents twenty Mitsui shares in Tokyo. This is something to keep in mind when you are comparing, for example, the prices of some British ADRs and the prices of the British company on the London Stock Exchange as quoted in the *London Financial Times*.

We'll now list the foreign stocks currently available in the United States through your regular American broker, and then go on to discuss ways of selecting stocks from the list where it might be worth investing your money at any particular time. Take note of where each company is listed, and remember that those on the New York Stock Exchange (NYSE) are pretty big ($100 million and up), those on the American Stock Exchange (ASE) may be medium ($20 million) to large, while the NASDAQ list contains everything from $2 million midgets to international giants. It may be prudent also to give preference to NYSE and ASE stocks on the ground that they are sponsored, while most of the NASDAQ ADRs are unsponsored.

Foreign stocks available in the United States are listed here by country. Figures in parentheses indicate how many foreign shares are represented by each ADR: 1:10 means one ADR equals ten foreign shares. If no ratios are given, the stocks are either original shares or in a 1:1 ratio. All stocks are traded over the counter unless they are marked NYSE or ASE.

### Australia

Acorn Securities Ltd.
Ampol Exploration Ltd.
Ampol Ltd.
Anglo Gold Mines (1:10)
A.R.I. Ltd.
Ashton Mining Ltd.
Asia Oil & Minerals Ltd.
Australia & New Zealand
  Banking Group Ltd.
Bass Strait Oil & Gas
Bell Resources Ltd. (1:3)
Black Hills Minerals Ltd.
Bond Corp. Holdings Ltd.
  (1:10)
Bougainville Copper Ltd.
Bridge Oil Ltd.
Broken Hill Proprietary
  ADR, NYSE, SP (1:2)
Brunswick Oil N.L.
Cape Range Oil Ltd. (1:10)
Central Norsemen Corp.
Central Pacific Minerals (1:2)

Charter Mining N.L. (1:4)
Claremont Petroleum N.L.
Condor Minerals & Energy
  Ltd. (1:10)
Consolidated Gold Mining
  Areas N.L.
Coopers Resources N.L.
CRA Ltd.
Cracow Gold Ltd.
CSR Ltd.
Delta Gold N.L.
Dominion Mining & Oil
  N.L. (1:2)
Eagle Corp. Ltd.
East West Minerals N.L.
  (1:10)
Eastern Petroleum Australia
  Ltd.
Elders IXL Ltd.
Emperor Mines Ltd.
Energy Oil & Gas N.L.
Enterprise Gold Mines N.L.

Expo Oil N.L. (1:4)
FAI Insurance Ltd.
Forsayth N.L. (1:10)
Geometals N.L.
Golconda Minerals N.L.
Gold Mines of Kalgoorlie
  Ltd.
Grants Patch Mining (1:10)
Great Australian Resources
Great Eastern Mines Ltd.
  (1:10)
Greenvale Mining N.L.
Griffiths Brothers Ltd.
Haome Northwest N.L.
HMC Australasia N.L.
Industrial Equity Ltd.
International Mining Corp.
Jimberlana Minerals N.L.
Jingellic Minerals N.L.
Jones, David, Ltd.
Kalbara Mining N.L.
Kitchener Mining N.L.
Lennard Oil N.L. (1:4)
Magnet Group Ltd. (1:4)
Meridian Oil Ltd.
MIM Holdings Ltd. (1:2)
Minefields Exploration N.L.
Mintaro Slate & Flagstone
  Co.
Monarch Petroleum N.L.
  (1:4)
Monier Ltd. (1:5)
Moonie Oil Co. Ltd.
National Australia Bank Ltd.
News Corp. Ltd. ADS,
  NYSE, SP (1:2)
Niugini Mining Ltd.

North Broken Hill Holdings
  Ltd.
Offshore Oil N.L.
Otter Exploration Ltd. (1:4)
Peko Wallsend Ltd.
Pelsart Resources N.L. (1:10)
Petrogulf Resources Ltd.
Philip Morris (Australia) Ltd.
Poseidon Ltd.
Queen Margaret Gold Mines
  N.L.
Regent Mining Ltd.
Samantha Exploration N.L.
  (1:4)
Samson Exploration N.L.
  (1:4)
Santos Ltd.
Sirius Corp.
Southern Goldfields Ltd.
Southern Pacific Petroleum
  N.L. (1:2)
Southern Resources Ltd.
Southern Ventures N.L.
Southwest Gold Mines N.L.
Swan Resources Ltd.
Tantalex Ltd.
Terrex Resources N.L.
Vamgas Ltd.
Victoria Exploration N.L.
Walhalla Resources Co. Ltd.
Western Mining Holdings
  Corp.
Westpac Banking Corp.
Woodside Petroleum Ltd.
Woolworth Ltd. (Australia)
Zanex Ltd. (1:10)

*Bahamas*

Commodore International Ltd., NYSE, SP

*Bermuda*

Minerals and Resources Corp., SP
Sea Containers Ltd., NYSE, SP

*British West Indies*

Club Med Inc., NYSE (5:1)

*Canada*

Agnico-Eagle Mines Ltd., SP
Ajax Resources Ltd.
Alaska Apollo Gold Mines Ltd.
Alcan Aluminium Ltd., NYSE, SP
AMCA International Ltd., NYSE, SP
American Barrick Resources Corp., SP
American Telecommunications Corp.
Amertek Inc.
ARC International Corp., ASE, SP
Asamera Inc., ASE, SP
Avino Mines & Resources Ltd., SP
Banister Continental Ltd., ASE, SP

Bell Canada Enterprises Inc., NYSE, SP
Bio Logicals Inc., SP
Bow Valley Industries Ltd., ASE, SP
Bralorne Resources Ltd., SP
Brascan Ltd., ASE, SP
Breakwater Resources Ltd., SP
Brican Resources Ltd., SP
California Gold Mines Ltd.
Cam-Net Communications
Campbell Red Lake Mines Ltd., NYSE, SP
Campbell Resources Inc., NYSE, SP
Canadian Marconi Co., ASE, SP
Canadian Occidental Petroleum Ltd., ASE, SP
Canadian Pacific Ltd., NYSE, SP
Carling O'Keefe Ltd., NYSE, SP
CDC Life Sciences Inc.
Central Fund of Canada Ltd., ASE, SP
Century Energy Corp.
Chieftain Development Co. Ltd., ASE, SP
Chieftain Development Co. 9.5% Conv. Pfd., ASE, SP
Chieftain Development Co. $4 Conv. Pfd., ASE, SP
Chieftain Development Co., warrants, ASE, SP
Citadel Gold Mines Inc.

City Resources (Canada) Ltd.
Cominco Ltd., ASE, SP
Consolidated Professor Mines
  Ltd.
Controlled Environmental
  Farming International Ltd.
Conversion Industries Inc.
Cortez International Ltd.
Crossland Industries Corp.
Cumo Resources Ltd.
Cusac Industries Ltd.
Daleco Resources Corp.
Davidson Tisdale Mines Ltd.
Develcon Electronics Ltd.,
  SP
Dickenson Mines Ltd. A,
  ASE, SP
Dickenson Mines Ltd. B,
  ASE, SP
Dome Mines Ltd., NYSE, SP
Dome Petroleum Ltd., ASE,
  SP
Domtar Inc., ASE, SP
Dumagami Mines Ltd.
Dune Resources Ltd.
Dusty Mac Mines Ltd.
E.A. Viner Holdings Ltd.
Echo Bay Mines Ltd., ASE,
  SP
ELXSI Ltd., SP
EMS Systems Ltd., SP
Falconbridge Ltd., SP
Ford Motor Co. of Canada
  Ltd., ASE, SP
Galactic Resources Ltd., SP
Gandalf Technologies Inc.,
  SP

Gemini Technology Inc.
Genstar Corp., NYSE
Geodome Resources Ltd.
Giant Bay Resources Ltd.
Giant Piper Exploration Inc.
Giant Yellowknife Mines
  Ltd., ASE
Glamis Gold Ltd.
Golden Knight Resources
  Inc.
Golden North Resource
  Corp.
Grandview Resources Inc.
Granges Exploration Ltd.,
  ASE, SP
Gulf Canada Corp., ASE, SP
Gulf Canada Corp. Series 1
  Pref., ASE, SP
Hemisphere Development
  Corp.
Highwood Resources Ltd.
Husky Oil Ltd., ASE, SP
IBS Technologies Ltd.
Imperial Oil Ltd., ASE, SP
Inca Resources Inc.
Inco Ltd., NYSE, SP
Inspiration Resources Corp.,
  NYSE, SP
Inter-City Gas Corp., ASE,
  SP
Inter-Globe Resources Ltd.
International H.R.S. Indus-
  tries Ltd., SP
International North Ameri-
  can Resources Inc., SP
International Standard Re-
  sources Ltd.

Interprovincial Pipe Line
Ltd., SP
Interstrat Resources Inc.
Javelin International Ltd.
LAC Minerals Ltd., NYSE
Lacana Mining Corp., SP
Laidlaw Transportation Class
A
Laidlaw Transportation Class
B
Lambda Mercantile Corp.
La Teco Resources Ltd.
Levon Resources Ltd., SP
Lifestyle Beverage Corp.
Lincoln Resources Inc.
Loadmaster Systems Inc.
London Silver Corp.
MacMillan Bloedel Ltd.,
NYSE, SP
Magna International Inc., SP
Malartic Hygrade Gold Mines
Canada Ltd., ASE, SP
Management Graphics Inc.
Massey Ferguson Ltd., NYSE
Maymac Petroleum Corp.
McIntyre Mines Ltd., NYSE,
SP
Mirtone International Inc.
Mitel Corp., NYSE, SP
Monogram Oil & Gas Inc.
Moore Corp. Ltd., NYSE,
SP
MSR Exploration Ltd., ASE,
SP
Murgold Resources Inc.
Muscocho Explorations Ltd.
Musto Explorations Ltd.

National Business Systems
Inc., SP
NETI Technologies Inc.
Ni-Cal Developments Ltd.
Nor Quest Resources Ltd.
North Canadian Oils Ltd.,
ASE, SP
Northern Telecom Ltd.,
NYSE, SP
Northgate Exploration Ltd.,
NYSE, SP
Nowsco Well Service Ltd.
N.R.D. Mining Ltd.
Numac Oil & Gas Ltd.,
ASE
Officeland Inc.
O.T. Industries Inc.
Paragon Resources Ltd.
Parkside Petroleum Inc.
Pegasus Gold Inc.
Pennant Resources Ltd.
Perle Systems Ltd.
Pilgrim Holdings Ltd.
Placer Development Ltd.,
ASE, SP
Plexus Resources Corp., SP
Prairie Oil Royalties Co.
Ltd., ASE, SP
Primrose Technology Corp.
Quebec Sturgeon River Mines
Ltd.
Quebecor Inc., ASE, SP
Ranger Oil Ltd., NYSE, SP
Rea Gold Corp.
Redlaw Industries Inc., ASE,
SP
Richport Resources Ltd.

Rio Algom Ltd., ASE, SP
Ruskin Developments Ltd.
Sand Technology Systems
 Inc.
Saturn Energy & Resources
 Ltd.
Saxton Industries Ltd.
Sceptre Resources Ltd., ASE
Scurry-Rainbow Oil Ltd.,
 ASE, SP
Seagram Co. Ltd., NYSE, SP
Shadowfax Resources Ltd., SP
SHL Systemhouse Inc.
Silver Eureka Corp., SP
Silver Hart Mines Ltd.
Silverado Mines Ltd., SP
Sonora Gold Corp.
Stake Technology Ltd.
Sterivet Laboratories Ltd.
Taurus Resources Ltd.
Terra Mines Ltd.
Texaco Canada Inc., ASE,
 SP
Total Erickson Resources Ltd.
Total Petroleum (North
 America) Ltd., ASE, SP
Total Petroleum (North
 America) Ltd. $2.88 Pfd.,
 ASE, SP
Tournigan Mining Explora-
 tions Ltd.
TransCanada Pipelines Ltd.,
 NYSE, SP
Tri Basin Resources Ltd.
TRV Minerals Corp.
United Hearne Resources
 Ltd.

U.S. Precious Metals Inc.
Varity Corp., SP
Veronex Resources Ltd.
Viscount Resources Ltd.
Vulcan Packaging Inc., SP
Westburne International In-
 dustries Ltd., ASE, SP
Westcoast Transmission Co.
 Ltd., NYSE, SP
Western Allenbee Oil & Gas
 Co.
Wharf Resources Ltd.
Zytec Computers Ltd., SP

### Denmark

Novo Industri A/S ADR,
 NYSE, SP

### Finland

Instrumentarium ADR, SP
 (4:1)

### France

Club Mediterranée (5:1)
Louis Vuitton (4:1)
Peugeot Citroen S.A. (5:1)
Société Nationale ELF Aqui-
 taine

### Germany

Bayer AG
Bayerische Vereinsbank AG
Hoechst AG (2:1)
Rheinisch-Westfaelisches
 Elektrizitaetswerk
Siemens AG (5:1)

*Great Britain*

In 1986 the British government levied a 1.5% tax on new issues of British ADRs, but the already existing ADRs listed below were not affected.

Barclays PLC ADS, NYSE, SP (1:4)
B.A.T. Industries Ltd. ADR, ASE, SP
Beecham Group ADR, SP
Bio-Isolates Holdings PLC
BOC Group PLC
Boots Co. PLC (1:2)
Bowater Indust. PLC ADR, NYSE, SP
British Airways ADS
British Petroleum Co. Ltd. ADR, NYSE, SP (1:4)
British Telecommunications PLC ADR, NYSE, SP (1:10)
BSR International PLC
B.T.R. PLC
Burmah Oil PLC, SP
Cadbury Schweppes ADS, SP (1:10)
Charter Consolidated PLC
Coats Patons PLC (1:4)
Courtaulds Ltd. ADR, ASE, SP (1:4)
De La Rue Co.
Distillers Co. PLC
Dowty Group PLC
Elan Corp. PLC ADS, SP
Fisons PLC ADR, SP (1:4)
Foseco Minsep Ltd.
Foseco Minsep Ltd. Preferred

Glaxo Holdings PLC ADR, SP
Govett Strategic Investment Trust PLC
Grand Metropolitan PLC
Great Universal Stores PLC
Great Universal Stores Ltd. A
Guinness (Arthur) & Sons PLC (1:5)
Hanson Trust ADS, NYSE, SP (1:5)
Hard Rock Cafe PLC
Harvard Securities Group (1:10)
Huntingdon International Holdings ADR, SP
ICL PLC
Imperial Chemical Industries PLC ADR, NYSE, SP (1:4)
Jaguar PLC ADR, SP
Ladbroke Group PLC
London International Group
Lonrho PLC
Metal Box PLC
National Westminster ADS, NYSE, SP (1:3)
Nimslo International Ltd.
Pentos PLC (1:5)
Pleasurama PLC
Plessey Co. Ltd. ADR,

NYSE, SP
Racal Electronics PLC
Rank Organisation PLC
    ADR, SP
Reuters Holdings PLC ADS,
    SP (1:6)
Rio Tinto Zinc Corp. PLC
Rodime PLC ADS, SP
Rothman's International PLC
Ryan Traders Distribution
    Ltd. (1:2)
Saatchi & Saatchi ADS, SP
    (1:3)
Sainsbury PLC
Sears Holdings PLC
Senetek PLC
Shell Transport & Trading
    Ltd. Co., NYSE, SP (1:4)
Sonic Tape PLC (1:10)
Swan Ryan International Ltd.
    (1:2)
Tate & Lyle PLC
Thorn EMI PLC
Tricentrol PLC ADR, NYSE,
    SP (1:2)
Turner & Newell PLC
Unilever PLC, NYSE, SP
    (1:4)
Universal Money Centers
Vickers PLC
Waterford Glass ADS, SP
    (1:10)
Whitbread & Co. (1:5)

## Hong Kong

Carrian Investments (1:10)
Cheung Kong Holdings Ltd.

China Light & Power Co.
Chuang's Holdings Ltd.
Conic Investment Co. Ltd.
    (1:5)
Evergo Industrial Enterprises
    Ltd. (1:5)
First Pacific Holdings Ltd.
    (1:10)
HK-TVB Ltd. (1:5)
Hong Kong & Kowloon
    Wharf & Godown Co.
Hong Kong & Shanghai
    Banking Corp.
Hong Kong Electric Holdings
Hong Kong Land Co. Ltd.
    (1:2)
Hutchinson Whampoa Ltd.
    (1:5)
Jardine, Matheson Holdings
    Ltd.
Sun Hung Kai & Co. (1:5)
Swire Pacific Ltd. (1:2)
Trafalgar Housing Ltd. (1:5)
Wah Kwong Shipping & In-
    vestment Co. (1:5)
Winsor Industrial Corp. (1:5)

## Israel

Alliance Tire & Rubber Co.
    Ltd., ASE
American Israeli Paper Mills
    Ltd., ASE
Aryt Optronics Industries
    Ltd.
Carmel Container Systems,
    ASE

ECI Telecom Ltd.
Elbit Computers Ltd.
Elron Electronic Industries
Ltd.
Elscint Ltd., NYSE
ETZ Lavud Ltd., ASE
IDB Bankholding ADR, SP
I.I.S. Intelligent Info. Sys-
tems Ltd.
InterfPharm Laboratories
Ltd.
Laser Industries Ltd., ASE
Optrotech Ltd.
OSHAP Technologies Ltd.
Rada Electronic Industries
Ltd.
Scitex Corp. Ltd.
S.P.I. Suspension and Parts
Industries Ltd.
Taro-Vit Industries Ltd.
Teva Pharmaceutical Indus-
tries ADR, SP (1:12)


## Italy

Fiat SpA
Fiat SpA Preferred
Italcementi Fabbriche Riunite
Cemento SpA
Montecatini Edison SpA,
NYSE
Olivetti SpA (nonconverti-
ble) (1:10)
Olivetti SpA (ordinary)
Olivetti SpA Preferred
Pirelli SpA

## Japan

Aida Engineering Ltd. (1:10)
Ajinomoto Co. Inc. (1:10)
Akai Electric Co. Ltd. (1:10)
Alps Electric Co. Ltd. (1:10)
Amada Co. Ltd. (1:2)
Asahi Chemical Ind. (1:10)
Asahi Glass Co. Ltd. (1:10)
Ashikaga Bank Ltd. (1:2)
Bank of Tokyo Ltd. (1:10)
Bank of Yokohama Ltd.
(1:10)
Banyu Pharmaceutical Co.
Ltd. (1:20)
Bridgestone Corp. (1:10)
Brother Industries Ltd.
(1:10)
Calpis Food Industry Co.
(1:10)
Canon Inc. ADR, SP (1:5)
Casio Computer Co. Ltd.
(1:10)
C. Itoh & Co. Ltd. (1:10)
Computer Services Corp
(CSK)
Daiei Inc. (1:2)
Dai-Ichi Kangyo Bank Ltd.
(1:10)
Daiwa House Industry Co.
Ltd. (1:10)
Daiwa Securities Co. Ltd.
(1:10)
Daiwa Seiko Inc. (1:10)
Ebara Corp. (1:10)
Eisai Co. Ltd. (1:10)

Fuji Bank Ltd. (1:10)
Fuji Photo Film Co. Ltd.
  ADR, SP (1:2)
Fujita Corp. (1:10)
Fujitsu Ltd. (1:5)
Furukawa Electric Co. (1:10)
Hitachi Cable Ltd. (1:10)
Hitachi Koki Co. Ltd. (1:10)
Hitachi Ltd. ADR, NYSE,
  SP (1:10)
Hitachi Metals Ltd. (1:10)
Hochiki Corp. (1:10)
Hokuriku Bank Ltd. (1:10)
Honda Motor Co. Ltd. ADR,
  NYSE, SP (1:10)
Industrial Bank of Japan
  (1:10)
Isuzu Motors Ltd. (1:5)
Ito-Yokado Co. ADR, SP
  (1:4)
Japan Air Lines (1:2)
Japan Steel Works Ltd.
  (1:10)
Jusco Co. (1:10)
Kajima Corp. (1:10)
Kanebo Ltd. (1:10)
Kao Corp. (1:10)
Kashiyama & Co. Ltd. (1:5)
Kawasaki Steel Corp. (1:10)
Kirin Brewery Co. (1:10)
Koakuen Co. (1:10)
Komatsu Ltd. (1:20)
Konishiroku Photo Industry
  (1:10)
Kubota Ltd. ADR, NYSE, SP
  (1:20)
Kumagai Gumi Co. (1:10)

Kyocera Corp. ADR, NYSE,
  SP (1:20)
Kyowa Bank Ltd. (1:10)
Makita Electric Works Ltd.
  (1:5)
Marubeni Corp. (1:10)
Marui Co. Ltd. (1:2)
Matsushita Elec. Ind. Co.
  ADR, NYSE, SP (1:10)
Matsushita Electric Works
  (1:10)
Meiji Seikai Kaisha Ltd.
  (1:10)
Minebea Co. Ltd. (1:5)
Mitsubishi Bank Ltd. (1:10)
Mitsubishi Chemical Ind.
  (1:10)
Mitsubishi Corp. (1:10)
Mitsubishi Electric Corp.
  (1:10)
Mitsubishi Estate Co. (1:10)
Mitsubishi Kakoki Kaisha
  Ltd. (1:10)
Mitsubishi Trust & Banking
  Corp. (1:10)
Mitsui & Co. Ltd. ADR, SP
  (1:20)
Mitsui Bank Ltd. (1:10)
Mitsukoshi Ltd. (1:10)
Nagoya Railroad Co. (1:10)
NEC Corp. ADR, SP (1:5)
Nifco Inc.
Nikko Securities Co. (1:10)
Nippon Kogaku K.K. (1:10)
Nippon Kokan K.K. (1:10)
Nippon Seiko K.K. (1:10)
Nippon Shinpan Co. (1:10)

Nippon Suishan Kaisha Ltd. (1:10)
Nippon Yusen K.K. (1:10)
Nippondenso Co. (1:4)
Nissan Motor Co. Ltd. (1:2)
Nisshin Steel Co. Ltd. (1:20)
Nitto Electric Co. Ltd. (1:10)
Nomura Securities Co. Ltd. (1:10)
Oji Paper Co. Ltd. (1:10)
Omron Tateisi Electronics Co. (1:10)
Onoda Cement Co. (1:10)
Pioneer Electronic Corp. ADR, NYSE, SP (1:2)
Ricoh Co. Ltd. (1:10)
Ryobi Ltd. (1:10)
Saitama Bank Ltd. (1:10)
Sanwa Bank Ltd. (1:10)
Sanyo Electric Co. (1:5)
SECOM Co. Ltd. (1:2)
Seksui House Ltd. (1:10)
Seven-Eleven Japan Co.
Sharp Corp. (1:10)
Shiseido Co. Ltd. (1:5)
Shizuoka Bank Ltd. (1:10)
Showa Sangyo Co. Ltd. (1:20)
Sony Corp. ADR, NYSE, SP
Sumitomo Bank Ltd. (1:10)
Sumitomo Electric Ind. Ltd. (1:10)
Sumitomo Metal Ind. Ltd. (1:20)
Suruga Bank Ltd. (1:10)
Taisei Road Construction Co. (1:10)

Taisho Marine & Fire Insurance (1:10)
Taiyo Kobe Bank Ltd. (1:20)
Taiyo Yuden Co. Ltd. (1:4)
TDK Corp. ADS, NYSE, SP (1:2)
Teijin Ltd. (1:10)
Toa Harbor Works Co. Ltd. (1:10)
Tokai Bank Ltd. (1:20)
Tokyo Land Corp. (1:10)
Tokyo Marine & Fire Insurance ADR, SP (1:50)
Tokyo Sanyo Electr. Co. (1:5)
Toppan Printing Co. Ltd. (1:5)
Toray Industries Inc. (1:10)
Toto Ltd. (1:10)
Toyo Suishan Kaisha Ltd. (1:10)
Toyota Motor Corp. (1:2)
Tsubakimoto Precision Products (1:4)
Tsugami Corp. (1:10)
Victor Co. of Japan Ltd. (1:2)
Wacoal Corp. (1:5)
Yamazaki Baking Co. Ltd. (1:10)
Yasuda Trust & Banking Co. (1:10)

## Mexico

Tubos de Acero de Mexico SA ADR, ASE, SP

## Netherlands

Advanced Semiconductor
  Materials
Centrafarm Group N.V.
Heineken N.V.
KLM Royal Dutch Airlines,
  NYSE (1:10)
Oce-van der Grinten ADR,
  SP (5:1)
Philips NV, NYSE
Royal Dutch Petroleum Co.,
  NYSE

## Netherlands Antilles

Divi Hotels N.V., ASE
Erbamont N.V., NYSE
Schlumberger Ltd., NYSE
Unilever N.V., NYSE, SP
  (1:4)
WTC International N.V.,
  ASE

## Norway

Norsk Data ADR B, SP

## Panama

Norlin Corp., NYSE
Syntex Corp., NYSE

## Philippines

Atlas Consolidated Mining
  Corp., ASE
Benguet Corp., NYSE
Philippine Long Distance
  Telephone, ASE

San Carlos Milling Co., ASE

## Singapore

City Developments Ltd.
Cycle & Carriage Ltd.
Development Bank of Singa-
  pore
Inchcape Berhad
Keppel Shipyard Ltd.
Malayan Credit Ltd.
Overseas Union Bank Ltd.
Pan-Electric Industries
Sembawang Shipyard Ltd.
Sime Darby Berhad
Singapore Land Ltd.
United Overseas Bank Ltd.

## South Africa

Afrikander Lease Ltd.
Anglo American Coal Corp.
Anglo American Gold Invest-
  ments ADR, SP (10:1)
Anglo-American Investment
  Trust Ltd.
Anglo-American South Afri-
  can ADR, SP
Anglovaal Ltd.
ASA Ltd., NYSE, SP
Barlow Rand Ltd.
Beatrix Mines Ltd.
Blyvoor Gold Mining ADR,
  SP
Bracken Mines Ltd.
Buffelsfontein Gold Mining
  ADR, SP
Consolidated Modderfontein
  Mines Ltd.

Daggafontein Mines Ltd.
DeBeers Consolidated Mines
ADR, SP
Deelkraal Gold Mining Co.
Doornfontein Gold Mining
Co.
Driefontein Consolidated
ADR, SP
Durban Roodepoort Deep
Ltd.
East Daggafontein Mines
East Rand Gold & Uranium
Co.
East Rand Proprietary Mines
Ltd.
Eastern Transvaal Consoli-
dated Mines Ltd.
Elandsrand Gold Mining Co.
Elsburg Gold Mining Co.
Free State Consolidated Gold
Mines
Genbel Investments Ltd.
General Mining Union Corp.
Gold Fields Property Co. Ltd.
Gold Fields South Africa
Ltd., SP
Grootvlei Proprietary Mines
Ltd.
Harmony Gold Mining Co.
Hartebeestfontein Gold Min-
ing Co.
Highveld Steel & Vanadium
Corp.
Impala Platinum Holdings
Ltd.
Johannesburg Consolidated
Investment Co.

Kinross Mines Ltd.
Kloof Gold Mining, SP
Leslie Gold Mines Ltd. (1:5)
Libanon Gold Mining Co.
Loraine Gold Mines Ltd.
Lydenburg Platinum Ltd.
Marievale Consolidated
Mines Ltd.
Middle Witwatersrand (West-
ern Areas) Ltd. (1:3)
Modder B Gold Holdings
Ltd.
New Wits Ltd.
O'Okiep Copper Co. Ltd.,
ASE
Orange Free State Invest-
ments Ltd.
Palabora Mining Co. Ltd.
Rand Mines Ltd. (10:1)
Rand Mines Properties Ltd.
Randfontein Estates Gold
Mining Co.
Rustenburg Platinum Hold-
ings
St. Helena Gold Mines
ADR, SP
Samancor Ltd.
Sasol Ltd.
Simmer & Jack Mines Ltd.
South African Breweries Ltd.
South Roodepoort Main Reef
Areas Ltd., Conv. Pre-
ferred
Southvaal Holdings Ltd.
Stilfontein Gold Mining Co.
Trans Natal Coal Corp.
Unisel Gold Mines Ltd.

Vaal Reefs Exploration &
Mining ADR, SP (10:1)
Venterspost Gold Mining Co.
Vlakfontein Gold Mining Co.
Welkom Gold Holdings
ADR, SP
West Rand Consolidated
Mines Ltd.
Western Areas Gold Mining
Co. Ltd.
Western Deep Levels ADR,
SP
Western Mining Holdings
Corp.
Winkelhaak Mines Ltd.
Witwatersrand Nigel Ltd.
Zambia Copper Investment
Ltd.
Zandpan Gold Mining Co.

### Spain

Banco Central ADS, NYSE,
SP

Compania Telefonica Na-
cional ADR

### Sweden

ASEA ADR, SP
Electrolux AB
Ericsson (LM) Telephone B
ADR, SP
Gambro AB ADR, SP
Pharmacia AB ADR, SP
(1:¾)
PLM AB
Volvo AB ADR B, SP

### Switzerland

Nestle SA (40:1)

### Zambia

Minerals & Resources Ltd.
ADR, SP

Make a special note of the stocks in the above list with the notation SP. These stocks are carried in *Standard & Poor's Stock Guide*, a monthly statistical publication providing the latest price, dividend, price-earnings, sales, and other data on more than 5,000 domestic and Canadian and seventy other foreign stocks traded in the United States. You can thus be assured of a constant flow of financial data on these stocks. The *Guide* is an astonishingly compact source of information considering that each company gets a one-line entry.

The line on Canadian Pacific, to take one example, tells you that the company's ticker symbol is CP; 234 institutional investors such as mutual funds and pension funds hold 60.5 million of its shares; CP is an integrated transportation system, the stock gets a B+ (average) rating from Standard & Poor's; its shares traded between $10 and $14⅝ in 1986, between $11⅝ and $15⅞ in 1985, and between $3½ and $15 in the previous fifteen years. Sales in the past month were 6.9 million shares at a range between $10⅞ and $11⅞, the last sale being at $11⅞. The dividend yield is 2.9% and the price-earnings ratio is 18. The company has paid a dividend every year since 1944, it currently pays a quarterly dividend of 12 cents a share on October 28, and the stock goes ex-dividend September 22. Dividends for the year totaled 48 cents a share, and for the year before 47 cents. The company has $523 million in cash equivalents, current assets of $4.98 billion, liabilities of $4.63 billion, long-term debt of $6.24 billion. The capitalization is $15 million in preferred shares and 298 million common shares. Earnings for the past five years were 87 cents a share, 66 cents, 1.75 dollars, 1.11 dollars, and 65 cents. For the latest twelve months they were 37 cents. Earnings for the last nine months were 20 cents a share compared with 94 cents in the same period of the previous year. All the above comes in one line of figures, updated monthly. A yearly subscription to the *Stock Guide* costs $84 a year (Standard & Poor's Corporation, 25 Broadway, P.O. Box 992, New York, NY 10275). A single monthly issue may be ordered for $10.

When looking up the latest prices of individual stocks, keep in mind that prices quoted on the New York Stock Exchange and the American Stock Exchange represent actual transactions, whereas NASDAQ quotations of over-the-counter stocks represent the amounts that a dealer making a market in a particular security would offer to pay (bid) or the price at which he would be willing to sell (ask). The over-the-counter market is not really a market in the physical sense of a building on Wall Street like the New York Stock Exchange or on Trinity Place, New York, like the American Stock Exchange. It is a countrywide network of dealers, each of whom makes a market in a number of stocks, and who keep in touch with each other by telephone and electronic terminals to buy and sell shares.

## · HOW TO SELECT YOUR STOCKS ·

In the list above you have your field of starters. The next question is which horse to bet on. The obvious thing to say is that you should do a thorough job of handicapping. Read everything you can on the international economy, business conditions abroad, how the dollar is doing on foreign exchange markets, the outlook for overseas stock markets, and the activities of foreign companies, in such periodicals as the *Wall Street Journal, Barron's* magazine, *Forbes, Business Week, Fortune, Dun's Review,* and the business section of your local newspaper. Also if possible, such foreign sources of information as the *Financial Times,* the *Economist,* and *Euromoney* of London, the *Financial Post* of Canada, the *Japan Times* of Tokyo, and whatever else you can lay your hands on in the way of international business literature.

However, subscribing to all these periodicals soon adds up to a sizable investment in money, and perhaps more time and attention than you can afford to give them.

Fortunately there is a better way. It takes up very little of your time, it concentrates precisely on what you want to know, and best of all it is free. All you have to do is ask for the latest quarterly reports of some of the closed-end funds or mutual funds whose addresses are given in the previous two chapters. Let us say, for example, that you are thinking of investing in Germany, Scandinavia, Italy, Australia, or Japan. Here is some of the information you can pick up in just a few minutes by reading the eight- to sixteen-page quarterly reports of the funds specializing in those countries.

At the time of writing, this is what Dr. Rolf-Ernst Breuer and Christian Strenger, chairman and president of the Germany Fund, have to tell you as investment professionals about the German economy and stock market. "The German economy is nearing its fifth year of cyclical recovery and well along into the expansion phase. . . . Reflecting the positive economic outlook, the German stock market rallied smartly from its three-month decline. . . . From July through September the Frankfurt stock index rose

16.2%, including the appreciation of the Deutsche Mark against the U.S. dollar over the same period. . . . The Fund's strategy has been to overweight investment in companies emphasizing German domestic activities. This policy reflected the German economy's transition from export-driven growth toward domestic expansion. The Fund, therefore, invested more heavily in companies specializing in consumer-oriented activities, as opposed to those exporters whose earnings were materially affected by the appreciation of the Deutsche Mark against the U.S. dollar."

There you have it from two pros who are laying their reputation on the line managing a $75 million investment fund. They give you a lot of other information in their report, including key statistical data on the German economy, and best of all, thumbnail sketches of the companies that are Germany Fund's biggest holdings. For instance: "ASKO—a fast-growing mass merchandising chain, this former co-op owns and operates self-service department stores, supermarkets, clothing stores, and a do-it-yourself builders' supply chain. It also operates stores in Switzerland and holds a participation in a Texas supermarket chain."

Unfortunately ASKO shares are not available in ADR form in the United States, but this company might be an interesting possibility to explore when we get to the chapter on buying foreign stocks in their own markets overseas.

Scandinavia Fund's quarterly report issued in January 1987 also contains a wealth of useful information in its sixteen pages: graphs of the Swedish, Danish, Norwegian, and Finnish stock market indexes over the past year; graphs of the four countries' currency exchange rates with the U.S. dollar over the past year; and economic data and comments on all four nations. Scandinavia Fund president Bjorn Carlson notes in the report that the fund has eliminated all its investments in Norway for the present, and has concentrated on buying Danish shares in the latest quarter. The fund now has 55% of its assets in Sweden, 35% in Denmark, and 10% in Finland.

Carlson remarks that the Norwegian economy was hurt by the falling price of oil, its major export, and a rising inflation rate. The reasons for buying Danish stocks look rather dubious to an outsider, since "after a strong 1985, the Danish market became overpriced and as a reaction risk capital was withdrawn." Nevertheless, Carlson adds, "Foreign investment in the Danish market has increased continuously."

The underlying reason for Scandinavia Fund's buying of Danish stocks might possibly be deduced from another statement in Carlson's report to stockholders: "Most Swedish and Finnish companies have two categories of common stock, 'free shares' and 'restricted shares.' Restricted shares can only be purchased by nationals of the particular country, while free shares, which generally represent 20 to 40% of a company's capitalization, can be purchased by any investor. Free shares generally trade at a premium to restricted shares."

With Norway out for general economic reasons, and Swedish and Finnish shares at a premium, the only remaining possibility is Denmark. Without knowing anything more about Scandinavia than what is in this fund's quarterly report, one is tempted to conclude that Scandinavia Fund might be trying to make the best of a temporarily bad situation.

However, the Scandinavia Fund report is a fertile seedbed of ideas for possible investments when the investment scene in the Scandinavian countries becomes more attractive. The fund has holdings in ASEA, Ericsson, Pharmacia, and Volvo of Sweden, and Instrumentarium of Finland, all of which are available as ADRs in the U.S. over-the-counter market.

Now let's see what we can get out of the quarterly report from Italy Fund, signed by Heath B. McLendon, chairman, and Mario D'Urso, president. It may give us some explanation for why the fund is selling at a discount. It seems that one reason could be politics, but the report comments that "while the recent political turmoil has left many foreigners shaking their heads in confusion, we feel the outcome is understandable and positive. . . . In Italian politics, it seems, the more things change, the more they are the same."

Meanwhile, "The economic situation remains unchanged: inflation continues to fall, the balance of trade continues to improve and the public sector debt remains a problem. . . . The case for the Italian equity market has not changed. Following a big increase last year we expect corporate profits will rise by 25% this year and up to 40% next year."

The Italy Fund report then tells you why it likes some of the main companies in its portfolio: "Benetton . . . a world leader in the fashion clothing business, with 3,200 outlets in 57 countries. . . . SAI, the third-largest insurance company in Italy . . . future growth likely to be concentrated in the life insurance sector. . . . CIR (Compagnie Industriale Riunite) is an industrial holding company of Carlo de Benedetti, who is thought by many to be the outstanding entrepreneur in Italy. CIR's growth has been very rapid in recent years. . . ." So there you have three more possibilities to explore when investing on your own in the Italian market.

Moving on to the Antipodes, this is what Sir Roden Cutler, chairman, and Brian M. Sherman, president, of First Australia Fund have to say in their latest quarterly report: "The Australian share market built on the strength shown in the September quarter. . . . The All Ordinary Shares Index rose 18.1% over the quarter to a peak of 1473 points at December 31. . . . The Australian dollar appreciated during the December quarter as against both the U.S. dollar and a trade-weighted basket of currencies . . . an increase of 5.8% in U.S. dollar terms over the quarter. . . . A fall in interest rates during 1987 will allow the economy to grow at a modest rate in 1987, with economic growth expected to average slightly under 3%. . . . Inflation is expected to fall throughout 1987 to an expected rate of 6.5% to 7% in the December 1987 quarter. . . . Australian shares continue to represent sound investment value within an international context. . . . The fund's emphasis within the industrial sector of the market remains on the service industries, in particular the financial services and media industries. . . ."

The First Australia Fund report then gives you a brief sketch of its main holdings, including "News Corporation Ltd. This company is a major world media group led by the dynamic Rupert Murdoch, now a U.S. citizen. Its major interests are in United

Kingdom newspapers as well as in the U.S. television markets through Metromedia. Growth has been outstanding and shareholders have been constantly rewarded through regular bonus issues."

Now, there is something you can follow up on—immediately if you think Australia Fund might be right about the media sector—for News Corporation Ltd. is listed on the New York Stock Exchange as well as the Sydney Stock Exchange.

And now for Japan Fund, whose latest quarterly report from O. Robert Theurkauf, president, and Jonathan Mason, chairman, notes that during the year "the Tokyo Stock Exchange Index and the Nikkei Dow Jones Average rose 48.3% and 42.6% respectively. The yen increased 26.7% (against the U.S. dollar), resulting in dollar-adjusted gains in these same indexes of 87.9% and 80.7%. . . . In November the election in the United States gave control of the Senate to the Democrats and increased the potential for restrictive trade legislation in 1987" to whittle down Japan's huge trade surplus with the United States.

"In line with the above conditions, the fund in 1986 reduced its participation in automobile shares and in the stocks of secondary export-oriented companies, while additions were made in banks, insurance, retail, consumer products, service and domestic infrastructure companies. . . . Will the Tokyo Stock Market remain strong and the Japanese economy continue sluggish in 1987? Most informed opinion seems to think so. . . . Fears that the Tokyo Stock Exchange may have gone too high are growing. . . . At the same time . . . we see world financial services as a new sector presenting opportunities for Japan to excel, as Tokyo assumes a leadership position in international banking. . . ."

The report also records Japan Fund's major changes of portfolio during the quarter, and it is interesting to note that new investments include 180,000 shares of Sumitomo Bank, which the fund apparently sees as a way of benefiting from Japan's push into the international financial field. It may be noted too that retail companies make up 10% of the fund's portfolio, and that the biggest holding in that sector is Ito-Yokado Co. Ltd., which has "the second-largest retail operation in Japan."

So here are two interesting possibilities to investigate further, for Sumitomo Bank is not only one of the world's biggest international commercial banks, it is also listed in the U.S. over-the-counter market. A quick check in the latest *Wall Street Journal* stock tables reveals that it is selling at fourteen times earnings. Since the average price-earnings ratio for Tokyo stocks is around 50, this stock might be a bargain. And Ito-Yokado Co. might also be worth a phone call to your broker to see if his research department has a report on this company even though it seems richly priced at its current sixty-seven times earnings. Japan Fund, incidentally, was a closed-end fund with a sterling investment record that converted itself into a no-load mutual fund in August 1987, and thus gave its investors a nice 20% gain by eliminating its market discount on the NYSE.

While you are extracting investment ideas from these fund reports, you may observe that they have a certain Panglossian tendency to see the best of all possible outcomes in the best of all possible worlds—which is only natural in view of their common interest in keeping their shareholders happy and satisfied with the fund management. Even so, they are an invaluable source of general information on the foreign stock markets you are interested in, and on particular foreign companies you might consider buying there. A few small investments in some of these foreign closed-end funds and mutual funds might well be rewarding simply to provide yourself with a steady stream of investment ideas, as well as quarterly status reports on how those individual foreign companies are actually turning out for the fund.

At any event, if a foreign company's ADR shows up in the portfolio of a fund, you may be reasonably sure that there is quite an active market for this stock, because a fund, particularly a mutual fund, is unlikely to buy a thinly traded ADR that it will have difficulty unloading.

You may, however, decide to buy an ADR for other reasons:

because of a favorable write-up in *Forbes* or some other business magazine. The first thing to do in that case is to check the daily trading volume in the stock tables in the *Wall Street Journal* or *Barron's*. If only a couple of hundred shares change hands daily this might well be a stock to avoid. It may be difficult to sell. If you are unable to find the stock quote, it could be that the stock did not trade that day, or that it is quoted in the "Pink Sheets" and doesn't get into the newspapers at all. The Pink Sheets are printed daily, giving dealers' bid and asked prices, and your broker will have a copy. But do you really want to buy such an obscure stock where you will have to call your broker every time you want to check its price?

Anyway, a thinly traded stock is unlikely to have much information available on it, simply because brokerage houses don't bother to follow it. Ask your broker if his firm has a research report on it. If they don't, try *Nelson's Directory of Wall Street Research*, an annual publication that sells for $249 (W.R. Nelson & Co., 11 Elm Place, Rye, NY 10580). If the price is too steep, your public library might have it (or get it for you; New Jersey and other states have statewide hookups to fish books out of other branches if your local branch doesn't carry the one you want).

*Nelson's Directory* lists about 500 stock market brokerage and research firms and the names of their analysts, together with the 4,500 stocks they cover, including hundreds of Canadian and other foreign companies. The *Directory* will tell you, for example, that Honda Motor Co. is followed by a dozen analysts in as many American brokerage houses, from Philip Fricke at Goldman Sachs to Wendy Beale at Smith Barney, whereas Hong Kong & China Gas Co. gets the attention of one single analyst, Sharon Li at Merrill Lynch.

*Nelson's Official Research Guide*, a monthly publication (yearly subscription $95) carries this one step further. It tracks research reports on every public company in the world, listing the newest reports each month as they come out. If you find a report on the company that interests you, you would have to contact the re-

search firm and find out whether you can get it free—brokers
hand them out sometimes to attract new customers—or how
much it would cost.

If you do buy some dogs after all this, you can console yourself
with the thought that you are in the best professional company.

And at the end of the year there is one last thing to keep in
mind. Look over all your ADR holdings to make sure that you
have all the necessary tax information from the custodian bank
or your broker. Most foreign countries have a 15% withholding
tax on dividends (except Hong Kong, which has no withholding). In most cases, where the United States has a double taxation treaty with the country involved, you are entitled to credit
on your U.S. tax return for the amount withheld abroad.

# CHAPTER

# FOREIGN STOCKS, AMERICAN BROKER

With a steady source of information from the reports of U.S.-based mutual funds and closed-end funds that specialize in foreign stocks, you may now feel ready to move on from ADRs and tackle overseas stock markets directly if you find a hot stock that is available only abroad.

There are foreign brokers aplenty that are eager for your business outside the United States, and we will discuss them in later chapters, but you do not need them just yet. An American broker, perhaps your current broker, will do to begin with. By dealing with a broker in the United States, you keep your transactions in this country and at least partly under the surveillance of the Securities and Exchange Commission, you deal on familiar terms with a familiar business partner, you save yourself the paperwork of opening a brokerage account in another country, you sidestep possible language problems when dealing with a non-English-speaking country, and you will probably settle all your accounts in dollars, avoiding the complications of foreign exchange transactions.

To begin with you have to play it by ear. When you are ready to buy a foreign stock, let us say for example Norsk Data, ask your present broker to buy it for you. If the brokerage is a small regional firm or a discounter you may be told straight out that it does not deal in foreign stocks quoted outside the United States. Or your current broker may run a somewhat bigger operation and might handle transactions in major markets like London or Tokyo, but be unwilling or unable to handle deals on minor and out-of-the-way markets like the Oslo Stock Exchange. Or he may split the business with a Norwegian broker, so that you end up paying a double commission.

In any case, if your current broker proves incapable of handling the business or charges inflated commissions, you will have to look elsewhere. This means to one of the big American brokerage houses with international operations, such as Merrill Lynch, which is a member of the London, Tokyo, and Toronto stock exchanges and is thus able to handle your purchases and sales through its own branches abroad.

Other American brokerages that operate on a worldwide scale are:

Bear, Stearns & Co.
55 Water Street
New York, NY 10041

Brown Brothers Harriman & Co.
59 Wall Street
New York, NY 10005

Dean Witter Financial Services Inc.
130 Liberty Street
New York, NY 10006

Dillon Read & Co. Inc.
535 Madison Avenue
New York, NY 10022

Donaldson, Lufkin & Jenrette Inc.
140 Broadway
New York, NY 10005

Drexel Burnham Lambert Group Inc.
60 Broad Street
New York, NY 10004

Goldman Sachs & Co.
85 Broad Street
New York, NY 10004

E.F. Hutton Group Inc.
1 Battery Plaza
New York, NY 10004

Kidder Peabody & Co. Inc.
10 Hanover Square
New York, NY 10005

Morgan Stanley & Co. Inc.
1251 Avenue of the Americas
New York, NY 10020

Oppenheimer & Co. Inc.
1 New York Plaza
New York, NY 10004

Paine Webber Inc.
1285 Avenue of the Americas
New York, NY 10019

Prudential Bache Securities Inc.
1 Seaport Plaza, 199 Water Street
New York, NY 10292

Salomon Brothers Inc.
1 New York Plaza
New York, NY 10004

Shearson Lehman Brothers Inc.
World Financial Center
New York, NY 10285

Smith Barney, Harris Upham & Co. Inc.
1345 Avenue of the Americas
New York, NY 10105

Thomson McKinnon Inc.
1 New York Plaza
New York, NY 10004

Wertheim & Co. Inc.
200 Park Avenue
New York, NY 10166

These firms have offices overseas, international experience and know-how, and extensive research operations. They are all equipped to handle your foreign investments if you have the investment clout to make it worth their while. Merrill Lynch, for example, conducts business in twenty-nine countries and employs 140 research professionals in seven offices around the globe. These analysts cover about 1,500 companies, including 250 non-American stocks. Merrill Lynch also offers its Cash Management International Account to investors seeking greater convenience and accessibility in managing their assets. This brokerage account—provided you have at least $25,000 to put in it—allows you to keep your money at work full time. All interest, dividends, securities, and sales proceeds and other idle cash are automatically reinvested daily in an interest-bearing account. You can write checks against this account and withdraw funds from it through a special Visa card. You can also borrow up to the full margin value of your shares and bonds. The securities in the account are insured up to $10 million per client. All your transactions are settled in dollars, saving you any foreign exchange hassles.

Merrill Lynch will even manage your international investments if you have at least $500,000 to invest and open a discretionary account through Merrill Lynch Asset Management, which has operations in New York, London, and Tokyo. Merrill Lynch portfolio managers will then take all the day-to-day decisions out of your hands. Merrill Lynch Asset Management currently manages $75 billion worth of investments.

If you are a small investor who is not eligible for these special services, the weak link in the chain is likely to be the person you deal with, your account executive. The AE is unlikely to have any special expertise in foreign securities or any great interest in them. Nor is it reasonable to expect your customer's representative to have an encyclopedic knowledge of every stock market and security in the world.

The bottom line is that you will have to take the initiative rather than depend on your broker to suggest any specific foreign investments. When you do propose buying an overseas stock, let us say Deutsche Bank, your account executive will see what information is available from the firm's research department. If you are dealing with Merrill Lynch it just so happens that Deutsche Bank is covered by analyst Bryan Crossley at Merrill Lynch Research.

Once you decide to go ahead, your account executive in the United States, let us say the Mr. Babbin we met in Chapter 1, contacts Merrill Lynch's representative in Frankfurt and gives him your order to buy Deutsche Bank, at the market, with a limit order, or whatever your instructions are. You get your confirmation slip in the mail a few days later ("It takes a little longer than a U.S. trade," Babbin says), and Merrill Lynch keeps your Deutsche Bank stock in street name. That is, the share certificate remains in the Merrill Lynch Frankfurt office, and your account in the United States is credited with a book entry. This arrangement minimizes the difficulties when you want to sell your Deutsche Bank stock, since no share certificates have to be shipped back and forth between Germany and the United States.

The Merrill Lynch Frankfurt office withholds whatever German tax it is required to collect in Germany, but otherwise considers that tax matters are the customer's primary responsibility. It is up to you, for example, to get yourself a credit on your U.S. income tax form for the German tax you have paid. The amount of the American tax credit you can get depends on whatever double taxation agreements are in effect between the United States and the other country involved (in the case of Germany and Deutsche Bank you could claim credit for 15% of the 25% German dividend tax you paid. You would also have to ask the German tax authorities for a refund of the other 10%).

The score or so of big American brokers listed above provide similar services, research, and methods of operation. There are also dozens of foreign brokerage firms that maintain offices in the United States and might well be lumped together with the American brokers, since your dealings with them are also governed by American laws and regulations. In New York City alone there are more than sixty, including ten from Great Britain, fourteen from Japan, nine from Canada, six from Australia, and smaller numbers from the Bahamas, France, Germany, Hong Kong, Israel, South Korea, the Netherlands, and Switzerland.

Most of these U.S. branches handle only institutional business—multimillion-dollar investments of U.S. pension plans and other financial behemoths. They are not interested in the nickels and dimes of retail brokering, unless you are what they delicately call "a high net worth individual," a vague term that apparently means that you have anything from $1 million to $10 million as a minimum amount for them to handle.

These foreign-based brokers would in any case only be useful for investments in their own particular country. However, Nikko Securities, the second-biggest brokerage in Japan, maintains branch offices in San Francisco, Los Angeles, and New York (140 Broadway, New York, NY 10005), from which it serves the accounts of about 3,000 individual American investors who are actively interested in the Tokyo stock market. Nikko notes that its main business in the United States is research, advice, and trading for big Japanese institutions investing in American securities, so that it is also well equipped to serve the American investor in the U.S. market. Each individual client is assigned an account executive knowledgeable in both the U.S. and the Japanese stock markets, as well as other Pacific Basin markets, particularly Sydney, Singapore, and Hong Kong.

You may be able to find other foreign brokers who, like Nikko, handle some retail accounts in addition to their main institutional business. But, like Nikko, they will probably be interested only in "high net worth individuals."

## · INFORMATION ·

It is obviously impractical to invest in stocks where you have no readily available means of checking periodically at the very least on their current prices, and ideally on other information too that may affect your company. The American press carries daily or weekly quotes on several hundred foreign stocks traded on exchanges abroad, but its news coverage of foreign companies tends to be rather ragged.

The *Wall Street Journal* carries daily quotes on about 400 stocks traded on foreign exchanges: about 160 in Toronto, fifteen in Montreal, forty in London, twenty-five in Johannesburg, forty in Tokyo, eight in Brussels, nine in Milan, five in Stockholm, fourteen in Paris, twelve in Zurich and Basel, fifteen in Amsterdam, eleven in Hong Kong, and sixteen in Sydney.

The *Wall Street Journal* also publishes two regional editions abroad: The *Asian Wall Street Journal* (AIA Building, 1 Stubbs Road, Hong Kong) and the *Wall Street Journal Europe* (P.O. Box 2845, 6401 DH Heerlen, the Netherlands). Subscription cost for United States–based readers is $325 a year each (there are also once-a-week editions at $225 a year). Both regional editions carry a lot more regional and international news than the regular U.S. *Wall Street Journal*, but they don't carry any more local stock quotes than the main American edition, except that the Asian *Journal* publishes some additional Far Eastern stock quotes (six Malaysian companies, sixteen Thai, ten Philippine, sixteen Korean, twenty-six Taiwanese, and ten New Zealand stocks) that you may not find elsewhere. The editors of the two regional editions apparently assume that their readers in Asia and Europe can get local stock quotes from the local press.

The *New York Times* has a somewhat shorter list of foreign stock market quotations than the *Journal*, but includes four Buenos Aires stocks.

*Barron's* magazine carries more than 600 stock quotations on a weekly basis, including six from the Singapore Exchange and twenty-five Swedish stocks from the Stockholm Exchange.

These lists tend to overlap the same companies as they all concentrate on the largest and most active stocks in each market. The quotations are all in local currencies.

*Barron's* magazine runs a regular feature titled The International Trader, but most of the American press tends to skimp on foreign stock market commentary in favor of U.S. business news.

The *Financial Times* of London (which as we mentioned in an earlier chapter is available on newstands in a number of American cities) is much more internationally minded in its news coverage. It carries the daily quotations of the entire London stock market list plus about 600 U.S. stocks, plus a further 600 or so stocks traded on other world markets, including eight Austrian stocks, thirteen Danish, ten Finnish, twelve Norwegian, and thirteen Spanish.

The *Financial Times*, the *Wall Street Journal*, the *New York Times*, and *Barron's* thus provide daily or weekly quotations on close to a thousand foreign stocks plus the entire London Stock Exchange list.

You can get the Tokyo Stock Exchange list daily (and a lot of Japanese news) by subscribing to the English-language *Japan Times* (5-4, Shibaura 4-chome, Minato-Ku, Tokyo, 4,960 yen a month airmail to the United States), and you can get weekly quotes by subscribing to the *Japan Stock Journal* (C.P.O. Box 702, Tokyo 100-91, $86.67 yearly airmail subscription).

As for news on foreign company and stock market developments, *Business Tokyo* (P.O. Box 1273, Grand Rapids, MN 55745) is another source of Japanese business news for $60 a year.

*Euromoney* magazine (Nestor House, Playhouse Yard, London EC4 5EX, England) is an excellent source of international financial news at $120 for twelve monthly issues.

A number of foreign banks also run newsletters on their respective countries and their economies. The Bank of New Zealand (P.O. Box 2392, Wellington, New Zealand) publishes *New Zealand Economic Indicators* monthly. Deutsche Bank (40 Wall Street, New York, NY 10005) publishes comments and news on the German economy in its *Atlantic Weekly* newsletter.

Foreign governments also publish periodical information on their national economies, among them the Canadian Government Publishing Center (Supply and Services Canada, Ottawa, KIA OS9), which publishes *The Economy in Brief* quarterly at $20 a year. The first place to inquire about such publications is the foreign country's U.S. consulate in New York or some other major American city.

You also have an assortment of commercial newsletters, among them *Japan Financial Report* (Far Eastern Economic Review Ltd., GPO Box 160, Hong Kong), a biweekly which claims to provide inside information on Japanese business developments for $495 a year.

John P. Dessauer, a former Citicorp international executive, publishes *Dessauer's Journal* (P.O. Box 1718, Orleans, MA 02653), a fortnightly survey of the international scene that provides some interesting investment ideas for $195 a year.

In Britain, the *Financial Times* publishes the *IC Stock Market Letter* (FT Business Information Ltd., Greystoke Place, Fetter Lane, London EC4 1ND), a weekly tipsheet on what British stocks to buy or sell. A subscription costs 110 pounds a year. The *Financial Times* has a whole catalogue of other publications, including a survey of the 500 biggest companies in Europe for 10 pounds.

A number of publications in the international investment field are aimed at the big institutions and are far beyond the average individual investor's budget. The *Investor's Guide* published monthly by Morgan Stanley Capital International Perspective costs $5,000 a year, for example. However, there are somewhat more modestly priced publications, such as *Securities International* (1221 Avenue of the Americas, New York, NY 10020), a weekly for $750 a year. Later chapters will give the names and addresses of publications and services that specialize in specific national markets.

And then, in this age of exploding computer technology, there are computer databases. Wright Investor's Services (Park City Plaza, 10 Middle Street, Bridgeport, CT 06604) offers *Worldscope*, a global company financial database featuring the world's major corporations, 2,000 American and 2,000 foreign companies based in twenty-four countries. The database includes 227 data variables, with six years of history for each company, updated monthly. This service is intended mainly for big institutional investors. The cheapest crack at it that an individual investor can get is by paying an $8,000 annual license fee. However, Wright also publishes *Worldscope Industrial Company Profiles*, a five-volume looseleaf set covering 3,000 worldwide industrial companies for $1,100 a year, including quarterly updates.

*Nexis* (Mead Data Central, P.O. Box 1830, Dayton, OH) lists *Barron's* magazine among its subscribers for financial and business data. This database provides computer access to 150 sources of information, ranging from the Associated Press news wire to articles from *Chemical Week* and the *Bond Buyer* magazine. If you want information on defaulted czarist bonds, for example, you punch into the computer the word "bonds" or "czarist" or "Russian" or "default" and see what it spits out—perhaps half a dozen AP stories and an article or two from the *Bond Buyer*.

*Nikkei*, Japan's leading economic daily (Nihon Keizai Shimbun Inc., 1-9-5 Otemachi, Chiyoda-Ku, Tokyo 100) now publishes an English-language edition in the United States and also provides *Nikkei Telecom*, a database on Japan and Japanese financial markets, as well as *Quick*, an online system for Japanese stock quotations and business news.

Perhaps the ultimate in electronic information is provided by Telemet America Inc. (325 First Street, Alexandria, VA 22314). For the price of a $395 beeper, which you carry around in your pocket, and a $330-a-year subscription fee, you have twenty-four-hours-a-day access to the latest quotes on the NYSE, ASE, and NASDAQ. This includes of course many of the foreign ADRs mentioned in the previous chapter. If you are rafting down the Mississippi or climbing Mount McKinley, don't worry about being out of touch; just punch out what you need and presto, there's the latest quote on Korea Fund or British Petroleum. As this book was going to press, Frederick Parsons, the president of Telemet, was planning to add the London Stock Exchange quotations to his beeper's offerings. Within a few years, the twenty-four-hours-a-day global stock market will no longer be a remote abstraction. You will be able to plug yourself into it permanently, whether you are playing eighteen holes of golf on a Sunday afternoon or tossing sleeplessly at 4 A.M. Monday morning.

# CHAPTER
# 8

## CANADA

At first sight, investing in Canada may seem merely like an extension of investing in the United States. But first appearances can be deceptive. To begin with, the similarities. Buying Canadian stocks is practically as easy as buying American stocks. There is really no unavoidable need even to have your brokerage account in Canada, since any American broker can execute trades for you in Canadian stocks. You can even use one of the U.S. discount brokers, who do not usually deal in foreign stocks (except U.S.-listed ADRs). Canadian securities are so similar to their American counterparts, moreover, that they trade in the United States in their original form, not as ADRs.

You may not even go through a Canadian stock exchange when buying Canadian stocks. Computer and communications technology is rapidly making traditional-type stock exchanges obsolete, and nowhere is this more evident than in United States–Canadian cross-border trading. In September 1985 the Toronto Stock Exchange and the American Stock Exchange in New York launched the first-ever two-way electronic trading link between two stock markets. And in June 1986 the TSE also established a computer linkup with the Midwest Stock Exchange. Canadian and American stocks can thus be dually or even triply listed on the three exchanges, and your order is executed wherever the price is most favorable to you at the time of your trade. Initially, six Canadian stocks were traded through this system. The project then expanded to include all thirty-six Canadian stocks inter-listed on the TSE and the ASE. It will eventually include all the stocks listed on either exchange. At that point buying a stock on the TSE will be technically indistinguishable from buying a stock on the ASE, whether the company is American or Canadian.

To take another example, if you buy a stock on the Vancouver Exchange, your trade might be routed by your broker through ACCESS (American and Canadian Connection for Efficient Securities Settlement), an electronic system that handles the reporting, clearance, and settlement of broker-to-broker trades between the United States and Canada. ACCESS is used by hundreds of American brokers and is available to any broker anywhere in either country. By making use of this fully automated two-way system, trades between American and Canadian brokers are settled in the normal five-day period. Some years ago the process might have taken as long as twelve weeks. All North American listed equities, including NASDAQ over-the-counter stocks, are eligible for settlement through ACCESS. A trans-border trade via ACCESS is identical to any other U.S. over-the-counter trade.

Canada has traditionally welcomed foreign investors, and you can use your money there as freely as if it were in the United States. There are no exchange controls restricting your right to take money in or out of the country, and as a result of this hospitable, laissez-faire atmosphere it is estimated that more than half of Canada's manufacturing industry is foreign-owned, as well as three-quarters of the petroleum and rubber products industries. About 75% of this foreign ownership is American. As many of the companies operating in Canada are subsidiaries of American corporations this has made the Canadian securities market relatively small in proportion to the Canadian economy. It has also led to some restrictions on foreign stock ownership of enterprises in sensitive areas, such as banks, some oil and gas corporations, and broadcasting companies.

The two nations have the largest binational trade in the world, and their economies are so closely intertwined that they tend to be in economic lockstep with each other. Canada had a yearly inflation rate of 13% in the early 1980s, for example, closely matching a similar affliction in the United States. Because of this close relationship, the American and Canadian stock markets also tend to move in the same general direction, if not exactly in unison. The Toronto Stock Exchange 300 Index usually takes the same general course as the American Standard & Poor's 500 Stock Index, although with some rather wilder swings than the S&P 500 in the last ten years or so.

If you were buying the market averages, therefore—by investing in Canadian mutual funds, for example—your results would probably not be too different from buying a U.S. mutual fund. Which removes the major incentive for investing outside the United States.

At this point, however, we come to the dissimilarities between the United States and Canada. The first of these is that the Canadian dollar is not at all the same thing as the U.S. dollar, a fact that may affect your investment results even if U.S. and Canadian stock markets do run in tandem. Back in 1976 the Canadian dollar was worth 2 cents more than the U.S. dollar. Since then—thanks to the declining price of Canadian oil, a burgeoning Canadian federal budget deficit, and a resultant speculative run on the Canadian currency—it has declined fairly steadily to a low of 69.24 U.S. cents in 1986 and its value of 75 U.S. cents at the time of writing. If you put your money into Canadian investments in 1976 at US$1.02 per Canadian dollar and got it back in 1986 at 69.24 cents, your end result is likely to have been highly unsatisfactory. You can, however, protect your investments against such declines in the future (or indeed speculate on a declining U.S. dollar) by buying Canadian dollar options on the Montreal or Vancouver stock exchanges. The options are quoted in U.S. dollars, and each contract is for $50,000, which would thus offset a similar amount invested in Canadian securities.

The next discrepancy is that although apparently an extension of the U.S. economy, the Canadian economy is markedly different in its high degree of dependency on world trade. United States–Canadian trade alone comes to more than $160 billion a year, the biggest binational trading relationship in the world. Canada exports more to the United States than Japan does, more than Germany, France, and Great Britain combined. Both nations are gradually establishing a common duty-free market, but the talks to remove almost all trade barriers have produced more controversy and argument than anything else in the past couple of years and the difficulties seem likely to continue despite the signing of an agreement in October 1987.

Meanwhile Canada is one of the world's largest trading nations with the rest of the world. More than 3 million Canadian jobs, a quarter of the work force, depend on exports, mainly of metals, oil and gas, cereals, and forest and industrial products. The Canadian stock market is thus heavily influenced by world prices for these natural resources and products, a characteristic shared with the Australian and South African stock markets. In fact, outbreaks of racial turmoil in South Africa and the resultant threat to South African gold-mine production tend to benefit Canadian gold-mining stocks particularly.

A further misconception arises from the huge size of Canada on the map. The world's second-biggest country, it is indeed the seventh-largest economy in the world, and perhaps the richest capitalist nation in natural resources to boot. But in actual demographic fact, Canada is only a populated strip about 200 miles wide extending from the U.S. northern border. Canada has only 25.3 million people, not much more than California, and about 80% of them live in this strip, one-third of them in only three metropolitan areas: Toronto, Montreal, and Vancouver. The rest of the country is largely Arctic and sub-Arctic wasteland. As a matter of demographic and geographic fact, therefore, Canada is likely to remain closely related economically to the United States. In terms of investment it will probably march in step with U.S. markets into the indefinite future, except for the fluctuating value of its dollar and its vulnerability to world trade fluctuations.

## · CANADIAN BROKERS ·

As a practical matter, your next concern is a broker for your Canadian stock trading. While your current broker or any other

American broker will do, they may not provide much in the way of Canadian expertise or stock market information. You will also probably find difficulty locating a Canadian broker in the United States, as they tend to deal only with institutional investors abroad. Wood Gundy Corp., for example, has thirty-five offices from coast to coast in Canada and 350 account executives, but its Wall Street office deals only with major institutional investors.

In Canada, you have scores of brokerage firms to choose from. More than seventy are members of the Toronto Stock Exchange, and some of them have considerable international capabilities, with offices in New York, London, Paris, Lausanne, Geneva, Zurich, Hamburg, Hong Kong, Tokyo, Nassau, and Grand Cayman Island. Dominion Securities (P.O. Box 21, Commerce Court South, Toronto, Ontario M5L 1A7) is the largest investment firm in Canada, with offices in all ten Canadian provinces as well as New York, London, Paris, Geneva, Lausanne, Hong Kong, and Tokyo. A member of all Canadian exchanges and of the New York Stock Exchange, Dominion Securities offers research material on most listed companies in Canada.

However, stockbrokers are not the only alternative. In its own version of London's Big Bang, Canada announced a series of sweeping changes for its securities industry in December 1986 and started putting them into effect in mid-1987. For the first time, banks, trust companies, insurance companies, and securities dealers were allowed to compete on an equal footing in many financial services. Investors can make money deposits, buy and sell stocks and bonds, arrange loans, and make other investments all at one institution. Canadian and foreign banks were allowed to buy brokerage firms and become Canadian stock exchange members as of June 30, 1987. The largest banks in Canada are the Royal Bank of Canada, Bank of Montreal, Imperial Bank of Commerce, Bank of Nova Scotia, Toronto-Dominion Bank, and National Bank, all of which have scores of branches throughout Canada and in many other countries.

Royal Bank of Canada (200 Bay Street, Toronto, Ontario M5J 2J5), the country's biggest with 1,500 branches across Canada and operating units in forty-five other countries, offers a

Private Banking Program for its more affluent customers that can function on a worldwide basis. Its services include offshore trusts, real estate financing, investment counseling, and portfolio management. Private Banking Program clients have access to Royal Bank offices in the Channel Islands, Switzerland, Germany, France, and Belgium. Royal Bank's captive Swiss bank, Royal Bank of Canada (Suisse), will take you on in Geneva if you have a minimum of 100,000 Swiss francs to invest.

However, perhaps the best solution for an American investor is to deal, either in the United States or in Canada, with an American broker that has a major interest in Canada and branch operations there. One of these is Merrill Lynch Canada (Merrill Lynch Canada Tower, 200 King Street West, Toronto, Ontario M5H 3W3). Merrill Lynch Canada trades for its own account as an odd-lot dealer and market-maker in Canadian securities. It provides publications such as *Spotlight*, a monthly survey of the Canadian investment scene, general studies of Canadian preferred shares and other market sectors, as well as research reports on individual Canadian companies. Each report, incidentally, notes whether the stock in question is subject to Canadian limitations on foreign ownership and alerts you to the fact that you should check whether it has been cleared for sale to American investors under the blue-sky laws of the state where you live.

Canadian brokers include:

Bache Securities Inc.
33 Yonge Street
Toronto M5E 1V7

Brink, Hudson & Lefever Ltd.
1500 Park Place
666 Burrard Street
Vancouver V6C 3C4

Burns Fry Ltd.
Suite 5000
First Canadian Place
Toronto M5X 1H3

Dominion Securities Pitfield Ltd.
P.O. Box 21
Commerce Court South
Toronto M5L 1A7

Levesque, Beaubien Inc.
150 York Street
Toronto M5H 3S5

Loewen, Ondaatje, McCutcheon & Co. Ltd.
7 King Street East
Toronto M5C 1A2

Wood Gundy Inc.
P.O. Box 274
Royal Trust Tower
Toronto Dominion Center
Toronto M5K 1M7

As one of the first results of Canada's Big Bang, in mid-1987 First National Bank of Chicago acquired a major stake in Wood Gundy.

Other brokers' addresses may be obtained from the Canadian Investment Dealers Association, 33 Yonge Street, Toronto M5E 1G4. The Association was formed in 1916 and has sixty-five members, who between them handle 95% of all Canadian securities transactions.

One advantage of a brokerage account in the United States, of course, is that you are covered by insurance against broker insolvency. In Canada, as soon as you open an account with a member of one of the Canadian exchanges or of the Investment Dealers Association your account is covered by the National Contingency Fund, which was set up by the investment industry to assist the individual investor in the event of any Canadian broker insolvency. It has a relatively small insurance fund of $30 million, but so far no broker has gone into bankruptcy.

If you want to take risks yourself and jack up your profit potential, margin trading is permitted to both Canadian and foreign investors. The actual margin depends on the security being traded and your broker's policy.

Brokerage commissions, which used to be fixed, have been deregulated in Canada, but as in other countries, deregulation has brought little benefit to the small investor. The average commission on orders of less than $5,000 is about what it was before deregulation. The minimum commission at many brokers is $50, although discounters may charge less. Typically, big institutions pay 0.3% to 0.6% and smaller investors 0.9% to 1.1% in commissions on both stocks and bonds. Most brokers also charge annual administration and safekeeping fees, but there are no stock transaction taxes. Securities regulation is in the hands of the ten provincial governments rather than the national government—the Vancouver Stock Exchange comes under the British Columbia Securities Act, for example—but regulations are very similar in all Canadian jurisdictions.

One curious aspect of investing in Canada, by the way, is that if you invest on a substantial scale you may also qualify as an immigrant. Under a program to attract entrepreneurs, investors, and self-employed people, the Canadian government has admitted several thousand immigrants a year who met the minimum requirements. As the regulations are liable to changes you should contact the nearest Canadian consulate or write Investment Canada, P.O. Box 2800, Station D, Ottawa K1P 6A5.

## · CANADIAN EXCHANGES ·

There are five stock exchanges in Canada—Toronto, Montreal, Vancouver, Winnipeg, and Alberta—the largest being Toronto with about 75% of the total business transacted. Montreal accounts for about 21%. There is also an over-the-counter market, where all Canadian bonds are traded.

These exchanges are the primary sources for any further information you may need. They all publish booklets, fact sheets, and periodicals. The Toronto Stock Exchange offers a whole catalogue of books, periodicals, and other publications, among them: the *Toronto Stock Exchange Review* (C$138 a year), a comprehensive monthly digest of investment information used by investment professionals; and the *Daily Record* (C$449 a year), a complete rundown of each day's trading, dividends declared, stock splits, and so on.

The exchanges' addresses are:

Toronto Stock Exchange
The Exchange Tower
2 First Canadian Place
Toronto, Ontario M5X 1J2

Montreal Stock Exchange
Stock Exchange Tower
800 Victoria Square
Montreal, Quebec H4Z 1A9

Vancouver Stock Exchange
Stock Exchange Tower
609 Granville Street
Vancouver, British Columbia V7Y 1H1

Alberta Stock Exchange
64300 5th Avenue South West
Calgary, Alberta P2P 3C4

Winnipeg Stock Exchange
955/167 Lombard Avenue
Winnipeg, Manitoba R3B 3V3.

### Toronto

Founded in 1852 by a group of Toronto businessmen who paid C$6 each for their seats (the price has since risen as high as C$166,000), the Toronto Stock Exchange has far outdistanced its older rival, Montreal. It is not only the predominant stock exchange in Canada, it is also a technological leader among the world's stock exchanges. Its Computer Assisted Trading System (CATS) was the first automated trading system in the world when it was introduced back in 1977. The system is now marketed internationally and has been leased to the Paris Stock Exchange in France. Under the CATS system, some stocks are traded solely by computer. Your buy order goes directly from your broker's computer into the Toronto Stock Exchange, whose computer then holds the order until a corresponding sell order comes in, then matches the two automatically. About half the stocks quoted on the TSE are now traded through CATS.

The TSE also uses other automated systems. The Market Order System of Trading (MOST) handles small market orders for up to 1,099 shares, filling all orders automatically at current bid and asked prices against the accounts of market-makers for each stock. The Limit Order Trading System (LOTS) is an automated trading facility that handles orders at prices on or just outside the current market range.

At the beginning of 1987, 1,087 companies were listed on the TSE, with a total of 1,570 separate issues of stock. These companies can be pretty small, however. The minimum listing requirement is only C$350,000 worth of publicly held shares and at least 200 public shareholders owning at least one board lot. A board lot may be anything from ten shares worth more than C$100 each to 1,000 shares worth 10 cents or less. But as most shares trade between C$1 and C$100, the standard board lot is 100 shares.

Trading on the TSE hit an all-time high in 1986 with 4.9 billion shares changing hands, worth C$63.6 billion. This was up nearly 50% from the record level of 1985. Average daily trading thus came to about 19.5 million shares a day in 1986, with an average share price of about C$12.50.

One peculiarity of the TSE is that it sets maximum spreads between bid and asked prices for individual stocks, based on their price and normal trading activity. For stocks included in the TSE-300 Index the maximum spread is around 29 cents, and for the top 150 stocks it is about 16 cents a share.

The TSE Composite Index of 300 Stocks is perhaps your most reliable guide to price levels in the Canadian stock market and might be compared to the Standard & Poor's 500 Stock Index in the United States. Its base value is 1,000 in the year 1975, so that at its reading of around 2,900 at the time of writing it indicates that Canadian stock prices have nearly tripled over the past dozen years. The TSE-300 Index is divided up into a number of subindices, such as transportation, pipelines, utilities, financial services, and other stocks, which you will find published in the Canadian financial press whenever you need to know how any particular section of the market is doing.

In January 1985 the TSE launched a separate High Technology Index, which comprises twenty-seven Canadian high-tech companies—seven computer firms, thirteen electronics corporations, and seventeen communications companies. The base level is 100 as of December 31, 1974. A list of all the component stocks of these indexes is to be found in the TSE's booklet *Everything You Ever Wanted to Know About the Toronto Stock Exchange*.

Option trading has grown vigorously on the TSE since it was first introduced in 1976. At the time of writing you can buy puts and calls on forty-two stocks, as well as on Canada Long-Term Bonds and a market index option known as TIX that is based on the TSE-300 Index. Each equity option represents 100 shares of the underlying security, while the index option represents 100 units of the index. Equity options are available in 3-, 6- and 9-month time periods, the index option in 1-, 2-, and 3-month periods. Like U.S.-style options, but unlike European options and some Montreal options, which we will get to later, TSE options can be exercised at any time.

The biggest companies listed on the TSE include: Bell Canada Enterprises, Imperial Oil Ltd., Northern Telecom Ltd., Gulf Canada Ltd., Pan Canadian Petroleum Ltd., Canadian Pacific Ltd., Alcan Aluminium Ltd., Texaco Canada Inc., Royal Bank of Canada, Toronto-Dominion Bank, and Thomson Newspapers.

### Montreal

Founded in 1817, the Montreal Stock Exchange was Canada's first stock market. The first also to introduce listed stock options and the only exchange in the world to trade precious-metals certificates, Montreal has a reputation as an innovator. Since 1985 it has been trying to establish itself in the worldwide trading of international stocks by setting up an International Division in which foreign stocks are listed under rules similar to those in their own home country. The project has got off to a slow start, however. The development of the Montreal Stock Exchange was hampered by Quebec's efforts to impose French as the official language of the province, as a result of which a number of corporations and financial institutions migrated to Toronto in the 1970s. However, trading has picked up in more recent years. The yearly total was C$15.9 billion dollars in 1986, about half again as much as the C$10.6 billion recorded in 1985.

More than 600 companies are listed on the Montreal Exchange—over 1,100 separate issues in all. About two-thirds of these are also listed in Toronto, and in fact nearly all major Canadian companies are listed on both exchanges.

The Montreal Stock Exchange publishes seven market indexes that complement the Toronto indicators: the Canadian Market Portfolio Index, as well as indexes of banking, forest products, industrial products, mining and minerals, oil and gas, and utilities stocks. The Exchange also publishes a *Daily Official News Sheet*, a *Montreal Options* monthly newsletter, and a *Monthly Review*.

Montreal is a convenient market to trade in gold, silver, and platinum, through the Exchange's precious-metals certificates. Each gold certificate represents 5 Troy ounces, the platinum certificate 10 ounces, and the silver certificate 250 ounces. The certificate in each case is a receipt for these quantities of precious metals held in insured storage for you in bar or wafer form in a central vault. The advantage of the certificate system is that you do not have to worry personally about storage and insurance against theft, the paperwork, and possibly the assaying involved in taking or delivering physical metals. It is particularly advantageous for silver, which is a bulky commodity to store in any quantity. There is also ease of trading. When you want to buy or sell, the precious metals certificates change hands like ordinary stocks. You can even buy them on margin. The certificates, by the way, are quoted in American dollars.

Montreal is also a link in a worldwide market for gold options, which are traded in 10-ounce lots in Montreal in conjunction with the Vancouver and Sydney stock exchanges and the European Options Exchange in Amsterdam. This global linkup permits trading almost around the clock. Daily closing quotations are published in major Canadian newspapers as well as the *Financial Times* of London and the Australian financial press.

Other options available in Montreal include options on more than twenty Canadian stocks, and—the most active option market in Canada—options on long-term Canadian government bonds. There are two such options, one on the 9½% October 2001 Government of Canada bond (ticker symbol OBA), and the other on the 10¼% February 2004 issue (ticker symbol OBD). Each bond option covers C$25,000 face value of the underlying bond, with expiry months in March, June, September, and December.

There is also a Montreal treasury-bill option contract which covers C$250,000 face value of three-month Government of Canada T-bills. This is a European-style option, which means you cannot exercise it at any time as you can with American-style options. It is only exercisable on its expiry date. This rigid system tends to favor the big institutional hedgers, who do not then run the risk of early assignment of their options. An individual speculator just has to sit there and possibly watch his profits evaporate at times without being able to do anything about it. Another feature of this market is that there is no delivery of T-bills. All contracts are settled in cash, which eliminates a lot of fuss and bother in the way of paperwork.

### Vancouver

The Vancouver Stock Exchange, founded in 1907 to raise capital for emerging resource companies in the Canadian West, has come to be the second-busiest exchange in North America—in share volume at least—after the New York Stock Exchange. An astounding 3.5 billion shares changed hands in 1986 in Vancouver, but at an average price of about C$1.30 a share, the monetary volume of C$4.5 billion was of course nowhere near New York's. Vancouver is one of the major venture capital markets of the world. The Exchange states quite frankly that it provides "predominantly high-risk, speculative offerings" since it is primarily a market "for junior companies to go public and raise risk capital."

The minimum listing requirement is that a company should have expended C$60,000 of its own assets as well as raising at least C$100,000 in seed capital and another $75,000 in its first public offering. If you have a small company and want to list it, ask for the *Vancouver Stock Exchange Membership Directory*, which will give you all the details on all VSE-member brokers and their minimum financing requirements. About a quarter of all VSE stock trading originates in the United States, and more than 200 of the 1,900 VSE-listed corporations are U.S.-based. Most of them are small high-tech companies. Nearly 100 are dually quoted with NASDAQ in the United States. The Canadian stocks are mostly involved in exploration and development of precious metals, although a growing number (about 30%) are high-tech or junior industrial firms. Listed stocks also include oil and gas companies and some larger industrial corporations. American brokers that are members of the VSE include Merrill Lynch, Bache Securities, Paine Webber, Dominick, and Dean Witter.

The VSE has also diversified into options trading in both equities and commodities. Together with Montreal it is part of the worldwide precious-metals options market and allows you to hedge your Canadian investments through its Canadian dollar option.

The VSE's monthly *Review* (C$65 a year) and its *Daily Bulletin* (C$475 a year) provide quotations, trading volume, and other information. Your broker can access VSE quotation devices through *Canadian Consolidated Data Feed*. American publications providing coverage of VSE stocks include *North American Gold Mining Industry News*, *Western Mining News*, the *National OTC Stock Journal*, and *Penny Stock News*, besides, of course, Canadian general financial periodicals and the *Northern Miner*.

### Alberta and Winnipeg

The two smallest Canadian exchanges, Alberta and Winnipeg, deserve at least a mention. The Winnipeg Exchange consists of a network of brokers who trade by phone, mostly in mining, oil, and energy stocks. You can also trade in precious metals and agricultural commodities in Winnipeg. The Alberta Stock Exchange, founded in Calgary in 1913 during the Turner Valley oil boom, has closed a couple of times since then due to ensuing busts in the oil and securities industries. Discovery of oil in the Leduc field in 1947 injected new life into it. It is a small-investors' market, with the retail trader accounting for most of the activity, which amounted to 370 million shares in 1986, with an average share price of only C$1.29. About 650 issues of slightly more than 500 companies are traded. You will find a lot of outfits with names like Petrohunter Energy Ltd. and Stellar Resources Corp. The *Alberta Stock Exchange Monthly Review* gives you a complete rundown of the latest prices and trading figures.

## · BONDS ·

Canadian bonds are not listed on any formal exchange but are quoted over the counter through a network of bond dealers' offices. Both bearer and registered bonds are available, and interest is paid semiannually. The usual denomination is C$1,000. Besides Canadian federal government, provincial, and municipal bonds, there are various kinds of corporate bonds known as mortgage bonds, collateral trust bonds, debentures, and notes. While we lack space to go into their various idiosyncracies, one important point to remember is that municipal bonds in Canada, unlike those in the United States, are not tax-exempt. This is one very good reason for the fact that their yields are usually higher than those of U.S. municipals. There are two firms that analyze the quality of Canadian bond issues, Canadian Bond Rating Service and the Dominion Bond Rating Service.

Other oddities of the Canadian market include extendable bonds, which allow the investor to hold the bonds and collect interest past maturity; and retractable bonds, which allow you to redeem your bonds early. A number of Canadian companies too have issued preferred stock with oddball features not found in the United States, such as the commodity-indexed preferred stock of Inco. These are exchangeable for the cash equivalent of a specified amount of nickel or copper, based on the average London Metal Exchange cash price.

## · TAXES ·

One welcome feature of Canadian bonds is that for nonresidents of Canada the interest and capital gains on Canadian government bonds are tax-exempt, and besides the lack of withholding tax there is also no stamp duty.

Otherwise, Canadian tax laws tend to favor equities over interest-bearing investments. For Canadian taxpayers interest is fully taxed as income. Dividends are treated more leniently, so that 33 cents of every dollar of dividend income is deductible from tax payable on other Canadian income. The government, trying to encourage equity investments by its citizens, allows every Canadian resident to earn up to C$500,000 in capital gains tax-free over one lifetime. Dividend income only attracts 6% taxes, and the average Canadian taxpayer pays 37 cents of every dollar of income in taxes. This is a considerable incentive to invest.

Foreign investors receiving Canadian dividends have a 25% withholding tax deducted at the source, unless they are residents of a country with a double-taxation treaty with Canada, such as the United States, in which case the withholding is reduced to 15%. Capital gains received by foreign investors are not subject to Canadian capital gains tax.

## · INVESTMENT FUNDS ·

Apart from the tax benefits, Canadian equities have tended to outperform Canadian fixed-income investments in recent years. The equity mutual funds qualifying for government-approved personal retirement plans achieved an average annual return of 16.4% in the 1980–1985 period compared with only 11.8% for term deposits and guaranteed interest rate investments in the same period.

There are about 200 investment funds, or mutual funds, in Canada, and more than 1.5 million Canadians have money in them. They include load funds, no-loads, and—another Canadian peculiarity—negotiable-load funds. The maximum load is 9%. Their performance records over the past few years are reported monthly in the *Financial Times* and the *Financial Post*.

The Investment Funds Institute of Canada (70 Bond Street, Toronto, Ontario M5B 1X2), which represents about 85% of the entire investment fund industry, can send you a list of funds and their addresses. Most of them are not registered with the SEC and may be reluctant to do business with you. If you are an expatriate who lives outside the SEC's jurisdiction, you might consider funds such as One Decision Fund, which splits its portfolio fifty-fifty between Canadian stocks and bonds, or Sentinel Canada Equity Fund, which invests in Canadian common stocks, or Sentinel Canada Bond Fund, which specializes in Canadian bonds. One fund that *is* available to American investors is Canada Fund Inc., 1 Wall Street, New York, NY 10005.

Besides making all your investment decisions for you in Canada, a mutual fund offers the additional advantage of a tax statement at year end, simplifying the complications you might run into by investing in Canadian stocks on your own.

## · INFORMATION ·

Besides the literature available from the Canadian stock exchanges, Canadian financial information is to be found in these publications, among others: the *Toronto Globe & Mail* (daily); the *Financial Post* (481 University Avenue, Toronto, Ontario M5W 1A7) and the *Financial Times* (920 Yonge Street, Toronto, Ontario M4W 3L5), both weeklies; *Canadian Bu$iness* (70 The Esplanade, Toronto, Ontario M5E 1R2, C$40 a year), *Report on Business*, and *Your Money*, all monthlies; and *Market Matters*, a newsletter published by the Toronto Stock Exchange.

# CHAPTER
# 9

## SWISS BANKS AND FOREIGN MONEY HAVENS

There comes a time for everything. The baby's umbilical cord is cut. The fledgling eagle flaps uncertainly off its parents' eyrie. The astronaut floats free in space. The young kangaroo crawls out of his mother's pouch. The twelfth-grader goes off to college. Eventually the time comes to do your own thing.

There are two basic reactions to these rites of passage. You feel that you are either facing a threatening, overwhelming universe out there or entering a new realm of opportunity and that the world is your oyster. You are either a pessimist or an optimist. There are quite evidently valid reasons for both points of view.

As an international investor venturing out on your own for the first time from the United States and Canada, you may quite legitimately be one or the other. If we had a crystal ball that was any better than yours we could tell you what to be. As we don't, this chapter is for pessimists, and the next chapter is for optimists. You will have to make your own choice.

If you take the gloomy view, as we plan to do in this chapter, you want the safest possible refuge you can find in this vale of tears and sorrow. The initial problem, in that case—if you live in the United States—is that in the opinion of many people abroad you already reside in one of the world's safest places. These foreigners see in the United States the most politically stable country in the world, the strongest power militarily, and the wealthiest economically. Hundreds of thousands of non-American investors around the globe look on the United States as the world's strongest bastion of capitalism, the safest place for

their money, and—if they could only get an immigration visa—
the safest place on earth for themselves and their families.

As a pessimist who has seen paradise from the inside, you may
have a different point of view. You may wonder at these foreigners' naive faith in a U.S. dollar that has lost a huge chunk
of its value against other currencies such as the Japanese yen,
the German mark, and the Swiss franc. You may worry about
the $2 trillion U.S. national debt that has doubled from $1
trillion in less than a decade, and that may double again in the
next ten years. Or the $250 billion the United States now owes
abroad. This growing burden makes it the world's biggest debtor,
outborrowing even such chronic $100-billion international dead-
beats as Brazil and Mexico—a sad decline when you consider
that Uncle Sam was up to only a few years ago the biggest creditor
nation in the world. Or you may see the chronic $150 billion-
plus U.S. foreign trade deficit that makes it unlikely that the
country will pay off its foreign debt any time soon. Or back-to-
back federal budget deficits in the $100 billion to $200 billion
range, which make it improbable that the U.S. government will
pay off its national debt in the foreseeable future. Or you may
be alarmed at the parlous state of the American financial system,
in which one out of every five commercial banks is losing money—
raising questions as to whether the Federal Deposit Insurance
Corporation will be able to pay off depositors against a growing
spate of bank failures now numbering more than 100 a year, the
highest number since the Great Depression. Or the even more
parlous condition of the savings and loan industry, where the
Federal Savings and Loan Insurance Corporation has already run
out of funds and so has refrained from liquidating technically
bankrupt thrift institutions, lacking the money to pay off their
depositors. As of this writing, nearly 400 of the nation's 3,200
savings and loans are overdue for mandatory liquidation.

With such a view of the American economy you may develop
a sense of impending doom and start looking around for a safer
haven for your money. What you need above all is a bank account
in a safer place than your savings and loan on Main Street,
U.S.A. After all, about half of all U.S. banks did collapse in

the Great Depression, and the government-imposed bank holiday in 1933 prevented depositors from getting their money out before many of the banks went under—unless they had the foresight to see what was coming earlier on and take precautions. Americans' gold holdings were confiscated by the government at that time too. The only safe place for your money and your gold back in 1933 was somewhere abroad.

If a similar panorama appears in your scenario for the future, you need a foreign bank account to hold at least some of your money and some gold abroad. The question is, where?

This is not really a question of weighing minor details—as you might in choosing a U.S. bank—balancing the merits of a 6% savings account in London against a 3% account in Zurich, for example, or mulling the relative convenience of a checking account in pounds rather than in German marks. What you need initially is a broad overview, a long-term perspective, and a satisfactory answer to the question, is this the safest place for my money?

You can of course open a bank account anywhere in the world from London to Tokyo (you can at least at the time of writing this, but foreign bank accounts may no longer be allowed by the U.S. government in the future if our gloomy scenario should actually unfold). However, there are about a dozen money havens that actively seek foreign funds through tax breaks, secrecy provisions, and other incentives. These havens include fair-sized nations, ministates, and even colonies. The biggest, ranked by the amount of foreign money stashed away there, is the Cayman Islands in the Caribbean. Luxembourg and Switzerland come next, running neck and neck, followed by Singapore, the Bahamas, Hong Kong, the Channel Islands, Bahrain, Panama, and Liechtenstein. Austria and other countries are also working busily to sweep up foreign money with anonymous numbered accounts and other attractions, but are nowhere near the multibillionaire status of the top ten havens mentioned above.

The front-runner is an astonishingly dark horse, a British crown colony consisting of three microscopic islands in the Caribbean between Jamaica and Cuba. These islets, covering all of

100 square miles, are inhabited by 22,000 natives—mostly the descendants of marooned pirates, shipwrecked sailors, and runaway slaves—who share their little tropical paradise with about 18,600 corporations, more than 450 international banks, 320 insurance companies, an unknown number of tax-free trusts, and a floating population of expatriate bank managers.

It is estimated that about $200 billion has sought refuge in the Cayman Islands, a ratio of about $9 million per islander. The attraction is that there are no taxes on personal income in the Cayman Islands, no corporate profits or capital gains taxes, no gift taxes, no estate duty or death taxes. It is a tax haven pure and simple. It also appears to have become a haven for illegal drug money, a matter that concerns the colonial authorities in London and has led them to cooperate with U.S. lawmen investigating large shipments of money from the United States to Grand Cayman by wire or on the weekly plane from Houston and Miami.

This is in a word a midget-size bolt-hole in the middle of nowhere, with practically no local autonomy that cannot be overridden by straitlaced bureaucrats in London, and that has come under the basilisk eye of U.S. drug-law enforcement officers and tax inspectors.

The Channel Islands—Jersey, Guernsey, Alderney, and Sark—just off the coast of France, are another little anomaly left over from the global sweep of British imperial history. They are the last remaining French legacy of William the Conqueror, the duke of Normandy who invaded England in 1066. William's successors on the British throne subsequently lost Normandy and all their other French possessions except the Channel Islands. The queen of England thus rules as the heir to William the Conqueror. But the Channel Islands never were and are not now a part of the Kingdom of Great Britain, or its welfare state, or its stifling income tax system, or its confiscatory death duties. The British Parliament's word is not law here. Because of all this, close to $60 billion in foreign funds are tucked away in the banks of Jersey and Guernsey, the two main islands. This is largely British expatriate and European money. The Channel Islands, however, are not all that secure from foreign interference. They were the only part of the royal domains to be occupied by Nazi troops in World War II.

Singapore, an independent city-state on a 238-square-mile island between Indonesia and Malaysia, used to be a British colony, the Royal Navy's main bastion in the Far East. It reinforces once more the impression that one of the British Empire's main historical functions was to leave a string of money havens around the globe. Singapore is now an independent nation peopled and run by highly competent Chinese who have turned a backward, underdeveloped colony into a modern industrial economy, and who realize that their ministate can only survive in the world on free trade and a competitive free enterprise system. Some of Singapore's government ministers sound like Asian members of the John Birch society when they talk about the Soviet Union.

Singapore has developed a strong manufacturing base, a sophisticated financial system, and a vigorous stock market. Foreign money in Singapore is estimated at more than $150 billion. But this ministate does not have a secure position in the world. The island was taken over by the Japanese in World War II and would probably be a strategic hotpoint in any future global hostilities because of its position at a chokepoint on the oil lifeline between Japan and the Middle East oil fields.

Hong Kong, an enclave on the coast of China, still is a British colony. It has duplicated the free enterprise manufacturing success of Singapore, and has even exceeded it in creating one of the major financial centers of the world. Unfortunately, as Britain has formally agreed to hand Hong Kong back to China in 1997, a bank account in Hong Kong means that your money will be under the jurisdiction of communist bureaucrats from Peking within another few years. This is probably the least alluring prospect of all the world's money havens. Nevertheless, Hong Kong is host to about $110 billion in foreign funds, whose owners presumably have rather a short-term perspective.

Bahrain, an oil-exporting island state in the Persian Gulf, has taken in about $50 billion in foreign, largely Arab, money. Small, defenseless against larger neighbors, dependent on the ups and downs of the world oil market, Bahrain can be discarded out of hand by Americans who are not working or involved in the Middle East, on the grounds of remoteness, language problems, and its exposed position in an Islamic world that is largely alien to Western business practices—Islam prohibits the payment of interest, for one thing.

Panama, with its $15 billion or so in foreign money, is Latin America's representative in the money-haven fraternity, and serves a mainly Latin American clientele, largely composed of South American businessmen and others who set up dummy Panamanian corporations to cover up the trail of flight capital on its way to Miami, New York, or Zurich. The country itself is no more immune to military coups and other political disturbances than any other Latin American republic.

Luxembourg, a 1,000-square-mile ministate of 360,000 people sandwiched between Germany and France, gave its name to Franz Lehar's operetta *The Count of Luxembourg,* and is in fact a grand duchy ruled by a real live grand duke, a businesslike blueblood who has been pushing his little country into the big global bank leagues as an alternative to the traditional and deeply depressed Luxembourg steel industry. The policy has achieved remarkable success. Ten percent of the population now gets its livelihood from banking in one way or another, the unemployment rate has shrunk in the 1980s to a minuscule 1.3%, and the grand duchy is awash in about $160 billion handled by hundreds of international banks that have set up shop there.

Luxembourg is perhaps the most serious contender of all the money havens we have discussed so far. Unfortunately, it was also the scene of the opening shots on the Western Front in World War I, was overrun by Hitler's panzers in World War II, and as a member of the North Atlantic Treaty Organization is almost certain to be involved in any future large-scale European hostilities.

Which brings us to the last major foreign money haven, Switzerland—and its politically independent economic appendage,

Liechtenstein. Ruled by an archduke, the 30,000 Liechtenstein-ers occupy 61 square miles between Switzerland and Austria. They run the little country on the revenue from postage stamps and do a thriving business registering dummy foreign corporations that operate out of post office boxes. They use Swiss money, and the Swiss handle their foreign affairs. Liechtenstein is probably the most politically stable country in Europe, one of its two parties being conservative and the other archconservative. They have not yet made up their minds whether to give women the vote.

In all this motley crew of foreign money havens, Switzerland stands out like a giant among pygmies. This is a decent, solid, middle-class, politically stable, financially responsible nation in the heart of Europe. Switzerland has not been involved in any foreign conflicts since the last of the Napoleonic Wars in 1815. It is so intent on preserving its neutral status today that it even refuses to join the United Nations, where it might have to vote on one side or the other of international disputes.

In the event of economic, political, or military disasters for the West, Switzerland would have to be the first and perhaps the only choice of an American seeking a place where his money would be safer than it is in the United States. Switzerland is practically immune to revolution and political upheaval. It has been a democratic republic for more than 600 years, and it prac-tices democracy at a grass-roots level that is unknown even in the United States, through citizen plebiscites on major national questions and in some cases through citizens' meetings in the town square to settle local matters. On the economic level, the Swiss currency is backed several times over by gold, the Swiss government is a model of fiscal responsibility in comparison with the profligacy of the U.S. Congress, and the banking system is on a much sounder footing than its American counterpart, bank failures being practically unknown. On the pure survival level, Switzerland, as a neutral nation, is not only considerably less likely to become embroiled in external hostilities than the United States, it is also more likely to survive the fallout of any nuclear conflict as well. The Swiss civil defense program provides for the survival, medical care, housing, and feeding of the entire population for one year after a nuclear exchange.

This prosperous neutral enclave in the center of Europe is an improbable conglomeration of 7 million ethnic Germans, French, and Italians who do not even share a common language. In a country half the size of South Carolina, with twice the population density of China and seven times that of the United States, the Swiss enjoy one of the highest living standards in the world despite a habitat one-quarter of which is barren Alpine slopes fit only for ski-slides and the remainder devoid of any natural resources except mountain streams for hydroelectric power.

Swiss neutrality is no mere pious declaration. It is backed up by a force that is unlikely to be challenged lightly. Every Swiss male citizen is required to be a part-time soldier from the ages of twenty to fifty. The citizen's employer pays his salary while he is on leave from his job for summer training or winter maneuvers. This system enables Switzerland to maintain at little government cost—about 2% of gross domestic product—an army strength equivalent to one-tenth of the entire population. The United States would have to maintain armed forces of 24 million instead of the current 2 million to match this proportion.

The Swiss citizen is obligated to maintain his army uniform, kit, and weapons throughout his life. So this is a country where citizens are actually required to keep automatic rifles in their homes, and yet the death rate by firearms is less than in some police precincts of New York City. It is also a country where 625,000 armed men can be in the field within forty-eight hours, where every bridge, pass, and tunnel on every possible invasion route has been prepared for demolition, where every major road is enfiladed by hidden artillery with fields of fire cut in swaths through the surrounding woods. Even Adolf Hitler, who was not squeamish in such matters, stayed on his side of the Swiss border.

If you are concerned not only with financial survival but also with actual physical survival in a nuclear-threatened world, this is the place. Switzerland is the country that will probably pick up all the pieces after a nuclear war. Should you try to move to

Switzerland, you will discover another peculiarity of Swiss democratic freedom. It is not the Swiss national government that will decide on your residence application but the provincial government of the canton where you want to settle. It is as though the state of Wyoming, not the federal government, were to decide to admit you or not as an immigrant to the United States.

However, immigration problems are beyond the scope of this book. We are concerned with finding a safe haven for your money, and the Swiss franc has been a considerably safer preserver of value than the dollar in the past few decades. Fifteen years ago the Swiss franc cost 25 U.S. cents. At the time of writing it is worth 72 cents. In the past sixty years, the Swiss franc has not lost value against any other currency (except briefly for a few years at a time).

What is behind this performance is solid gold backing (the Swiss franc is not formally exchangeable for gold at a fixed rate, but the government has more than enough gold to redeem all its paper money for gold if it ever had to), a perennially balanced budget, a small national debt, a sizable foreign trade surplus, low unemployment, one of the highest economic growth rates among industrialized nations, and, as a result of all this, one of the lowest inflation rates in the world—0.75% in 1986 and a little over 1% in 1987.

This sort of political and economic background has attracted a flow of foreign money into Switzerland from all over the world for many years now, and the Swiss have built up an internationally oriented banking industry specifically geared to handle the influx. There are 593 banks in Switzerland, one for every 1,200 citizens. Despite this overcrowding, their failure rate is very low. In the United States, 120 banks failed in 1985—the highest number in a single year since the Great Depression. But 1985 was not to hold that dubious distinction for long—138 banks failed in 1986, and more than 200 in 1987. Over 20% of all American banks are losing money at the time of writing in 1987, and about 1,000 troubled American banks are on a U.S. bank regulators' "watch list." In Switzerland, three banks have failed in the past thirty years.

Swiss banks might seem riskier because the Swiss national banking system has no national depositor insurance like the Federal Deposit Insurance Corporation (FDIC) in the United States. However, Swiss bankers point to their own record as proof that Swiss banks are as safe as or safer than American banks. The FDIC insurance fund, in fact, represents less than 2% of all U.S. bank deposits. It is adequate to cover the depositors of a string of small failed banks in Oklahoma or upstate New York or wherever, but it would be swamped if a couple of the major New York City banks were to go under as a result of their multibillion-dollar loans to major debtor countries like Brazil and Mexico. The FDIC's sister organization, the Federal Savings and Loan Insurance Corporation, is already out of funds and unable to liquidate a number of technically insolvent thrifts.

Otto Roethenmund, formerly vice-chairman of the board of the Foreign Commerce Bank of Zurich, adds also that "FDIC officials claim that insured depositors have never lost a dime, but that misses the point. Thousands of partially insured depositors have lost money because the FDIC covers only the first $100,000 of deposits in American banks."

Roethenmund, who now runs his own New York–based international money-management firm, says, "I know of no Swiss banks that are on any danger list of the Swiss bank authorities. Swiss tax laws encourage banks to accumulate reserves. Unlike U.S. banks, Swiss banks set aside the maximum possible reserves every year. In any of the leading Swiss banks you'll see assets to liability ratios three or four times those at the best U.S. banks, and Swiss bank balance sheets are almost always understated when it comes to their reserves."

In addition to safety, Swiss banks have also traditionally offered secrecy, to the point where the Swiss numbered bank account became a staple of spy fiction and popular folklore. Political leaders in bad odor like Ferdinand Marcos of the Philippines and Jean Claude Duvalier of Haiti have reportedly used anonymous numbered accounts to stash away billions of dollars in Switzerland. This is highly embarrassing to the Swiss, who originally set up their bank secrecy provisions to protect foreign refugees from political persecution, not to shelter deposed dictators.

The Swiss Banking Law of 1934, which still governs Swiss banking secrecy, was passed specifically to protect the deposits of foreign customers, particularly from Germany. Under the Nazi regime it was an offense punishable in some cases by death to send money out of the Third Reich. Businessmen, democratic opponents of the Nazis, Jews, and others who crossed the border to open Swiss accounts were then extremely vulnerable. Nazi agents and ordinary blackmailers would try to bribe Swiss bank employees to reveal the foreign depositor's identity and threaten dire consequences to the depositor himself if he still lived in Germany or to his relatives there if he had managed to flee abroad. The 1934 Swiss law made it a criminal offense to deliberately reveal a client's identity, punishable by six months in jail and a 50,000-franc fine. A mere unintentional slip of the tongue can cost a Swiss bank employee a 30,000-franc fine. Even after leaving the bank's payroll he is still bound by bank secrecy for the rest of his life.

To a fundamentally decent country like Switzerland, however, it has become an embarrassment to have the likes of Marcos and Duvalier, as well as the protagonists of American and British insider stock market deals, American CIA agents, international drug dealers, Mafia dons, and other shady characters taking advantage of the bank secrecy law. The Swiss government has ordered the banks to collaborate with foreign authorities in the Marcos and Duvalier and some other cases, raising fears that the bank secrecy law is not much good anymore. Nevertheless, despite all the cooperation from the Swiss government, even the Marcos case—where the Swiss government council did not even wait for a formal request for assistance from the Philippines before it pressured the banks to freeze the Marcos assets in Switzerland—seemed destined to remain tied up in the law courts for years. In fact, it seemed uncertain that the Philippine government would ever be able to crack Swiss banking secrecy and recover the money it said Marcos had embezzled. Marcos's lawyers raised a barrage of appeals, and the Swiss federal authorities admitted they could not lift bank secrecy until all these legal disputes were settled, which were in for a long run, with appeals expected all the way up to the Swiss Supreme Court.

For ordinary run-of-the-mill foreign customers, Swiss bankers insist that the bank secrecy law is as strong as it ever was. As an average citizen, your major concern is likely to be a charge by the IRS that you are using your foreign bank account to evade U.S. income taxes. In this case the Swiss position is that tax evasion may well be a criminal offense in the United States, but it is only a misdemeanor in Switzerland, and Swiss banks will open their records to foreign authorities only by court order in cases where the foreign customer has committed an act that is considered a crime under Swiss law.

As for the famous "Swiss numbered bank account," you might as well leave it to people like James Bond. There are no anonymous bank accounts in Switzerland. Every Swiss bank is required to establish its customer's identity. Roethenmund states flatly that the numbered account "is more trouble than it's worth. All the numbered account means is that when the paperwork moves through the bank, it carries a number instead of a name. The name of the client is available only to the manager and one or two other officers. But otherwise there is no difference from an ordinary Swiss bank account, which has the same protection from the Swiss bank secrecy law. It also has two big disadvantages. You actually have to go to Switzerland to set up an account. And you have to go there in person to make cash deposits and withdrawals."

## · OPENING A SWISS BANK ACCOUNT ·

To open an ordinary Swiss bank account you can do it all by mail. If secrecy is what you want, do not deal with the Swiss bank's American branch (if it has one) because it operates under U.S. laws just like any American bank. And if bank secrecy is a major concern to you, choose a bank without any American branches; it will be less amenable to U.S. government pressure. Write directly to the head office in Switzerland.

For that matter, do not deal either with an American bank branch located in Switzerland. It will probably be much more disposed to cooperate with U.S. authorities, if that is on your mind, and it probably doesn't want you as a customer anyway. Merrill Lynch, for example, runs its own Swiss bank, Merrill Lynch (Suisse) S.A. in Geneva, but it requires a $250,000 minimum deposit for new accounts (most customers have much more than that according to international director William Waters), and it refuses to take on American clients. ("We don't want to get involved in possible U.S. insider stock traders' deals or anything like that," says Mr. Waters.)

As for Swiss banks you might consider as a convenient parking place for your money, the general rule appears to be: the bigger the Swiss bank, the smaller the customer it is interested in. The big three are Union Bank of Switzerland, Bahnhofstrasse 45, 8021 Zurich; Swiss Bank Corporation, Paradeplatz 6, 8022 Zurich; and Credit Suisse, Paradeplatz 8, 8001 Zurich. The next two in size are Bank Leu, Bahnhofstrasse 32, 8000 Zurich; and Swiss Volksbank, Bundesgasse 26, 3001 Bern.

All five are publicly owned and their shares are quoted on Swiss stock exchanges. "These banks are clearly the best for people who wish to open small accounts, as they have almost no minimum amounts to open an account. Other Swiss bank minimums can go up to $1 million," says Roethenmund.

An intermediate-size bank is Julius Baer & Co., Bahnhofstrasse 36, 8022 Zurich, which will open an account for you with a minimum of 250,000 Swiss francs (about $180,000). For a 1-million-franc minimum, Baer will open a discretionary account and manage your investments for you.

Private Bank & Trust Co. of Zurich is another bank with an established reputation, located at Barengasse 29, 8001 Zurich. It started business in 1938 and has long experience in handling discretionary accounts. The minimum investment in such an account is 400,000 francs (about $290,000).

As a rule of thumb, if you want your Swiss bank to manage your investments for you, you can expect a minimum requirement of $100,000 to $250,000 in your account.

If you have in excess of $1 million to ship over to Switzerland you might try one of the privately owned Swiss banks. There are about twenty of them, they deal with a much snootier clientele, and they will probably give you a lot more personal attention than the publicly owned banks. Private banks include: Lombard Odier & Cie., Rue Corraterie 11, 1200 Geneva; Pictet & Cie., Rue Diday 6, 1200 Geneva; and A. Sarasin & Cie., Freiestrasse 107, 4000 Basel. The partners who own these private banks have unlimited personal liability for the bank's assets. They don't publish their accounts and don't reveal how much money they control. Analysts say their client portfolios may total $100 billion.

Whether you have a few hundred dollars or several million, you may be sure that there is a Swiss bank eager for your business, even though they do not solicit customers in the United States. It's only a question of finding the appropriate bank for your particular means and needs. "Swiss banks do business with people from all over the world and from all walks of life," says Roethenmund. "Within some degree of reasonableness, they will do anything you request, provided you're willing to pay for the extra service. Some people like to be met at the airport by a bank limousine. No problem. Just expect to pay for it."

Whatever financial level you are beginning at, you start out by writing to several banks in Switzerland and explaining in general terms what it is you want—a checking account, a savings account, a trading account to buy precious metals, or a securities account to buy stocks and bonds.

All correspondence and application forms are in English (although you can request German, French, Italian, or Spanish if you prefer). The bank will require that the signature on your application form be verified by an officer of your local bank or a Swiss consular official or one of the Swiss bank's own customers. That is all there is to opening a Swiss bank account. All further correspondence and bank statements will also come in English.

There are a lot of things you can do with a Swiss bank account. There is no separation between banks and brokers in Switzerland, as there is in the United States, so your Swiss bank can buy stocks, bonds, precious metals, and commodities for you. With their worldwide capabilities, the major Swiss banks can act as your broker in all the world's stock markets. We will get into all that in the next chapter. In this chapter we are considering Switzerland, Swiss banks, and the Swiss franc exclusively as the ultimate refuge for your money in times of trouble. You will therefore play it safe and keep all your investments within Switzerland, either in Swiss francs or in precious metals. This means you will probably need (1) a checking account, (2) a savings account, (3) a precious-metals account, and (4) a securities account for the purchase of Swiss bonds and shares exclusively. Let us consider these one by one.

### Swiss Current Account

This is basically no different from your U.S.-bank checking account. You even write out your checks in English. You can withdraw your money without any time restrictions, but you don't collect any interest. At some banks there is an extra feature that can be a boon to an American traveler in Europe; even though your account is in Swiss francs, you are allowed to write out checks in British pounds or Italian lire, or other European currencies. This simplifies paying hotel bills and frequently gets you a better exchange rate than the hotel's rate.

### Swiss Deposit Account

This is similar to your U.S.-bank savings account. You will want a Swiss franc account in this case, but you can also open a deposit account in dollars, pounds, marks, or other currencies. The interest rate varies according to the currency involved, the lowest rate almost always being on the Swiss franc account—at the time of writing between 2% and 3% at various banks. Despite this low interest rate you will usually come out ahead in the long run with a Swiss franc account rather than some other currency, thanks to the habitually low Swiss inflation rate and the appreciation of the Swiss franc over the years. Whichever currency you choose, a 35% withholding tax is deducted from your interest. You should claim credit for this tax on your U.S. income tax return as it will entitle you to a 90% refund.

There are time limits on withdrawals from deposit accounts that vary from one bank to another. One bank might allow withdrawals of $1,500 per month without advance notice to the bank, for example. Retired people who travel a lot tend to use this type of account so as to maximize savings while making limited monthly withdrawals.

### Securities Account

This type of account enables you to trade in stocks and bonds. You can keep control of this account in your own hands or, if you are a big enough customer, make it a discretionary account empowering the bank to trade for you. You communicate your buy and sell orders in writing, by wire or telex, or by telephone if you want to pay overseas phone bills and can remember the time zone differences between the United States and Switzerland so as not to catch your banker at home in bed. Most banks will make loans with your stocks and bonds as collateral.

Through your securities account you can buy Swiss-franc bonds issued by the Swiss federal government, by the various Swiss cantons, municipalities, industrial and financial corporations. The interest on all these bonds is subject to the 35% Swiss withholding tax on dividends and interest. You can avoid this tax, however, by buying the Swiss-franc bonds of non-Swiss issuers such as the World Bank or the European Development Bank and other AAA-rated securities of international organizations, as well as the Swiss-franc bonds of top-flight American, European, and Japanese corporations. Scores of Swiss-franc bond issues are available, with the foreign-based issues exempt from withholding tax and yielding somewhat more than the purely Swiss issues. But you will have to resign yourself to the low yield of Swiss franc bonds in general. That is the price of seeking safety for your money in a strong currency. Your Swiss bank should be able to recommend the best bonds to buy at any particular time.

When you consider Swiss stock investments, your bank should

also be able to provide a plethora of information. Union Bank of Switzerland publishes an annual *Swiss Stock Guide*, a 188-page manual with essential information and the latest figures on Switzerland's sixty major companies. The *Guide* is available free from UBS investment counselors.

### Precious-Metals Account

This is the Swiss bank account you use to trade gold and silver bullion and coins, platinum, and palladium. The bank handles the details of storage and insurance as well as buying the metals for you. It will lend you money with your metal holdings as collateral (up to 50% of their market value), which is a thing few U.S. banks will do. In some cases you can even write checks against this account and the bank reduces your balance by the appropriate number of ounces of gold or silver—a somewhat easier solution than selling a whole bar of gold or silver when you need only half their cash value. The precious-metals account usually provides for safekeeping of your bullion at the tax-free, high-security storage facility at Zurich International Airport, where all deposits are insured against loss. Precious-metals purchases are tax-free in Switzerland.

## · BIG SWISS BANKS ·

Here are specific examples of the services available from some of the big Swiss banks at the time of writing:

### Union Bank of Switzerland

If you have at least 250,000 francs for the bank to manage you can open a discretionary account and let the bank handle all your Swiss investments according to the guidelines you give your bank officer. If you want to handle matters yourself, you open a cash account and a securities safekeeping account. The minimum amount for the cash (checking) account is 1,000 francs, and for the securities account it is 20,000 francs. You use the securities account to buy individual stocks and bonds, which are held for you by UBS in Switzerland. Mutual funds run by UBS can be bought separately from the securities account. UBS monitors information on stockholders meetings, new share issues, bonds called for redemption and other such matters, and collects interest payments and dividends.

You can also open a checking account, and a savings account which yields 2 ½% a year. However, if you have less than 100,000 francs for the bank you are pretty much limited to these options: a checking account; a savings account (or medium-term three-to-eight-year notes that pay a slightly higher interest rate); the UBS investment trusts, which include funds investing in Swiss stocks and real estate. You can also buy UBS shares—bearer shares without voting rights, the only kind available to non-Swiss investors. They sell at a premium over the registered shares available only to Swiss investors. You can also buy gold. The minimum purchase is 1 kilo (32.15 troy ounces).

Pony up more than 100,000 Swiss francs, and UBS gives you these additional options: time deposits of at least 100,000 francs each (available in other currencies too besides Swiss francs); fiduciary deposits of 100,000 francs or more outside Switzerland, in Swiss francs or other major currencies, with maturities of one to twelve months; bonds issued by the Swiss federal government, cantons, municipalities, industrial and financial companies. The smallest denomination is 1,000 francs per bond. Bonds denominated in Swiss francs are issued by non-Swiss governments such as Australia, cities such as Tokyo, or non-Swiss corporations such as Dow Chemical Corporation (one bond, as an example, being Dow's 4.75% 1987–1999 issue of 200 million Swiss francs). These foreign issues are exempt from the 35% withholding tax. UBS will send you a list of high-quality issues on request. UBS will buy silver bullion and gold coins for you in the following minimum amounts: 5 kilos (160.65 ounces) of silver; 30 Krugerrands, Maple Leafs, or Mexican 50-peso gold coins; 50 Vreneli (Swiss 20-franc) gold coins or new British sovereigns (the Elizabeth II coinage). The Krugerrands and Maple Leafs contain 1 ounce of gold, the Mexican 50-peso contains 1.2 ounces, the Vreneli 0.19 ounce and the sovereign 0.24 ounce.

## Credit Suisse

Credit Suisse offers these accounts at this time:

Current account—no minimum deposit, no restrictions on withdrawals, no interest paid. Semiannual maintenance fee of 10 francs, plus postal fees for correspondence.

Savings account (in Swiss francs)—no minimum, no maintenance charges, interest of 3.5% (minus 35% withholding tax) on amounts up to 250,000 francs, 1% interest on balances over that amount. Withdrawals of up to 10,000 francs per month without prior notice; six months' notice required on larger withdrawals.

Private account—no minimum deposit, interest rate 2.5% less 35% withholding, maintenance fee 1 franc per month, withdrawals up to 25,000 francs a month without notice, three months' notice on larger amounts. You use the private account to buy securities and precious metals.

## Swiss Bank Corporation

To complete the picture of the Big Three banks with Swiss Bank Corporation, we might as well take this member of the trio as a spokesman of the Swiss banking industry, and note in doing so that it adopts a punctiliously Swiss attitude toward American customers and U.S. tax laws. "We are seeking long-term customer relationships," said a Swiss Bank Corporation official in New York, "and we are selective in choosing our clients." After reading the Swiss chapters of this book, he added: "References to tax havens, gangsters, Mafia types, drug dealers, inside stock traders or deposed dictators detract from the standard of the book. Switzerland is not a tax haven. It is a country with a different tax system. If we become aware that a person wishes to deposit funds in our bank for the purpose of avoiding tax liabilities we refuse to entertain a request for the opening of an account.

"Your information should not suggest or give the impression to the reader that reporting of income and capital gains is a matter of choice," the bank spokesman commented. "It should be clearly noted that all income and capital gains accruing to U.S. citizens and residents are reportable for tax purposes." In any case, he observed, "whatever method he selects, a U.S. resident cannot transfer funds abroad without leaving a paper trail in the United States. Given this fact, there is no reason not to deal with a U.S. branch of a Swiss bank."

At the Swiss Bank Corporation's New York office (4 World Trade Center, New York, NY 10008), you can open an account with a minimum of $100,000 and get the bank to manage your portfolio if you like. You can choose three types of portfolio management: growth, growth and income, or income and growth. And in all three cases you can specify whether you want a global or a purely U.S. portfolio. The annual management fee ranges from 0.75% of the first $1 million under management to 0.5% for assets in excess of $2 million in the case of the two growth-oriented portfolios. The income portfolio pays a flat 0.5% a year in management fees. If you plan to include a checking account in your program, it comes free but incurs a $20 monthly charge for any month in which the average balance drops below $3,000. On a savings account no interest accrues if the balance drops below $10,000.

If you open an account in Switzerland, Swiss Bank Corporation offers a menu of checking, savings, fixed-term, short-term money market, precious-metals, and investment accounts similar to those of its big competitors. It provides safe custody for securities traded in Europe, Asia, or the United States. On most of these Swiss-based accounts you can figure on an initial minimum deposit of $50,000. When buying gold coins the minimum lot is 5 Krugerrands, Maple Leafs, or American $20 Eagles, so you can reckon on minimum trades of $2,000 or so.

With regard to taxes, Swiss Bank Corporation stresses that the crucial point is the U.S. government's insistence on having all income of U.S. citizens and residents reported to the IRS, whether it originates in the United States or abroad, and regardless of whether this income is actually remitted to the United States or not. Since you are stuck with this situation, the bank says, the important thing is to get all the tax benefits you can through the U.S.-Swiss double taxation treaty. The first order of business then is dealing with the Swiss 35% withholding tax.

You apply for a refund of the withholding on Swiss tax form R82, which you file with the Federal Tax Administration of Switzerland (Eigerstrasse 65, CH-3003 Bern). A refund of 20% in the case of dividends and 30% for interest is then made directly to your Swiss bank account. The remainder (that is, 15% for dividends and 5% in the case of interest) you claim as a foreign tax credit in the United States on IRS form 1116, in which case you of course have to itemize your deductions on your 1040 tax form.

## · DEATH AND TAXES ·

And now an unpleasant fact that you may tend to overlook. As Mr. Roethenmund remarks, "Even Swiss bank clients die, and you should make preparations to avoid problems. Bank accounts in the United States, Switzerland, or anywhere else can be tied up for a long time in court proceedings. You can avoid these if you execute a power of attorney between spouses, so that on the death of the account-holder the account can be transferred immediately to the surviving spouse. It's also a good idea to give your children a power of attorney. The document is still valid after your death, and even if the children are minors they can still exercise the power of attorney in Switzerland and have the account transferred to their own names."

Although the Swiss government levies taxes on savings account income and dividends and also applies other taxes such as stock transfer fees, Roethenmund notes that "there are no inheritance taxes or capital gains taxes or any other government charges applicable when the holder of a Swiss bank account dies."

## · BIG BROTHER ·

It is now our disagreeable duty to bring to your attention another unwelcome fact: Big Brother is watching you. You had better heed this reminder from Mr. Roethenmund: "Don't forget that it is mandatory for you to declare on your U.S. income tax form that you do have a foreign bank account."

The Internal Revenue Service, as you might have imagined, takes a professional interest in your banking activities in Switzerland and elsewhere abroad. If you itemize your deductions when filing your U.S. income tax returns, form 1040, schedule B, inquires whether you have a foreign bank account, yes or no. Just fail to answer this question and you may be penalized with a $1,000 fine or one year in jail or both. One further result of noncompliance is that you are no longer covered by the three-year statute of limitations. All your previous income tax returns then become liable for IRS audit. More than half of all U.S. taxpayers ignore this question, apparently without ill effects, so the rule is evidently not too rigidly enforced. Nevertheless, the IRS could theoretically put most of the country in jail on this technicality.

If your answer to the foreign bank account question was yes, your next worry is form 90-22.1. You have to fill this thing out if your foreign bank account "exceeded $1,000 in aggregate value at any time during the calendar year." The form then demands details about your foreign bank account, its number, the amount of money in the account, and other specifics if all your foreign bank accounts amounted to more than $10,000 during the year.

Reporting your foreign bank account is entirely your own responsibility. Your Swiss bank is certainly not going to report it for you to the IRS, which wants to make sure it is getting every last penny in tax due on your foreign income. If you are not a drug dealer, or an inside stock trader, or a Mafia type, or a deposed dictator, if you are a stickler for being on the up and up with Uncle Sam, if you are the nervous type who likes to sleep well at night, we would recommend that you report it and pay the U.S. tax due. The purpose of your Swiss bank account in any case is not high income or tax evasion, it is safety of principal in a strong currency. And furthermore, reporting your bank account is the only way you are going to get your U.S. refund on the Swiss dividend or interest withholding tax you paid.

There are other legal requirements, designed mainly to catch gangsters, couriers with hot drug money, and other criminals. Whenever you cross the U.S. border, coming or going, you have to report any monetary instrument worth $10,000 or more that you may be carrying. Whenever you withdraw more than $10,000 from your U.S. bank account (for whatever purpose, by the way—to transfer to Switzerland, to buy a new car, or for any other reason, whether the money involved is a domestic or international transaction), the bank has to file with the IRS form 4789, Currency Transaction Report. Ditto when you deposit $10,000 or more. Banks are also required to microfilm every one of your checks worth more than $100.

So you will reduce your visibility to the IRS if you (1) keep your Swiss bank account below $1,000 (this may seem self-defeating, but need not necessarily be so, as we shall see further on), (2) don't transport more than $10,000 in or out of the country when traveling, (3) keep your bank transfers below $10,000, and (4) don't use personal checks—buy a cashier's check or a money order instead; they are not so easy to trace.

At the other end, the Swiss too have their little rules, some formal, some informal. One informal rule is that Swiss banks will not solicit or collect your money in the United States. It is your business to get it to them in Switzerland. This is the outcome of a gentleman's agreement made between the Swiss banks and the Swiss National Bank in 1977—relations between these parties are largely governed by gentleman's agreements. Up to that time Swiss bank agents working in nations with exchange control or capital export restrictions used to collect and transfer to Switzerland the currency of clients in those countries. The gentleman's agreement stipulated that thenceforth the client in France, for example, would have to get his own money out past the French government's restrictions by his own efforts. The Swiss banks could still accept the money in Switzerland, but they thus avoided any unpleasantness with the French government. France is a major source of Swiss bank deposits as the government is in the habit of cracking down on its wealthier citizens every few years.

The Swiss have also tried to make things difficult for drug

dealers and others who habitually deal in large amounts of cash. The Swiss Bankers Association suggested in March 1987 that it could tighten up on anonymous bank fund movements by requiring customers to identify themselves at bank windows when depositing or withdrawing more than 100,000 Swiss francs. A previous informal agreement between the Swiss banks and government had set the limit at 500,000 francs.

However, if you happen to be adamant on maintaining your incognito, you can always try to avail yourself of yet another layer of Swiss secrecy: that between a Swiss lawyer and his client. If you get a Swiss lawyer to handle your dealings with the bank, he can claim the client-lawyer privilege to protect the confidentiality of your relationship with him. A few lawyers have specialized in this kind of business, going so far in some cases as to provide banks with their stationery and legal forms so that the banks can sign up customers under this legal cover—at a nice fee for the lawyer, of course.

But none of these evasive tactics is really necessary to achieve the purposes we are discussing in this chapter—a safe Swiss refuge for your money. You can avoid the Swiss withholding tax and you can avoid reporting a foreign bank account on your U.S. income tax return—all this on unlimited amounts of money and perfectly legally—by buying a Swiss insurance policy.

· SWISS ENDOWMENTS AND ANNUITIES ·

Let us go back to our basic premise. The attraction of investing in Switzerland is not the rate of return, which is usually low and subject to tax, but the strength of the Swiss franc, which has been outstanding for the past few decades, thanks to the responsible management of the Swiss economy. As the Swiss are continuing to run their economy on the same sober basis at this time—no huge U.S.-style trade deficits or budget deficits or national debts—it seems reasonable to anticipate more of the same for the next few decades.

The divergent economic policies followed by the two countries have resulted, as we noted earlier, in the franc rising from 25 U.S. cents in 1972 to as high as 72 cents during 1987. The effect on a Swiss bank account is beneficial, to say the least. Consider now the impact on a Swiss insurance policy.

Compare the results of two annuities sold in 1971, the first paying $1,000 a year, and the second the equivalent of $1,000 a year at that time but in Swiss francs. The annuitant collecting in U.S. dollars would have received $15,000 by 1986, while the annuitant paid in Swiss francs would have collected $27,500 as the Swiss franc rose in value over those same fifteen years.

Check the income you can get in U.S. dollars from an American insurance company annuity and compare it with the income in Swiss francs offered by a Swiss insurance company. At age sixty-five a man buying a Swiss annuity for a single premium payment of 100,000 francs should get a guaranteed income for life ranging from 6,071 francs a year (with refund of remaining cash value at death) to 7,149 francs a year with no refund. If the American company's dollar-based annuity offers approximately the same terms, the Swiss franc policy will most probably turn out to be the better buy in the long run.

Swiss insurance companies are required by law to guarantee 3% a year on the savings portion of each premium they receive. They also pay their policyholders dividends, which have ranged from 0.5% to 1.5% in past years, for a total annual return of 3.5% to 4.5%. This is not only better than the 2% to 3% paid on Swiss bank savings accounts, it is also exempt from the Swiss 35% withholding tax. Also, unlike foreign bank accounts, foreign insurance policies need not be reported on any U.S. tax return.

One further advantage of a Swiss insurance policy is that you can make a lump-sum premium payment and then immediately borrow up to 85% of the cash value at Swiss commercial interest rates, usually about 0.5% to 1% above your insurance policy return.

We are not necessarily talking about enormous amounts of money. If you buy an endowment policy, let us say to finance your baby's college education eighteen years from now, you can start out with very small amounts. If you pay annual premiums, the minimum is 1,000 francs a year. If you pay a single lump-sum premium, the minimum is 10,000 francs. Raise the ante, and further possibilities open up. If you buy a single premium endowment policy of at least 100,000 francs, you can then get a Swiss bank to manage the 85,000 francs you are entitled to borrow against the policy. According to Jurg Lattmann, a Swiss insurance broker, one Swiss bank managed to achieve an 18% return for its clients on the borrowed money.

Switzerland levies no taxes on Swiss endowments or annuities. The United States does: a 1% tax on your premiums, which is to say $100 on a $10,000 annuity premium. It is your responsibility, however, to report that you have bought a Swiss policy and to pay the tax on it. Swiss insurance companies, which have their own secrecy code, do not report anything to U.S. tax authorities on their operations in Switzerland.

You can pay your insurance premiums either directly to the Swiss insurance company or through a Swiss bank. This second alternative opens up one more interesting possibility: the nonreportable Swiss bank account. The way this works is that you open a "premium deposit account" with a Swiss bank (or the insurance company itself) for the specific purpose of paying your insurance premiums out of it. You cannot use this account to buy gold or securities or anything else; it is exclusively intended to pay the insurance company. It is therefore an insurance transaction rather than a bank operation, and is thus not reportable to the U.S. tax authorities, Lattmann says.

However, this account has other advantages: it pays about 1% more than a regular Swiss savings account, it is not subject to Swiss withholding tax, and you can predeposit as much as you want so as to maximize your interest return and enjoy the other advantages while the money is awaiting transfer to the insurance company.

When the time comes to collect your annuity, which may be of the immediate or deferred type, the Swiss insurance company will convert your annuity payments into dollars or any other currency you may prefer before sending them to you.

There are twenty Swiss insurance companies, solid institutions on a par with Swiss banks, the biggest being Swiss Life & Pension Co. (40 General Guisan Quai, Zurich), which was founded in 1857. Rather than contacting a number of companies to get the best policy, it is easier to try a Swiss insurance broker. This won't make the insurance any more expensive as the brokers collect their commissions from the insurance company, not from you. One broker who is experienced in international business is Jurg M. Lattmann A.G., Volkmarstrasse 10, P.O. Box 209, 8033 Zurich. Lattman provides a sixty-eight-page booklet for $10 explaining in English the details of various Swiss insurance policies.

## · FINAL WARNING ·

One last word. If you are a true believer in the gloom-and-doom school of thought, don't wait until The Crisis (a U.S.-Soviet clash in the Persian Gulf or whatever it turns out to be) is actually upon us. Get your money into Switzerland in good time, before the headlines start screaming and before television news analysts begin announcing the imminence of World War III. The point of this warning is that there is sometimes such a flood of scared money pouring into Switzerland that the government actually has to set up barriers to keep the funds out, such as slapping a charge on new Swiss bank accounts for nonresidents or banning outright the purchase of Swiss securities by foreigners. These measures were actually taken during the 1973 Arab oil crisis, when the post–World War II system of fixed exchange rates came to an end, and when the tattered U.S. dollar lost the last remaining fig leaf of its gold backing under President Richard M. Nixon.

# CHAPTER
# 10

## SWITZERLAND FOR
## THE OPTIMIST

In the foregoing chapter we took a gloomy look at the world, and a look at Switzerland as the ultimate refuge for the pessimist who believes that the United States, and probably a large part of the world with it, is headed for runaway inflation or a rerun of the Great Depression, financial collapse, and other unforeseen economic calamities, plus possibly World War III as well. If you skipped that chapter because gloom-and-doom scenarios don't appeal to your sunny, optimistic nature, you might turn back a few pages and read part of it anyway, where it explains how to open a Swiss bank account, and discusses how to choose a Swiss bank that might prove suitable for you as a larger or a smaller investor.

If you are basically an optimist who foresees a flourishing world economy and many years of peace ahead, that same Swiss bank account can become not a hideout but a springboard from which you can jump into investment opportunities around the world.

Mr. Roethenmund, the former Swiss bank official and present international investment adviser whose opinions provided an inside view of Swiss banking in Chapter 9, notes that "for over 200 years Swiss banks have been managing client funds on an international basis. You can buy or sell stocks, bonds, currencies and silver and gold on any exchange in the world through a Swiss bank account.

"Because they have been doing this for so many years, and because the Swiss banking industry depends on their continued success in managing money, Swiss bankers have developed enormous experience in handling client funds, not only on Swiss and European markets but on a worldwide scale."

There are big British, Canadian, and European banks through which you can also channel worldwide investment activities, but as the *London Financial Times* commented in February 1987, the major Swiss banks "are among the few banking institutions left in the world which qualify for the top-class AAA rating."

The main reason for the newspaper's comment was that many of the biggest American, European, and Japanese banks have tarnished their credit ratings by their reckless lending to Third World nations in the past decade. The lending spree started in the 1970s when the price of oil quadrupled and billions of dollars from the newly rich oil-exporting nations poured into the coffers of the international commercial banks.

Swamped by this torrent of deposits from members of the Organization of Oil Exporting Nations, and under extreme pressure to do something—anything—with all this cash, the banks started lending on an international scale to practically any borrower in sight. They even competed hotly with each other for the privilege of lending to financially shaky countries like Brazil, Mexico, and Argentina. These and other Third World nations now owe a total of more than $1 trillion and have very little hope of ever paying much of it back. But most of these loans are still hopefully carried as assets on the books of Citicorp, Bank of America, Chase Manhattan, and other big international banks, an exercise that appears to have more to do with wishful thinking than with realistic accounting.

Roethenmund says that "it's true that many Swiss banks participated in the lending spree of the 1970s, but they have made major efforts to reduce their exposure by writing off these loans, to the point where they now represent only a minor portion of their loan portfolio." The big American banks only started this process of facing reality in 1987.

It is for this reason that we are concentrating here on a Swiss bank account as the base for your worldwide investments. In other chapters we mention Canadian, British, and other international banks you might use for the same purpose if you have particular personal reasons for preferring them.

An account with a major Swiss bank in Switzerland gives you access not only to the Zurich and other Swiss stock exchanges but also to all the world's stock markets, since the big Swiss banks or their brokerage subsidiaries are members of stock exchanges from Amsterdam and Frankfurt to Tokyo and Hong Kong, or have representatives there. Open a futures trading account and you widen the scope of your activities to the commodities exchanges in London, Sydney, Singapore, and other markets around the globe where you can trade in everything from gold and silver to aluminum, zinc, wool, natural rubber, and palm oil.

Here are some specific examples of what Swiss banks can offer on world markets:

Union Bank of Switzerland, which as we mentioned in the previous chapter is the biggest of the Swiss banks, has assets of $87 billion, 2 million bank accounts at 300 branches in Switzerland, and foreign offices around the globe served by 19,000 employees. UBS accounts for about one-third of the total turnover on Swiss stock exchanges and is also custodian for the Intrag stable of mutual funds, whose assets of 8.4 billion francs constitute about 40% of all investment trusts in Switzerland. UBS owns UBS Phillips & Drew in London, a brokerage firm that contributes to UBS's worldwide economic and investment research as well as serving individual accounts.

UBS runs an assortment of mutual funds. Bond funds include Swiss Franc-Invest (Swiss-franc bonds issued by foreign companies), Helvetinvest (Swiss-franc bonds of Swiss issuers), D-Mark Invest (German-mark bonds), Dollar-Invest (U.S. and Canadian dollar bonds), Yen-Invest (Japanese-yen bonds), Bond-Invest (bonds in several currencies), and Convert-Invest (convertible bonds in several currencies). Stock funds include Globinvest (worldwide stocks), Amca (U.S. and Canadian stocks), Eurit (European stocks), Pacific-Invest (Japanese and Australian stocks), Rometac-Invest (worldwide raw material and energy stocks), Fonsa

(Swiss stocks), Brit-Invest (British stocks), Canac (Canadian stocks), Espac (Spanish stocks), Francit (French stocks), Germac (German stocks), Itac (Italian stocks), Japan-Invest (Japanese stocks), Safit (South African stocks), Sima and Swissreal B (Swiss real estate). Income from the non-Swiss funds is exempt from the 35% Swiss withholding tax if you are not a Swiss resident. The sales commission on the funds is 5%.

Minimum amounts and other specifics of UBS accounts in Switzerland were detailed in Chapter 9. For well-heeled customers (in the millionaire class) who prefer to centralize their worldwide investment operations in the United States, UBS offers private banking facilities at its New York branch (299 Park Avenue, New York, NY 10171). This branch provides a checking account and custody services for U.S. and foreign securities and precious metals, executes purchases and sales, collects stock dividends, and so on. You can give the bank full authority to manage your investments (the fee is 1% a year of assets under management), or (for a 1.25% yearly fee) have it provide an investment advisory service in which you approve every purchase or sale before the bank goes ahead with it. There is a minimum fee of $5,000 for these two discretionary and advisory services. There is also a fee for just about everything else you do: a 0.15% custody fee for securities held in New York, and up to 0.45% for securities held abroad. In addition to your brokerage commissions you pay UBS $20 to $50 for every purchase and sale of securities held in New York, $50 to $75 on securities that UBS holds for you abroad. You are billed also for transferring funds ($10 in the United States, $20 abroad), for retrieving copies of bank statements ($25), for having your mail held, and for physical shipment of securities certificates.

At the other end of the size scale from UBS, Bank Julius Baer has only about 10,000 investors worldwide, two-thirds of them outside Switzerland. Most of the funds entrusted to Baer are also invested outside Switzerland. The bank's staff of more than 600 is responsible for the management and safekeeping of several billion dollars. Baer may be considerably smaller than the Swiss

Big Three banks, but you name your needs and this bank will do it. Some of the services Baer offers:

- A checking account in Swiss francs or any other major currency
- A savings account in Swiss francs
- One- to twelve-month time deposits
- Individual investment advice and portfolio management on a worldwide scale
- Purchase and sale of securities as brokers/dealers in Zurich, New York, and London, and execution of stock market orders worldwide through a network of correspondents
- Subscription to and participation in new stock or bond issues in Swiss and international markets
- Purchase and sale of foreign exchange in all major currencies
- Futures dealings in currencies
- Purchase and sale of put and call options in currencies
- Financial futures contracts
- Purchase and sale of gold, silver, platinum, palladium, and gold coins, as well as futures contracts in these metals
- Put and call options on gold, silver, and platinum
- Limit orders around the clock worldwide and advice to clients on buying and selling precious metals
- Purchase and sale of treasury bills, certificates of deposit, and other short-term money market paper
- Placement of short-term deposits of at least $100,000 with major international banks in all major currencies
- Payments involving bank transfers or bank and postal checks
- Purchase and sale of banknotes of all major currencies' travelers checks and Eurocard services
- Safe custody of securities, valuables, and documents

- Safety deposit boxes

- Securities administration, including collection of interest and dividends, collecting bonds at maturity, exercising bond or stock subscription rights, and monitoring of securities drawings in case your holdings are redeemed.

Baer will even set up an investment program insured by the FDIC in the United States by buying $100,000 certificates of deposit distributed among American commercial banks and thrifts. Baer mutual funds include Equibaer Europe, Equibaer America, Equibaer Pacific, Conbaer (Swiss and non-Swiss convertible bonds), as well as funds for Swiss-franc, German-mark, and U.S.-dollar bonds.

If you think we unjustly slighted some of the tax havens mentioned in Chapter 9, such as Luxembourg, the Channel Islands, or the Cayman Islands, you can use a Swiss bank there too. Bank Baer, for example, has a subsidiary in the Cayman Islands (Julius Baer Bank & Trust Co., Ltd., Butterfield House, P.O. Box 1100, Grand Cayman, British West Indies) which will incorporate a company for you there if you have need of such a thing, provide a registered office for it, as well as a secretary, directors, and officers, and, of course, accounting services. The registration and incorporation will cost you $2,100 initially plus yearly services thereafter of $1,600 and up. For an initial fee of $750 and subsequent yearly fees of $1,000, Baer will set up and manage a trust for you which is not subject to any form of taxation in the Cayman Islands and whereby "the incidence of taxes and duties in high-tax countries may be reduced or deferred." We might add that you may need a U.S. lawyer and a tax adviser to make sure you will have no problems with the IRS, the SEC, and American lawmen in general with your foreign corporations and trusts.

You might also need the expertise of an international adviser such as Mr. Otto Roethenmund, whose Inter-Nation Capital Management Corporation (230 Park Avenue, Suite 2600, New York, NY 10169) acts as consultant on Swiss banking, inter national investments, foreign currencies, blocked funds, precious metals and other commodities, mergers, and acquisitions.

## · U.S. LAWS ·

At this point we might well clarify what foreign securities an American citizen or resident can or cannot buy without the buyer or the seller running afoul of the SEC. You may wonder about this when you see a prospectus—from Credit Suisse, for example, for its international stock fund or bond fund and notice the warning "Units of this investment fund may be neither bought nor held directly or indirectly by investors who are domiciled in and/or citizens of the United States and its territories, nor is the transfer of units to such persons permitted."

Foreign mutual funds (open-end investment companies whose shares are sold directly to the investor by the fund sales organization) may not be sold to American citizens or residents at any time, either inside or outside the United States, unless they have been registered with the SEC. Very few foreign funds are registered, so that excludes almost all of several thousand funds around the world. As there is no lack of mutual funds in the United States, and as the foreign-angled members of this American mutual fund fraternity cover many countries and areas of the world, the exclusion is no great hardship, particularly since most of the foreign funds are of the load variety.

However their exclusion is not 100% effective anyway because some foreign fund managements may not be so punctilious as Credit Suisse. The attitude of those managements is that if your bank account is in Ruritania or wherever and the fund you are buying is Ruritanian and the transaction takes place in Ruritania under Ruritanian laws and regulations, then it is none of the SEC's business. The risks arising from that attitude, by the way, are mainly theirs and not yours. SEC penalties would apply to the sellers.

Closed-end funds, which are traded on foreign stock exchanges rather than being sold directly to investors by fund sales organizations, are treated less severely than mutual funds by the SEC. They have the same rules applied to them as apply to the shares of foreign companies. The stock of a foreign company may be sold to U.S. citizens and residents in the United States or abroad without restriction if it is registered with the SEC. If the stock is not registered, it may not be sold to them during the initial offering period (during which it is first brought to market and the investor has to buy it from the underwriter launching the issue). After the initial subscription period is over, and once the stock is trading on the open market, any U.S. citizen or resident may buy it, provided the transaction complies with the blue-sky regulation. Blue-sky laws were passed by various American states to protect American investors against securities fraud.

All the above rules apply regardless of the location of the U.S.-based investor's account, whether it is set up in the United States or abroad. However, if your account is abroad, it is obviously rather difficult for American authorities to enforce SEC and blue-sky laws.

## · SWISS STOCK EXCHANGES ·

Armed with a Swiss bank account you are now ready for the Swiss stock exchanges. You have no need of a broker because your bank is your broker. There are seven stock exchanges, at Zurich, Geneva, Basel, Bern, Lausanne, Neuchatel, and St. Gallen, the biggest being Zurich, with about 60% of all Swiss securities turnover. Geneva is strong on foreign shares, Basel lists a lot of pharmaceutical and chemical stocks, while Zurich is the main market for Swiss industrial, bank, and insurance shares (banks, chemicals, and insurance stocks account for about two-thirds of the total market value of all Swiss stocks).

These three big exchanges are linked together by television so that orders can be executed on either of the other two if the price is better there. The three cities also have largely unregulated over-the-counter markets for unlisted shares, mostly of new companies awaiting listing. Brokers, which in Zurich include twenty-four banks, are also at liberty to make their own deals off the exchanges. In a typical feature of Swiss decentralization, there are no federal laws governing Swiss securities trading. Each canton regulates its own exchange.

In Zurich, to take the biggest market, bonds far outnumber stocks, by about 2,300 to less than 500 stock issues. On a purely Swiss level you have a choice of about 1,400 bond issues of Swiss borrowers. They include forty-five Swiss federal government issues, 200 cantonal bonds, and about eighty municipal bonds of Swiss cities, plus hundreds of bonds issued by Swiss banks and other financial institutions, utilities, and industrial concerns.

Without abandoning the Swiss franc as the medium of investment, however, you can also internationalize your holdings and improve your yield a bit by investing in any of about 900 Swiss-franc bonds issued by about forty foreign countries, states, and cities and more than 100 non-Swiss corporations. Of particular interest are more than 100 bond issues of international lending institutions such as the World Bank and the European Development Bank, which have AAA credit ratings on a par with United States government obligations and are exempt from Swiss withholding tax.

Swiss stocks offer a more limited choice: on the Zurich Exchange you will find thirty-five banks, seventy-nine other financial institutions, twenty-one insurance companies, eight transportation companies, and eighty-nine industrial corporations. Here too you can internationalize your holdings by investing in an additional list of non-Swiss companies: 110 American and Canadian stocks, thirty-two German, ten South African, thirteen British, fourteen Dutch, eight Japanese, and thirteen from other countries—enough to build up a substantial worldwide portfolio without ever leaving the Zurich Stock Exchange.

However, from a practical point of view it makes sense to buy only Swiss stocks whose price you can monitor regularly in whatever periodicals you usually read, which presumably means such English-language publications as *Barron's* magazine, the *Wall Street Journal*, the *New York Times*, or the *Financial Times* of London. Once you venture beyond that short list you will have to depend on Swiss newspapers such as the German-language *Zurich Schweizerische Handelszeitung* or the *Neue Zurcher Zeitung,* or the French-language *Journal de Genève.* Or you will have to subscribe to the stock exchange's quotation sheet.

The American financial press does provide you with daily Swiss stock market indexes (the main ones being those compiled by Swiss Bank Corporation, Credit Suisse, and the Swiss National Bank) to give you a general idea of the current level of Swiss stock prices.

Another useful source of information is a free 84-page booklet from the Zurich Stock Exchange (5 Bleicherweg, CH-8001 Zurich) explaining in English and in minute detail its methods of operation. Further information in English is available from the Basel Stock Exchange (Freiestrasse 3, CH-4001 Basel) and the Geneva Stock Exchange (10 Rue Petitot, 1211 Geneva 11). All the major Swiss banks also produce analyses of major Swiss and foreign corporations that are available free to their customers; Credit Suisse, for example, regularly publishes 240 corporate studies.

## · SWISS STOCK PECULIARITIES ·

As a foreign investor you may in some cases feel discriminated against in Switzerland because of the structure of the market. There are basically two kinds of shares. Registered shares are restricted to Swiss citizens. Bearer shares are what you have to buy as a foreigner, and they usually sell at a premium; at the time of writing the average premium is about 25%. This does reduce your yield, but you might reflect that your shares will still command a premium when you sell them. Shares of the registered type are issued by fifty-seven companies and they account for about one-third of the total capitalization on the Zurich market. During World War II they were a useful way of proving that a Swiss company was in fact a Swiss company and not, for example, a Nazi German front. Nowadays they are mainly a protection against a takeover of the Swiss company by foreign predators.

Switzerland is a small country and feels it has to defend itself against larger foreign powers.

Some Swiss companies offer an intermediate kind of stock, "participation certificates" or "Genussscheine," which have no voting rights, and tend to sell at a price between that of registered and bearer shares. Price comparisons are frequently confusing, however, as the three types of shares sometimes have different par values. Anyway, one way to avoid the higher price of the bearer shares is to invest in a Swiss mutual fund such as Actions Suisses, FONSA, or Swissvalor. These Swiss funds are allowed to buy the lower-priced registered shares.

Mutual funds also provide an entry into Swiss real estate. Switzerland is an overcrowded country, and the authorities make it very tough for foreigners to buy property there. However Swiss real estate funds are open to foreigners. They include Interswiss, Swissimmobil, and SIMA, run by the big three banks.

The yield on Swiss stocks tends to be low, an average 2.2% at the time of writing compared with 3.6% for stocks in the United States. It might be a mistake to let this put you off, however. Swiss companies are more inclined to squirrel away profits into their hidden reserves rather than pay them out in dividends. A Swiss stock yielding 2.2% might thus be a better bet in the long run than an American stock yielding 3.6% because it is plowing more of its profits back into the business, may appreciate more in price, and may benefit also by appreciation of the Swiss franc against the dollar.

The most actively traded Swiss stocks are Ciba-Geigy, Nestlé, Oerlikon-Buhrle, Alusuisse, Jacobs Suchard, BBC Brown Boveri, Sandoz, Swiss Bank Corporation, Union Bank of Switzerland, and Swissair.

If you are an aggressive investor you can trade on margin in Swiss stocks. The margins required vary, but the rate is generally about 60%. The securities in your account serve as collateral. In the matter of dividends and interest, however, you will have to be a patient investor: in Switzerland these payments are usually made annually, not quarterly or even semiannually.

Swiss brokerage commission rates are on the low side. On a

transaction of 50,000 francs or less you can expect to pay a 0.6% commission on a bond trade, 0.8% on Swiss shares, and 1.0% on non-Swiss securities, with a minimum in each case of 30 francs per transaction. For larger trades, commissions decline to as low as 0.15 to 0.2%. Safekeeping fees come to about 1.5 francs per 1,000 francs of the securities' value, with a minimum of 6 francs per book entry. You can expect to pay extra, of course, on securities held for you by your Swiss bank outside Switzerland.

Like Swiss stocks, Swiss bonds are traditionally low-yielding. The highest yield ever recorded on Swiss federal government bonds was 7.4% in 1974. But in spite of that, Swiss-franc bonds have easily outperformed dollar bonds in price appreciation over the years, thanks to the rising dollar-exchange value of the franc. The crucial point of comparison to watch in dollar bonds or Swiss-franc bonds or indeed any foreign currency bonds is the "real" rate of interest. The real rate is the local market rate of interest (let us say 8% on U.S. government bonds) minus the local rate of inflation (which, if the U.S. inflation rate is also 8%, becomes a nice fat zero). Swiss bonds have consistently yielded a small but positive real rate, while U.S. bond yields have dipped into minus territory for years at a time as the U.S. inflation rate outrageously outstripped the bond yield. Bondholders were thus actually getting a negative yield, which is a polite way of saying that as a bondholder you were paying borrowers like Uncle Sam for the privilege of lending them your money.

Swiss-franc bonds offered by foreign issuers (who are evidently taken in too by the apparently low cost of borrowing in Swiss francs) tend to provide somewhat higher yields than purely Swiss bonds, and they have the additional advantage of being exempt from the 35% Swiss withholding tax on interest. High-quality AAA issuers such as the World Bank are particularly interesting because of the tax exemption.

Lists of the latest bond quotations are available from the major Swiss banks. Credit Suisse publishes a fortnightly list of selected bonds denominated in other currencies as well as Swiss francs, with their current prices, yields, interest payment dates, and other details. The bank's quarterly English-language *Bulletin* also contains a select list of Swiss and foreign borrowers.

We will get to other foreign-currency bonds besides the Swiss-franc variety in a later chapter on Luxembourg, which has become a major trading center for international bonds. But your Swiss bank can be useful there too if you decide to make your Swiss account the central base for your worldwide investments. Credit Suisse, for instance, operates in Luxembourg through its Credit Suisse (Luxembourg) subsidiary. It would handle your stock or bond trades through Credit Suisse Buckmaster & Moore in London, through Schweizerische Creditanstalt (Deutschland) AG in Germany, through Credit Suisse France in Paris, and through Credit Suisse Trust & Banking Co. in Tokyo.

And finally, for one reason or another, you may be tempted to use your Swiss bank to buy American securities on U.S. stock exchanges. If so, a word of caution. Because you are an account-holder in Switzerland, your Swiss bank may well take the position that any transactions involving that account come under Swiss law and are beyond the jurisdiction of the SEC. However, this does not generally extend to transactions on United States stock exchanges. The problem here is insider trading. There are no specific laws against insider trading in Switzerland, but after a few U.S. insider trading scandals involving Swiss banks and a subsequent memorandum of understanding in 1982 between the United States and Swiss governments, the Swiss banks agreed to a so-called Convention XVI. This convention allows inspection of the banking records of a client suspected of U.S. insider trading, which incidentally is the misuse of privileged information on forthcoming mergers or other unpublished company developments on the part of company insiders to make a killing in the company's stock.

So if you were thinking of using your Swiss bank account to do some insider trading on the New York Stock Exchange, you had better think twice about it (or use your mother-in-law's account at another bank) because your Swiss bank is likely to balk.

# CHAPTER 11

## LONDON

London is usually listed in third place among the leading financial centers of the world, behind New York and Tokyo. It may be so in terms of stock market activity. But overall, when you include foreign exchange trading (in which London is the undisputed world leader), insurance (where Lloyd's of London is globally preeminent), financial futures markets, and such commodity exchanges as the London metals, coffee, cocoa, and sugar markets, the British capital looks more like the world's number-one financial center. Foreign exchange trading alone accounts for more than $20 billion a day.

To illustrate how London is habitually underestimated, annual trading on the London Stock Exchange comes to about $600 billion dollars a year, but London Eurobond trading, a loosely organized network of private dealers in unregistered international securities, amounts to a whopping $2.5 trillion a year. The Eurobond market raised about $200 billion for new international bond issues in 1986, while the London Stock Exchange raised only $7 billion in new capital for listed securities. London's Eurobond market grew from nothing in 1963 to its current status as the biggest financial market in the world.

The London Stock Exchange, which was the world's biggest up to World War I, has mounted a determined campaign to recapture the number-one spot. In 1986 the Exchange merged with a 187-member trade group that includes most of the biggest securities firms in the world and, making no secret of its global ambitions, renamed itself the International Stock Exchange. The

Exchange's governing council is now dominated by foreigners, such as Merrill Lynch, Nomura Securities, and Deutsche Bank.

Impelled in part by these giant foreign institutions seeking to market their own wares, the Exchange plans to become the world's leading marketplace for internationally traded shares. It aims to develop a new trading system in which about 200 securities marketing firms will eventually be able to display prices for about 1,500 non-British equities, London being the center of operations for these stocks as it already is for Eurobonds, foreign exchange, and insurance. The Euroequities market, as this system of stock offerings across national borders is known, quadrupled in two years, with trading volume up to $11.3 billion in 1986.

D-Day in London's campaign for world stock market dominance was October 27, 1986, the day of the Big Bang, when the Stock Exchange implemented a ruthless set of reforms to break up the cozy, clubby world of old-style London brokers and jobbers, exposing them pitilessly to the full ferocity of worldwide competition from Swiss and Japanese banking giants, cutthroat American discount brokers, and Australian takeover artists.

Farewell to two-hour lunches, afternoons watching cricket matches at Lords, chummy deals in the old-boy network over dinner at the club, and a juicy tip or two picked up over the three-day weekend at Lord Chuzzlewit's country house. The London Stock Exchange is now open from nine to five, a full eight-hour day compared with the New York Stock Exchange's relaxed six and a half hours, and the Tokyo exchange's gentlemanly four-and-a-half-hour session.

Since the Big Bang, the days of the gentlemen in pinstripe suits, bowler hats, and furled umbrellas, the jobbers who dealt only with brokers, and the brokers who dealt only with clients—for a nice double commission between them—are gone forever. Even the Exchange's trading floor, where up to 2,000 bustling dealers raised a hubbub where you could scarcely hear yourself think, is now silent and empty. Brokers have abandoned it to hunch over the glowing SEAQ (Stock Exchange Automated Quotations) electronic terminals in their own offices. The new London broker is more likely a whiz-kid type, a computer freak, a sixteen-hour-a-day workaholic who gets up early, stays up late to watch after-hours trading in New York, who is in the office to watch the Saturday morning session of the Tokyo Exchange, and who makes a yearly income in the six-figure range in sterling.

London was a much wider and more international market than New York to begin with. With its 7,000 stocks and bonds, the London Stock Exchange easily surpasses in number the New York Stock Exchange's 1,500 stocks and 1,000 bonds. The London total includes more than 5,000 stocks, of which about 600 are European, Japanese, American, or other non-British companies. To this must be added more than 500 British government and British public authority bonds, nearly 200 foreign public sector securities, and more than 1,200 Eurobonds. Since 1985 there has also been an Unlisted Securities Market, where about 300 smaller companies are traded, and a further Third Market was added in January 1987 for yet smaller companies. The London stock market has come a long way since the first brokers set up shop in Jonathan's coffee house in Threadneedle Street back in 1773.

The number of shareholders has mushroomed in Britain in recent years too as a result of the privatization of huge British state enterprises such as British Gas (the biggest one-time stock offering ever made in the world at $8 billion), British Telecom, British Airways, Britoil, and Rolls Royce, which were snapped up by nearly 5 million small first-time investors. Since coming to power in 1979, Prime Minister Margaret Thatcher has mounted a determined campaign to restore capitalism in Britain, a campaign that has placed the United Kingdom in the forefront of a worldwide wave of denationalizations of state industries. As the Labor Party has pledged to renationalize many of the privatized concerns, a Labor victory at the polls could be taken as a massive blow to the stock market, but capitalism has gained a solid new constituency as the number of British shareholders soared from less than 3 million to nearly 9 million under Mrs. Thatcher.

However, the Thatcher privatization campaign stumbled badly in the October 1987 stock market crash. In the last two weeks of October—almost at the first anniversary of Big Bang—the

*Financial Times* 100-share index shed 26% of its value, a fall worse than any other European stock exchange. Brokers, swamped by a record trading volume of 3.5 billion pounds on Tuesday, October 20—nearly double the usual rate—said that only the Big Bang reforms enabled the London Exchange to withstand the avalanche of selling. But they said the increased efficiency achieved under Big Bang had also increased the market's volatility. And the stock market had great difficulty digesting the biggest offering to date in Mrs. Thatcher's privatization program—$12.43 billion worth of British Petroleum Co. shares, the British government's remaining one-third stake in the oil giant. The October crash left the underwriting brokers holding the bag: they had bought more than a billion BP shares at 120 pence each from the government and now had to sell at a market price of 87 pence to the public. There was also a perceptible cooling of enthusiasm among small investors for any further government offers of stock as they saw the value of their British Airways, British Telecom, and Rolls Royce shares shrinking daily. Meanwhile, for American investors in British stocks, the pain caused by London's precipitous decline in October was tempered by the fact that the British pound soared against the American dollar.

Under the new Big Bang dispensation, British securities trading is governed by the Financial Services Act of November 1986 and by the Securities and Investments Board, a supervisory body paid for by the brokerage community. For the first time in Britain, all the country's investment markets, including Eurobonds, domestic and international equities, commodities, and life insurance, came under one regulatory umbrella. The Board's ten members are appointed from the public and the financial services industry by the Bank of England's governor and the secretary of state for trade and industry. It is essentially a self-regulatory system, and—also for the first time in Britain—it makes it a criminal offense to carry on investment business without authorization. The new system ran into some tough problems almost immediately in early 1987 with insider trading scandals that led among other things to the resignation of top directors at Guinness PLC, a major brewer.

Surveillance has improved considerably since the Big Bang

because the new SEAQ network, which operates much like the NASDAQ over-the-counter dealer quotations network in the United States, monitors and stores all trading information, thus enabling the Stock Exchange to build up a complete surveillance system. With this technology available, if a market-maker has filled a client's order from shares held by his own firm he may be forced to show that he could not have done better for the customer elsewhere.

The stock market is not strictly speaking the London Stock Exchange, it is the International Stock Exchange of the United Kingdom and the Republic of Ireland, with centers in London, Belfast, Birmingham, Bristol, Dublin, Glasgow, Leeds, Liverpool, Manchester, and Newcastle. Two unusual international aspects of the London Exchange are that it incorporates the Irish stock exchanges (even though Ireland has a different currency, the punt), and that it is linked by computer to an office in Johannesburg so as to facilitate the transfer of the scores of South African securities listed in London.

One of the first consequences of the Big Bang was that the abolition of fixed brokers' commission rates unleashed ferocious competition and just about halved the brokerage houses' commissions from their previous levels of about $1 billion a year. Competition became so fierce that a large part of total trading is now without any commission at all. Brokers make their money merely on the difference between their bid and asked prices.

Unfortunately this is unlikely to be of much benefit to you or me. What happened in London was a rerun of May Day in New York when fixed commissions were eliminated in 1975. The big institutional investor got big reductions, and the little guy kept on paying as much as before, or even more. A number of British brokers merely left their previous rates in place for the small individual investor.

The fact is that the British market is dominated by big institutions. Pension funds hold 27% of all quoted shares, insurance companies 21%, closed-end and open-end investment trusts another 11%. Individual stockholders, with only 28% of the market, don't have much clout.

Nevertheless, transfer taxes have been cut in Britain after the

Big Bang, and it may well be cheaper now to buy a European stock in London than to buy it in its home country. The spread on the bid and asked price of Electrolux shares, for example, might be only 40 cents or so in London, compared with perhaps $1.50 in Stockholm because of Swedish taxes. As a result of this, by some estimates London brokers were taking as much as 15% of the business away from some brokers in Switzerland, Germany, and France, shortly after the Big Bang. The other countries made hasty attempts to meet the threat. The Netherlands abolished fixed commissions, France planned to open the Paris Bourse to foreign brokers, and Switzerland was also taking measures to become competitive again.

Now, how do you personally fit into the London stock market? In two possible ways: either to buy British stocks or to benefit from lower transaction costs when buying stocks of other nations. As to your method of operation, you can always trade through a United States–based broker, as discussed in Chapter 7. But if for any reason this proves unsatisfactory, you can move your British investment operations to the United Kingdom.

## · BRITISH BANKS ·

One solution is to open an account with a British bank and consolidate all your foreign checking, savings, and investment activities in one place. Some of the major British banks are:

Barclays Bank
54 Lombard Street
London EC3P 3BS

Lloyds Bank Ltd.
71 Lombard Street
London EC3P 3BS

Midland Bank Ltd.
27-32 Poultry
London EC2P 2BX

National Westminster Bank
41 Lothbury
London EC2P 2BP

These are their head offices, but they all have scores of branches
throughout the country, any one of which might be more convenient for you. You can either go it alone or enlist your bank's
help in investing. National Westminster, for instance, which
prides itself on its services to individual customers, offers a Premium Investment Management Service. This includes cash management, investment, and tax planning.

You can deal with other banks too, among them Bank of
Scotland, which offers among other things a high-yield money
market checking account, either on its home turf at 101 George
Street, Edinburgh EH2 3JH, or at its Channel Islands branch,
4 Don Road, St. Helier, Jersey. "By having assets held in Jersey,"
the bank notes, "as opposed to the United Kingdom, non–United
Kingdom–domiciled individuals can hold United Kingdom assets
without the risks of creating a United Kingdom estate in the
event of death. It also avoids withholding tax complications."
There are no inheritance taxes in the Channel Islands, and bank
interest paid to nonresidents is nontaxable.

The Channel Islands advantage is also offered by Lloyds Bank
International (Guernsey) Ltd., Sarnia House, Le Truchot, St.
Peter Port, Guernsey. Lloyds offers a wide range of services to
nonresidents of Guernsey, including checking and savings accounts, investment management, trusts, and company forma-
tion. You can establish an interest-bearing deposit account in
most major currencies as well as the pound sterling, with a minimum deposit of 2,500 pounds. You can also open an investment
account in which the bank holds your securities, collects dividends, and so on. You can also invest in money market funds
denominated in currencies ranging from Swiss francs to New
Zealand dollars or European Currency Units. (Yields at the time
of writing, incidentally, were 2.73% on Swiss francs, a whopping
22.45% on New Zealand dollars, and 6.51% on ECUs.) The
bank also manages investment portfolios for investors with at

least 100,000 pounds and no time or inclination to manage the money themselves. Lloyds will also set up a company for you on the Channel Islands, or in Panama, Gibraltar, Liberia, or elsewhere for about 2,000 pounds and a 500-pound yearly fee. Through Lloyds in Guernsey you can also set up a type of trust to avoid taxation and death duties in which the deed is not recorded in any public register and in which the beneficiaries are known only to the trustees, and thus maintain complete anonymity.

## · BRITISH STOCKBROKERS ·

The second alternative is to deal directly with a British stockbroker. The list below gives the addresses of some brokers who are ready and even eager to deal with smaller private investors. We have added a few words on each firm's idiosyncracies that might be of interest to you.

Astaire & Co. Ltd.
117 Bishopsgate
London EC2M 3TD
UK and overseas equities, Eurobonds, currencies.

Barclays de Zoete Wedd
Ebbgate House
2 Swan Lane
London EC4R 3TS
International investment specialist of the Barclays Bank
    Group.

Beale, Sheffield & Co.
15 South Mall
Cork, Ireland
Domestic and international markets.

Blankstone Sington & Co.
Martins Building
6 Water Street
Liverpool L2 3SP

Tax planning for the individual and family in the UK and overseas.

Bloxham, Toole, O'Donnell
11 Fleet Street
Dublin 2, Ireland
Irish government-fund specialists.

Charles Stanley & Co.
18 Finsbury Circus
London EC2M 7BL
In business since the reign of King George III and the American Revolution. Stresses service to the private client. Minimum commission 10 pounds.

Chase Manhattan Securities
Portland House
72-73 Basinghall Street
London EC2V 5DP
Portfolio management for the personal investor in the UK or overseas (minimum 30,000 pounds).

County Securities Ltd.
Drapers Gardens
12 Throgmorton Avenue
London EC2P 2ES
UK, European, Japanese, Hong Kong, Australian, and U.S. securities.

Discount Brokers International
17 Lincoln's Inn Fields
London WC2A 3ED
American discount broker, claims to be the cheapest in Britain.

Earnshaw, Haes and Sons
17 Tokenhouse Yard
London EC2R 7LB
Taxation advice for residents and expatriates, insurance.

Fidelity Investments Group
Lovat Lane
London
American discount broker.

Hoare Govett (Channel Islands) Ltd.
35 Don Street
St. Helier, Jersey, Channel Islands
Offshore fund accounts, Eurobonds, tax and financial planning.

James Capel & Co.
6 Bevis Marks
London EC3A 7JQ
Discretionary portfolio management (minimum 75,000 pounds).

J. and E. Davey
60–63 Dawson Street
Dublin 2
Irish equities and government bonds.

Kitcat & Aitken & Co.
The Stock Exchange
London EC2N 1HB
International investments, discretionary accounts for 50,000 pounds and up.

Lyddon & Co.
113 Bute Street
Cardiff CF1 1QS, Wales
Welsh companies.

Magennis & Co.
43 Lower Mill Street
Newry, Ireland
Irish mining companies.

Mercury Rowan Mullens
33 King William Street
London EC4R 9AS
Advises 3,000 private clients and more than 150 charities, managing investments worth about 3 billion pounds.

Merrill Lynch Ltd.
Merrill Lynch House
27 Finsbury Square
London EC2A 1AQ
International securities, minimum portfolio 25,000 pounds.
If you live in London, or indeed elsewhere abroad, another Merrill Lynch office (153 New Bond Street, London W1Y ORS) offers a Cash Management Account Service for Overseas Employees, which is set up to handle the problems of the expatriate American, such as gaining immediate access to a paycheck that may take ages to clear through a U.S. bank back home. This service is oriented mainly toward Stateside investments. The minimum portfolio is $5,000 and the annual fee (U.S. income tax–deductible) is $100.

Penney Easton & Co.
24 George Square
Glasgow G2 1EB
Several offices in Scotland, minimum commission 8 pounds.

P.H. Pope & Son
6 Pall Mall, Hanley
Stoke on Trent ST1 1EU, England
Traditional and traded options.

R.J. Thompson & Co.
1 Salisbury Buildings
London Wall
London EC2M 5RH
Minimum portfolio 1,000 pounds.

Robert Ramsden & Co.
Estate Buildings
Railway Street
Huddersfield HD1 1NE, England
Gilt-edged and foreign fixed-income securities, convertibles, options. Small investors welcome, no minimum trade or portfolio.

Savory Milln
3 London Wall Buildings
London EC2M 5PU
UK and overseas, especially European, securities.

T.C. Coombs & Co.
5–7 Ireland Yard
London EC4V 5EE
Norwegian, French, South African, Australian, and Far
    Eastern securities, Japanese Euroconvertibles, UK-traded
    options.

Wood Mackenzie Private Client Services Ltd.
Kintore House
74–77 Queen Street
Edinburgh EH2 4NS, Scotland
Services to private investors worldwide.

Until the 1986 Big Bang, commission rates were fixed, and
came to 16.50 pounds for a 1,000-pound purchase or sale and
132 pounds on a 10,000-pound transaction. Now it is a "free-
for-all" and depends on what you can arrange with your broker,
which will probably not be very advantageous if you are a small
investor. After Big Bang, Savory Milln, for example, stuck to
the original Stock Exchange fixed-rate commission scale for their
private clients (while their big institutional investors got a 50%
reduction), so that on a 7,000-pound transaction in ordinary
shares the individual client's commission is 1.65%. On larger
deals the commission is progressively reduced, so that a 30,000-
pound purchase would pay 0.5%, or 150 pounds in commissions.
Savory Milln is also an example of how in many cases commissions have been eliminated completely for big institutional investors. In the stocks where it is a market-maker (such as Barclays
Bank or Bank of Ireland), Savory Milln offers the shares on a
net basis to big buyers, pocketing only the small difference between the bid and asked prices.

   In the new competitive environment in London, discount
brokers see a golden opportunity. "Big Bang is a bonanza for us,"

says Gerard Troncin of Discount Brokers International, a New York Stock Exchange member firm that has become a member of the London Exchange and set a commission rate at about half the pre–Big Bang fixed-rate of the London full-service brokers, some of whom, according to Troncin, "face disastrous profitability" in the new free-for-all competition.

"We are one of a handful of UK brokers operating on a discounted basis," says Troncin. "We also happen to be the cheapest, and we deal on the UK side for investors worldwide." DBI charges 25 pounds on a 2,000-pound transaction, 33 pounds on a 4,000-pound trade, 66 pounds on a 10,000-pound deal. DBI is also able to deal in overseas securities from London if you want to operate worldwide from a London base. As a discount broker it, of course, offers no research or investment advice.

## · TRADING IN LONDON ·

Having selected your broker you are ready for business—but perhaps not ready for some peculiarities of the British stock market scene. The first of these is politics, which looms much larger than it does in the United States. The installation of a Democratic or Republican administration in Washington usually makes very little difference on Wall Street. In Britain the difference between a Conservative government, under a Mrs. Thatcher vigorously pursuing the restoration of capitalism, and a Labour government, ideologically committed to renationalize everything that Mrs. Thatcher denationalizes, is likely to be considerable in investment matters—particularly if you own shares in such renationalization candidates as British Telecommunications or British Gas.

A change of government in London carries other implications. As soon as she came to power in 1979, Mrs. Thatcher lifted all the exchange controls that had been in force in Britain since World War II, so that there have been no restrictions on taking your money in or out of the United Kingdom in her scheme of things. This situation would be likely to alter under a Labour government, which stresses keeping capital and dividends in the country—although it must be said that the restrictions in the past have applied to Britons and British residents rather than to foreign-based investors.

At the practical level there are further discrepancies with the American way of doing things. Apart from the fact that stock prices are quoted in pence (600 pence rather than 6 pounds), stock quotations do not follow the usual American style in the British press. The major difference in the *Financial Times* of London is the absence of the usual American high, low, and close figures for each stock. There is only one quote given and it is not even a real price; it is an indication of the going price, usually the midpoint between the bid and asked prices. One useful feature of the British quotation table, however, is the "Cover" column. This gives you the ratio between a company's total profit and the amount of profit it distributes to shareholders. A company earning 60 pence per share and paying a 10-pence dividend would thus have its dividend "six times covered," and you might consider your dividend safer than with another company paying a 10-pence dividend on 10-pence earnings.

British company dividends are paid after deduction of a corporate tax of 52%. On your U.S. income tax statement you can claim a reduction of this to 15%. There is no British withholding tax on corporate bond interest or on most government gilt-edged stocks if you have held them for one month.

This brings us to some British traps for the unwary. A British government stock is in fact a bond in U.S. terminology, and a government stock, or Gilt, is thus the British equivalent of a United States government bond. A debenture in Britain is a corporate bond, but unlike an American-style debenture, it is backed by collateral. What Americans call a debenture is in Britain an Unsecured Loan Stock.

Billing procedures in Britain differ too from U.S. practice. The Stock Exchange year is divided into account periods, which are normally ten working days, but may vary because of bank holidays. You have to pay before Settlement Day (also called Account Day) because that is when your broker settles up with the market-maker for all business done during the account period. Settlement Day usually comes six working days after the end of the account. The actual date is always shown on your broker's contract note, and you will see a daily reminder of it in the *Financial Times*.

Like American investors, who are protected against losses through U.S. brokerage house failures by the Securities Investor Protection Corporation, investors in Britain are covered by a Compensation Fund. The Fund is run by the Exchange, which boasts that since 1951 no investor has lost money in Britain through fraud or financial failure of a member of the Stock Exchange. Complaints against brokers are handled by an independent ombudsman, who may be reached at the Exchange, London EC2N 1HP.

Before starting an excessively active trading plan in Britain you might keep in mind that your transaction costs are inflated by a 0.5% stamp duty (it used to be 1% until Big Bang), and by the imposition of Value Added Tax (15% on each of your brokerage commissions). Before cashing in your gains it is useful to know too that you will pay a 30% capital gains tax, but the first 6,300 pounds in yearly profits are exempt from the capital gains levy. All the above, of course, should be read in the understanding that taxes, rules and regulations, and other circumstances may change between the time this book is written and the time you read it.

## · GILT-EDGED INVESTMENTS ·

As the *Financial Times* is likely to be your daily guide as to current prices and news developments, let us make a broad survey of the main sections of the newspaper's quotation lists.

The first section, headed British Funds, comprises the Gilt-Edge market of securities issued by the British government. The term "Gilt" is sometimes loosely and incorrectly used to cover also the securities of lesser British public authorities that do not carry the guarantee of the British government any more than municipal bonds carry the guarantee of the U.S. federal government. Curiously, the Gilt certificates issued by the Bank of England are not edged with gilt and apparently never have been.

The United Kingdom government spends about 120 billion pounds a year, and its usually considerable shortfall in raising this sum is met by selling Gilts. There are thus 130 billion pounds' worth of Gilts currently on the market and about one billion pounds' worth change hands every day. Treasury bills, repayable in three months, are issued at the rate of about 100 million pounds a week. The other categories, as listed in the *Financial Times*, are "shorts," which expire within five years; "mediums," five to fifteen years; "longs," over fifteen years; "undated," which have no expiration date; and "index-linked," which are indexed to the rate of British inflation. There are more than 100 different issues, known variously by such names as Treasury, Exchequer, Funding, or Conversion Stock Loans, but they are all covered by the generic term "Gilt."

Nominal interest rates vary from 2% to 15.5% and the going prices of the different issues vary accordingly. Interest is paid twice a year and is at a fixed rate except for the Index-Linked Gilts. One exceptional feature of the Gilt market is that it works on the basis of "cash settlement." No leisurely account periods here. Make a bargain today and you will have to pay, or deliver your Gilts, tomorrow. Gilt prices are quoted on the basis of a 100-pound nominal-value certificate, with the prices given in pounds and fractions of a pound (99½ thus being 99 pounds 50 pence). The amount due is adjusted to take into account the accrued interest.

Traditionally, the government sold Gilts directly to the general public, announcing each new issue on the Stock Exchange on Friday afternoons through the Government Broker (the senior partner of Mullens & Co.), but it is now moving toward the U.S. system, in which the government auctions off each new issue to the highest bidder. This system is dominated by huge securities dealers, but if you read the announcements in the British press you can bid for the new issues just as a small investor can in the U.S. treasury bill auctions. The minimum amount of a bid is 100 pounds' worth of bonds, and the announcement includes instructions on how to apply for exemption from U.K. income tax if you are a foreign investor. Foreign investors are a big factor in this market, particularly when it seems the pound sterling is likely to appreciate against other currencies.

A number of Gilts are exempt from all British taxation to nonresidents of the United Kingdom. They include the 3½% War Loan, Treasury 10% 1993, Treasury 15¼% 1996, Treasury 15% 1998, Conversion 9% 2000, Treasury 8% 2002/06, and about two dozen others which you will find listed in *The New Gilt-Edged Market*, by Patrick Phillips of Barclays de Zoete Wedd, a firm that specializes in British government securities.

On the other Gilts, British income tax at the basic rate of 29% is deducted from the interest before you receive it. As a U.S. resident you then have to make a claim for a tax adjustment on your U.S. income tax statement.

A number of Gilts have distinct peculiarities. The undated issues, which include the 2½% Consolidated Stock (known as Consols) issued in 1883, behave on the principle that there will always be an England, since they have no expiration date and will pay you interest forever. Variable-rate Gilts are linked to the current rate on short-term U.K. treasury bills.

Index-Linked Gilts, the most interesting variety, have their interest and capital payments linked to the United Kingdom's General Index of Retail Prices. They thus offer the British investor protection against the ravages of inflation, and consequently yield considerably less than other Gilts—about 3% at the time of writing against 7% to 9% for the fixed-interest variety. The basic interest rate on the index-linked stocks is the rate fixed when it was first issued (for example 2% on the 1992 Treasury stock issued in February 1987).

This is an innovation the U.S. government might have thought of too to protect its long-suffering bondholders against inflation, but Uncle Sam never came up with the idea. For the American investor, unfortunately, the British index-linked Gilts are not particularly attractive because they afford no protection against future declines in the exchange value of the British pound. Sterling is a currency that has dropped from a value of $2.80 to as low as $1.10 in the past quarter-century, so that risk must be recognized as considerable. British index-linked Gilts have another curious feature. They are linked to the inflation rate prevailing eight months previously, so for the last eight months of their lives they do not provide any protection against inflation.

If you want to jump into this market, Barclays de Zoete Wedd turns out a useful four-page daily list of U.K. Gilt prices, detailing their accrued interest, net yields at various tax rates, and other data. There are also a number of investment funds that will deliver a portfolio of Gilts to you in one neat package. One of these is Asset Global Funds Ltd. (Abacus House, Mona Street, Isle of Man), whose U.K. Gilt Fund is specifically aimed at the international investor seeking high regular tax-free returns from U.K. Gilts and other sterling fixed-interest securities with a minimum of risk.

Whatever you plan to do, it is advisable to keep in mind that for the non-British investor the performance of sterling on foreign exchange markets is likely to outweigh any interest rate considerations. When you buy Gilts you are in fact gambling that British pounds are going to be worth more against dollars in the years ahead. The shorter the term of your Gilt, the lower your risk on that particular bet.

## · BRITISH ORDINARY SHARES ·

When you come to the general stock market list you will note that the *Financial Times* divides it up into separate sections, such as electricals, industrials, engineering, building, banks, insurance, leisure, tobacco, newspapers, shipping, and textiles, rather than using the single alphabetical list of New York Stock Exchange stocks to be found in U.S. newspapers. As your eye runs down the columns it may come to rest on such exotic categories as Plantations. These are subclassified into Tea Plantations or Rubber and Palm Oil Plantations. There are also Overseas Traders, South Africans, Canadians, and Americans. The South African Gold Mines are neatly separated into Central Rand, Eastern

Rand, Far West Rand, and O.F.S. (Orange Free State) mines. There are also clumps of Australian and Central African mining stocks, as well as clusters of tin and diamond and platinum mines.

When you get down to studying a stock in any particular area of the market a separate table of stock market indexes headed "FT-Actuaries Indices" gives you a useful overall guide to the current status of that specific area of the market—the Oil and Gas shares index, for example, if you are thinking of buying British Petroleum. You will find in this table market indexes for leisure stocks, stores, banks, investment trusts, and another three dozen categories of stocks.

Incidentally, for an overview of the whole market's performance, the *Financial Times* 30-Share Index is the British equivalent of the Dow Jones 30 Industrials in the United States. The FT-All Shares Index covers 739 stocks and might be compared with the Standard & Poor's 500 Stock Index. The newest market measure is the FT-Stock Exchange 100-Share Index (the FT-SE100, also known as Footsie), which is calculated every minute of the Stock Exchange session.

The most actively traded stocks on the London Exchange include British Telecom, British Petroleum, Shell Transport and Trading, Glaxo Holdings, ICI, Marks & Spencer, BAT Industries, General Electric, BTR, and Cable & Wireless.

General Electric, incidentally, has no connection with the American General Electric. However, as lack of space prevents us from giving further details or exploring all the more exotic corners of the London Stock Exchange let us concentrate on one section that allows you to achieve a widely diversified London portfolio with just one or two investments, and that may also offer unusual opportunities for profit.


## · BRITISH INVESTMENT TRUSTS ·

Some of the best bargains on the London Stock Exchange are to be found among the investment trusts listed in the section headed "Trusts, Finance, Land" in the *Financial Times* stock market table. These investment trusts are similar to American closed-end trusts, which you will recall were discussed in Chapter 5. There are about 200 of them in Britain, with total assets exceeding $20 billion, double the number of U.S. closed-end funds. As a group they represent about 6% of the capitalization of the London stock market. The American funds account for less than 1% of U.S. stock market capitalization.

Like their American counterparts, these trusts can usually be bought at a large discount from their net asset value. At the time of writing the average discount is about 25%. They are also much more internationally oriented than the U.S. closed-end funds, and they thus enable you to put together a global portfolio by investing in just a handful of trusts.

Just as with the American closed-end funds, however, one crucial piece of information, the current premium or discount, is missing from the daily quotes you will find in the *Financial Times* or other British dailies. To obtain this information you will have to buy either the *Financial Times* or the *London Daily Telegraph* on the fourth Saturday of each month. (The *Financial Times* is available in the U.S. cities listed in Chapter 4; the *Daily Telegraph* may be bought at a few newsstands in New York, Washington, San Francisco, and Boston.) The Saturday edition in question carries a table of investment trust data put together by the Association of Investment Trust Companies. It gives the latest price and the net asset value of each fund, from which you can see which are selling at a premium and which at a discount. This table features another interesting detail in a column headed "Gearing Factor." "Gearing" is the British term for leverage and in this case the figure given indicates the percentage amount by which the net asset value per share would rise if the value of the equity assets increased by 100%. The gearing factor depends on how much borrowing a trust has done or how much stock it has outstanding in the way of debentures, loan stocks, or convertible loan stocks (bonds or convertible bonds in U.S. parlance). A highly leveraged trust will give you a wilder ride for your money, with a bigger profit potential on the upside and a larger loss potential on the downside.

Other useful information in this monthly table includes the yield and the geographic spread of each trust's portfolio. If you are looking for a trust that concentrates on British companies, for example, you might pick out Fleming Claverhouse, which is 100% invested in U.K. companies. If it is Japanese exposure you want, you could choose Baillie Gifford Japan or another seven trusts specializing in Japanese securities, making your selection on the basis of their performance over the past five years (which is also given in this table) or the size of their current discounts. A number of Scottish investment trusts (that have a reputation for shrewdness, although it doesn't shine particularly brightly in their performance record) concentrate on American stocks. Other possibilities for a worldwide portfolio include Foreign & Colonial Eurotrust (77% invested in Europe), German Securities (100% in Germany), Nordic (85% in Scandinavia), Australia (100% in Australian stocks). There are half a dozen trusts that go in for oil stocks in a big way: Viking Resources, Winterbottom Energy, New Darien, City and Foreign, North Sea Assets, and TR Natural Resources. There are also trusts that specialize in growth stocks, commodity and income stocks, smaller companies, real estate, and other specialized niches such as the Plantation Trust, which you might consider if an individual tea plantation in India seems too much of a risk. You also have split-capital stocks, similar to the American dual funds, in which the capital shares take all the trust's capital gains while the income shares take all the trust's income.

Some of the closed-end investment trusts offer you monthly investment plans or similar ways of saving on stockbrokers' commissions. Foreign & Colonial Investment Trust, for instance, has an arrangement whereby the Royal Bank of Scotland makes a single monthly investment for participating individual shareholders and thus reduces their investment costs considerably.

One practical way to invest in British investment trusts is through Thomas J. Herzfeld & Co., 7800 Red Road, South Miami, Florida 33143, an American brokerage that specializes exclusively in closed-end funds, the only U.S. broker to do so. The firm's owner, Thomas Herzfeld, has spent his entire working life on closed-end funds, and his strategy is to play the discount angle for all it is worth: buy a fund when it sinks to a deep discount and sell it when the discount shrinks or even rises to a premium. There are times when the average discount on U.S. closed-end funds narrows, and Herzfeld then moves his game over to the investment trusts in London, if the discounts are larger there. His advisory firm, Thomas J. Herzfeld Advisors, Inc., turns out a constant stream of research on individual trusts, and will manage your portfolio for you for a 1% to 2% fee if you are in the millionaire class. If you want to run your own investment program concentrating on closed-end funds, Herzfeld recommends a minimum initial stake of $100,000 to do it properly. Transaction fees in London, he says, have shrunk considerably since the 1986 Big Bang and are now less than in the United States.

To get started in the field of British investment trusts, write to the Association of Investment Trust Companies, Park House, 16 Finsbury Circus, London EC2M 7JJ. The Association can provide you with a complete starter package: its annual *How to Make IT* (which contains the portfolio, historical record, and other details of member trusts); a monthly record of the performance statistics of the various trusts, including a listing of the top twenty performers over the past one, two, three, five, seven, and ten years; the addresses of member trusts; a list of British stockbrokers who deal in investment trust shares, their addresses, commissions, and minimum portfolios; a list of trusts with dividend reinvestment plans; and the monthly trade newsletter *Investment Trusts*.


## · UNIT TRUSTS ·

While investment trust quotations take up a little more than a column of the *Financial Times*, unit trusts, the British equivalent of American mutual funds, occupy about fourteen columns. There are more than a thousand unit trusts at the time of writing. About 150 new ones were launched in 1986, and in 1987 the total unit trust assets under management came to 39 billion pounds, twice as much as the British investment trusts. Nevertheless, despite their growing numbers and their 2 million investors, the British unit trusts share a common characteristic with American mutual funds—the average unit trust does not keep up with the market average any better than the average U.S. fund does. In the ten years up to 1986 the average unit trust turned 1,000 pounds into 7,077 pounds. It looks impressive, but the *Financial Times* All-Share Index rose from 1,000 to 8,100 in that period.

There is no reason to expect unit trusts to perform any better or worse than an investment trust or vice versa, but the brokerage commission on the investment trust is usually less than the usual 5% sales commission on the British unit trust. The closed-end investment trust also offers an additional advantage if it sells at a discount, as it usually does, since you then get a better income yield than you would from a unit trust—25% better at the time of writing since the average investment trust discount is 25%. The investment trust also charges a yearly management fee of about 0.4% of assets, which is better than the standard 1% charged by unit trusts.

Why then do unit trusts outsell the investment trusts? For the same reason that U.S. closed-end funds are less popular than mutual funds with American investors: lack of advertising and sales effort. British investment trusts are forbidden to advertise without issuing a full prospectus. They also do not pay commissions to investment advisers. Unit trusts pay brokers and banks 1% or more in commissions for the business they introduce, and up to 3% to investment advisers. So if you deal with any of these intermediaries you will have to insist that they refrain from their natural inclination to buy unit trusts.

There is an even more compelling reason to give preference to investment trusts over unit trusts. Unit trusts are theoretically off-limits to American investors under SEC regulations. However the attitudes of British unit trusts to these regulations vary. Target International, for example, states flatly that its stable of funds is "not open to nationals or residents of the United States. A declaration to that effect is a condition of application for shares."

Another management outfit says, however, that "if U.S. residents have London offices or other addresses in the United Kingdom, such as banks, there is no problem about using that as the unitholder's registered address. It is then up to the investor to have the mail forwarded to him." A few may even send you their literature and application forms without further ado.

Only a few unit trusts are registered with the SEC in the United States. They include GAM International, GAM Global, and GAM Tokyo (Global Assets Management Corp., Commerce House, St. Peter Port, Guernsey, Channel Islands). Also SEC-registered are Transatlantic Fund, Transatlantic Growth Fund, and Transatlantic Income Fund run by Kleinwort Benson International Investment (200 Park Avenue, New York, NY 10166). Despite their names they are actually global funds.

The other unit trusts seem to cover every investment purpose under the sun. There are funds to invest in Thailand, Korea, Singapore and Malaysia, New Zealand, Taiwan, Hong Kong, Brazil, and India. There are funds to invest in commodities, British real estate, smaller Japanese companies, long-term Eurobonds, metals and minerals, Scottish investment trusts, Norway, and the Philippines, as well as a multitude of purely British sector funds. There is even an Islamic Fund, which eschews interest-bearing investments because of Islam's ban on interest.

The Unit Trust Year Book gives details on over 1,000 trusts offered by more than 150 management groups, including their performance records and other data (available from the *Financial Times*, 102 Clerkenwell Road, London EC1M for 29 pounds). For a free copy of the Unit Trust Association's booklet *Everything You Need to Know About Unit Trusts*, write to the Association at P.O. Box 8, Stroud, Glos. GL6 7AT, England. The *Unit Trust Newsletter* (3 Fleet Street, London EC4Y 1AU), published monthly, recommends which unit trusts to buy or sell. Hargreaves Lansdown, Embassy House, Queens Avenue, Clifton, Bristol BS8 1SB, runs *Unit Investor*, a monthly publication, as well as offering investment management.

Unit trusts listed in the *Financial Times* are divided into two sections, Authorized Unit Trusts, which are for United Kingdom residents, and Offshore Overseas Unit Trusts, which include funds for expatriate Britons as well as foreign, mainly European, mutual funds. The offshore funds are off-limits for United Kingdom residents as well as United States residents.

For Americans, however, there may be a way around the SEC, if you have the necessary wherewithal. For example, Rothschild Asset Management (C.I.) Ltd., St. Julian's Court, St. Peter Port, Guernsey, Channel Islands, which runs a number of international money market funds and other investment funds, politely refuses U.S. inquiries. But it adds, "We can accept substantial subscription from U.S. investors in circumstances which will qualify as private placements and not offend SEC regulations." The minimum for a private placement, Rothschild says, is 100,000 pounds. If you qualify, you can then put the legendary Rothschild name to the test in international finance: Rothschild Asset Management will switch your money market funds among its stable of funds into whatever currency it feels is going to do best.

## · BONDS ·

Apart from the British government bonds mentioned earlier in this chapter there are also hundreds of international bonds available in London that are denominated in several other major currencies besides the British pound. However, for practical purposes you are pretty much limited at the time of writing to a couple of hundred whose prices are carried daily in a *Financial Times* table headed "International Bond Service," and another three dozen or so in the main stock market list under the headings "International Bank and Overseas Government Sterling Issues," "Commonwealth and African Loans," and "Foreign Bonds and Rails."

The "International Bond Service" quotations are provided by the Association of International Bond Dealers. They include issues quoted in yen, Luxembourg francs, Dutch guilders, Canadian dollars, European Currency Units, and Australian dollars as well as sterling and U.S. dollars. These are issues in which there is active trading and you will find a buyer or a seller when you need one without much trouble. On this list you will find such familiar names as Walt Disney, with its 8¾% 1994 European Currency issue, or Pepsico, with its 5¼% 1995 German mark issue, as well as World Bank, New Zealand Government, and Kingdom of Sweden bonds in various currencies that are not necessarily their own.

Other Eurobonds are pretty much inaccessible at the time of writing due to lack of public quotations, but that may have improved by the time you read this book. Eurobond trading up to 1987 was pretty much a private preserve for big international securities firms that made secretive deals with each other. Early in 1987 came the beginning of a rudimentary price reporting system in which the big Eurobond dealers gave the Association of International Bond Dealers the daily closing price of issues in which they trade. The Association, like the London Stock Exchange, was to become a recognized exchange for Eurobonds under the new United Kingdom regulatory structure. It was envisioned as a market for professional traders and big institutions rather than for small investors, but the market was expected to provide greater price information, including actual transaction prices as well as the day's highs and lows.

When selecting a foreign currency bond, a good place to start out is a table in the *Financial Times* headed "Eurocurrency Interest Rates." This gives the going rate for various periods of time, ranging from overnight to one year, and provides a basis of comparison for the yields you can expect in one currency or another. At the time of writing, for example, the one-year yen rate was 3.75% and the Italian lira rate 10.5%. Before you start looking for lira bonds to buy, however, you will have to decide whether the Italian currency is going to appreciate by 60% against the dollar, as the yen did in the 1985–1987 period, or whether it is going to lose in value and so wipe out all the advantage of the higher interest rate. Exchange rate fluctuations between the world's major currencies have been so violent in recent years that they may considerably outweigh the importance of the interest rate yield.

## · FINANCIAL FUTURES ·

We move now into an area that is mainly a preserve for big investors and high-rolling gamblers, the financial futures market. You might make use of this market if you have an investment of at least 50,000 pounds in Gilts that is giving you sleepless nights, or, at the opposite end of the scale, if you simply have a couple of thousand pounds you are willing to gamble on a Gilt futures contract. This high-stakes financial game is played on the London International Financial Futures Exchange (Royal Exchange, London EC3V 3PJ), which in 1982 opened a market for futures contracts in long-dated gilt-edged contracts. Each contract is for 50,000 pounds nominal value of twenty-year British government bonds with a 12% interest rate. (The interest rate is purely notional or theoretical; in practice any long-term Gilt with an equivalent value may be delivered against the contract no matter what interest rate it bears.)

If, as a big-time investor in Gilts, you are worried about your 50,000-pound Gilt portfolio sinking in value because of an anticipated rise in British interest rates, you can sell a long-dated Gilt futures contract at the going rate today and lock in your price for as long as nine months ahead. The futures contract delivery dates are spaced three months apart in March, June, September, and December. Margin rates vary but you would probably only have to put up 1,500 pounds initially to buy your 50,000-pound futures contract, and you might consider this cheap to purchase peace of mind about possible losses on your long-term Gilt investments. Contrariwise, if you are a gambler and want to speculate on falling British interest rates, you use those 1,500 pounds to buy a long-term Gilt futures contract, expecting to sell it within three, six, or nine months at a higher price. If you find all this hard to grasp or cannot spot the errors in the above statements you might take it as a good indication that the futures market is not for you. Gilt futures are in any case appropriate only for investors who have prior experience in the U.S. financial futures markets for treasury bonds or other financial futures—as well as being either unusually rich or exceptionally daring.

The LIFFE market also has a short-life Gilt futures market in which the small investor may feel even less welcome. The contract is for 100,000 pounds nominal value of a Gilt issue with a three- to four-and-a-half-year maturity and a nominal coupon rate of 10%. Trading volume is considerably lower in this market. It also makes things thoroughly confusing for the neophyte investor by using an apparently similar but in fact different pricing system from the long-term Gilt contract. Price variations of both long-term and short-term Gilt futures contracts are quoted in "ticks." But a tick in the long Gilt contract is one-thirty-second of a point (0.03125 pounds) while a tick in the short Gilt contract is one-sixty-fourth of a point (0.015625 pounds). This was done so as to make the tick on the 50,000 long Gilt contract equal in value to the tick on the 100,000 short Gilt contract. When you look up the latest prices in the *Financial Times* tables headed "Financial Futures" and see the long-term March Gilt quoted at 127.16, this means 127.5 pounds whereas 127.16 in the short Gilt table means 127.25 pounds. If you find this difficult to follow take it as one more hint that this might be a market to stay away from.

There are a number of other futures markets on the London Stock Exchange and the LIFFE, including the FT-SE 100 Index, on which you can either hedge your London stock market investments if you are a big and prudent investor, or you can simply speculate on future market trends if you are a gambler. The FT-SE 100 Index is an average of the top 100 shares traded on the London Stock Exchange. The FT-SE 100 futures contract is valued at 25 pounds per point. That is, when the FT-SE 100 Stock Index is at 2,000, the futures contract has a value of 50,000 pounds. So take a look at the current level of the FT-SE 100 index, multiply by 25, and if the figure you get is about the value of your London portfolio of stocks then one futures contract would be an adequate hedge against a drop in the market. Divide the figure by 50 and that is approximately the amount you would need for initial margin as a speculator. In either case, if the market moves against you, you may be called on to put up a lot more margin. You then have the choice of putting up more money or else being wiped out. Like the Chicago futures markets, this game is not for pikers or for the faint of heart.

Other futures markets in London include Three-month Sterling, which trades in lots of 500,000 pounds, Three-month Eurodollars, where each contract is for $1 million, and LIFFE-Sterling, which goes for a mere 25,000 pounds a shot.

All these markets attract an astonishing amount of activity, mainly from big institutional investors. Average turnover on the LIFFE is about 42 billion pounds a day, although the margin amounts actually put up are of course only a small fraction of that.

## · OPTIONS ·

In the same "Financial Futures" section of the *Financial Times* you will find the daily quotations of half a dozen option markets. These are markets where you may feel less out of your depth as a small individual investor. The beauty of the option markets is that your maximum loss is whatever you put up initially to buy your option. You cannot be dragged deeper and deeper into the swamp to be swallowed by the crocodiles—as you can in the futures markets, where as noted above you may face the choice of either meeting a margin call or having your whole investment liquidated involuntarily.

To take the Gilt options first, there are options for short-dated Gilts and for long Gilts, each contract being for 50,000 pounds nominal value. You buy a put if you expect Gilt prices to fall, you buy a call if you expect them to rise, and you can place your bets for as low as 100 pounds or so if you are willing to gamble on far-out-of-the-money contracts. You will find the daily quotations in the *Financial Times* in a table headed "London Traded Options."

There is also an active LIFFE market where you can buy and sell options on the long-term Gilt futures contract, and another where you can trade U.S. treasury bond futures. Both the LIFFE and the Stock Exchange run dollar-pound option markets where you bet on the rise or fall of the dollar's exchange rate against the pound. The LIFFE's Eurodollar options market enables you to gamble on Eurodollar interest rates, and its FT-SE 100 Index Futures option market gives you a chance to wager on the future price levels of the London stock market. Daily quotations of all these options markets are to be found in the "Financial Futures" section of the *Financial Times*.

As in the United States, you can also buy options on individual stocks. But in London, options come in two kinds, "traded options" and "traditional options." The traditional option is a static, passive kind of investment that you cannot sell once you have bought it. You just have to sit on it until it expires and then collect your money, if there is any money to collect. Prices of traditional options are quoted in the *Financial Times* under the heading "Options, Three Month Call Rates." Puts are not quoted.

Traded options are quoted in a table headed "London Traded Options." They are similar to U.S.-style options in that you can sell them at any time before the expiration date if that should be a profitable proposition. As in the United States, you can buy three-month, six-month, or nine-month options. The fifty or so traded stock options available vary from such financial pillars of the community as Midland Bank to Ladbroke, a national betting shop. All these option prices are quoted on a per-share basis, but each contract is for 1,000 shares, so that you have to multiply by 1,000 to arrive at the amount of money involved in each contract.

We have no space in this book to go into explanations of all these futures and options contracts—and you shouldn't be in them anyway if you need such explanations and haven't had prior experience in the U.S. futures and options markets. Explanatory literature and the technical details on each contract are available from the LIFFE and the London Stock Exchange. Among brokers specializing in futures and options we might mention that Petley & Co. Ltd., Dunster House, Mark Lane, London EC3 7AR, offers a "limited liability contract" under which it claims you can never lose more cash than you commit to any particular trade thanks to the use of "stop loss" orders. We would suggest that you limit your trading to options, where it is indeed a fact that you cannot lose more money than you put into a trade. On futures contracts, judging by United States markets and the general fallibility of stop orders, we would be more skeptical.

## · COMMODITIES ·

The list of commodity futures you can trade in London is just about as long as the roster of U.S. commodity markets in Chicago and New York. It includes aluminum, copper, lead, nickel, zinc, silver, gold, gold and platinum coins, coffee, cocoa, freight futures, wheat, barley, potatoes, soy meal, sugar, oil, and gas oil. Prices of all these are quoted in the *Financial Times* under the heading "London Markets." These markets are so highly specialized, and there are so many of them, that it is impossible to do them justice in a book of this size. A good starting point for the budding international commodities trader is to write for information to the London Metal Exchange, Plantation House, Fenchurch Street, London EC3, or the London Futures and Options Exchange, 1 Commodity Quay, St. Katharine Docks, London E1 9AX, which deals in coffee, cocoa, and sugar futures and options.

The London Metal Exchange has been recovering from the debacle of the world tin market collapse of 1985, which revealed a fatal flaw in its method of operation. This is in fact an important point worth checking before you deal in any futures market. The LME did not operate as a central clearing house that guarantees to you the fulfillment of every transaction even if the buyer or seller you are dealing with should fail to perform his part of the bargain. LME ring (market) members dealt directly with each other, and ran into a spate of bankruptcies and lawsuits when the International Tin Council, a cartel of tin producers, ran out of money to prop up the market and the world price of tin came crashing down. In May 1987 the London Metal Exchange set up a new system under which all LME transactions are cleared by the International Commodity Clearing House, an independent organization owned by Britain's five biggest banks. You can thus trade on the LME with a great deal more confidence than before.

## · INFORMATION ·

You cannot do anything in any market without adequate sources of information. We have mentioned the *Financial Times* of London as a source of daily prices and general news. The *London Times*, the *Daily Telegraph*, and the *Guardian* offer somewhat more limited daily price lists. The *Economist, Euromoney*, and the European edition of the *Wall Street Journal* are publications that add background information. Other sources include the *Investors Chronicle*, a weekly that runs a World Markets report in each edition (subscription 74 pounds a year, Greystoke Place, Fetter Lane, London EC4 1ND). If low-priced speculation is your game, *Penny Shares Focus* (biweekly, 59.50 pounds a year, 11 Bloomfield Street, London EC2M 7AY) may have some interesting ideas. The *Financial Times* Marketing Department, 102 Clerkenwell Road, London EC1M 5SA, also offers a number of publications and books such as *Investors Guide to the Stock Market*, which details the changes brought about by Big Bang. The *Financial Times* has a whole stable of specialized newsletters with the latest developments in various fields, such as *International Banking Report, Euromarket Report, North Sea Letter, Mideast Markets*, and *World Commodity Report*. They run about 15 pounds a month per report. The list also includes IC Stock Market Letter, a weekly tipsheet on stocks to buy, for 110 pounds a year.

The London Stock Exchange provides free of charge general literature on the market, on Gilts and options, a list of stockbrokers, and other brochures. For a fee you can also get publications such as the *Monthly Fact Sheet*, the *Stock Exchange Quarterly*, and the *Stock Exchange in Ireland*.

In addition to the literature of the firms mentioned previously in this chapter, Allied Dunbar (Allied Dunbar Centre, Swindon SN1 1EL, England), an insurance and private banking concern, has a useful booklet on the tax aspects of investing in the United Kingdom for both residents and nonresidents.

# CHAPTER
## 12

## AUSTRALIA AND NEW ZEALAND

## · AUSTRALIA ·

Australia has the eighth-largest economy in the noncommunist world, and its stock market ranks among the top ten. Rich in natural resources, Australia is one of the world's greatest producers of energy, minerals, and agricultural products. About the size of the United States, this continent-nation has a population of around 16 million, considerably less than New York State's. Most of these Antipodeans are bunched together on the fertile East Coast, the parched and arid interior being probably the largest expanse of nothing in the entire globe.

Economically and politically, Australia is something of a paradox. A highly developed industrialized nation, it still depends heavily on half a dozen raw materials for most of its foreign earnings. Coal is the biggest export, and Australia is the world's biggest coal exporter. The country's economy thus gets hurt when the world price of petroleum drops, sharpening competition with its coal. It also gets hurt when the world steel industry slumps, thus reducing global demand for Australian coal. Coal, iron ore, wool, wheat, and beef represent more than 40% of Australian exports; manufactured goods account for only 20%.

This combination landed Australia with one of the global stock market's booby prizes in 1987. In the October world stock market crash investors suddenly took a gloomy view of the outlook for world economic growth, took another look at Australia's heavy dependence on natural resource exports, and started selling stocks in Sydney. Australia's relatively small industrial base on the global scene and its rather thinly traded stock market exacerbated the decline, and Australian stocks lost about half their value in the last two months of 1987. However, Australia's stock market advance in the first ten months of the year had been so fast and furious that even this calamitous plunge only meant that Australian stock prices had been knocked back to a level that was still 10% higher than in October 1986.

Although a former colony of Britain, Australia has been slipping out of the British (and U.S.) economic orbit in recent years to become ever more closely integrated with the economies of the Far Eastern nations, the group to which it belongs geographically. Japan takes more than 25% of Australian exports, the United States only 10%, and Britain even less. Meanwhile Australia has been forced out of some of its wheat markets, such as the Soviet Union, by farmers in the United States and Western Europe, who are deep in a political war with each other over their subsidized grain sales to the Russians. Australia is thus becoming perforce a part of the fast-growing Asian-Pacific region. Nevertheless, Australia has been plagued by big foreign-trade deficits in recent years as the prices of its major exports plunged on world markets. This, and a relatively high inflation rate approaching double digits, weakened the Australian dollar against other currencies. These two factors caused interest rates to soar. The Australian bank prime lending rate climbed to 21% in 1986, more than double the rate in the United States.

The fact is that apart from its raw material export woes Australian industry has been made uncompetitive against Asia's lean and mean little tigers like Korea, Taiwan, and Singapore by highly paid beach-loving Aussies and their featherbedding labor unions.

The result of all this was a nasty economic recession in the early 1980s and a curiously Australian political reaction to it. The more conservative of Australia's two main political groups, the Liberal National Country Party, in power for seven years up to 1983, when the recession touched bottom, was booted out by the electorate. The incoming Labour Party, despite its socialistic left-wing image, then undertook a vigorous reformation oriented toward free enterprise. The utterances of Australia's treasurer,

Paul Keating, began to sound more like Ronald Reagan's than those of a British-style Labour leader.

The Australian Labour government removed all currency controls, initiating a vast economic liberalization program and financial overhaul that allowed foreign banks and other international competitors into the long-protected Australian economy. The removal of almost all restrictions on investment in Australia opened the floodgates to a torrent of new foreign money into Australian companies. Ownership of stock brokerage firms was also deregulated and opened up to foreigners. The result of this has been an internationalization of the Australian securities industry. Many of Australia's 100 or so brokers are now part of big worldwide organizations, with offices in world financial centers, offering a full range of financial services. Citicorp of New York, for instance, owns 100% of Clarke Vickers Ltd., an Australian brokerage firm, as well as Vickers da Costa in London, and has set up teams of Australian stock specialists abroad to sell Australian stocks to American, British, and European investors.

The market value of all Australian stocks nearly tripled from 1984 to 1986, and in early 1987 stood at A$180 billion before they were halved again by the October crash. Market activity more than tripled, climbing to A$40 billion in 1986. Australian companies such as Broken Hill Proprietary, News Corporation, Pacific Dunlop, and Brambles have expanded their operations out of Australia into the United States, Europe, and Asia, becoming major international corporations. Boral Ltd., Australia's leading construction industry supplier, with A$1.3 billion in sales, is also the biggest brickmaker in the United States. Goodman Fielder Wattie, Australia's biggest food company, owns a big chunk of Rank Hovis, the biggest British food supplier, and also has $300 million in sales in the United States.

In this newly invigorated atmosphere, the Australian stock market has undertaken a major spending program to set up a sophisticated technology with which it plans to make the Australian securities market a world leader in the global stock exchange league. One step in the campaign was the consolidation of the six Australian stock exchanges (Sydney, Melbourne, Adelaide, Brisbane, Hobart, and Perth) into one national market, the Australian Stock Exchange. This new national exchange now claims to have the only futures market in the world facilitating trade in individual stocks. Its options market is linked up to markets in Canada and the Netherlands. And a "Second Board" has been created to make room for smaller emerging companies that previously did not qualify for stock exchange listing.

Technologically, the major innovation is the Stock Exchange Automated Trading System (SEATS), which is progressively removing market activity from the traditional stock market trading floor to computer terminals in brokers' offices. Another novelty is CENSAS, a computer system to eliminate much of the paperwork in settling trades. All going according to plan, it is anticipated that in the next couple of years SEATS and CENSAS will transfer all Australian stock trading to computer screens and book entry settlement instead of the old-fashioned milling crowds of shouting brokers and the shuffling of stock certificates from one investor to another.

As the new system develops, Sydney—which together with Melbourne accounted for more than 90% of all Australian stock trading before the consolidation—is well on the way to becoming a major world financial center in the Asia-Pacific region. Most of the world's biggest financial institutions are now represented there, and a growing number of foreign companies are expressing interest in listing their stocks on the Australian Exchange. The Sydney Futures Exchange has also achieved outstanding success and is now even trading U.S. treasury bonds and Eurodollars among its futures contracts.

As the Australian trading system ties into the world's financial markets, Australian bankers and foreign-currency dealers are getting up earlier and earlier. By starting work at 6 A.M. they can mesh in with the final hour of trading on the U.S. West Coast.

Sydney is fifteen hours ahead of New York, a time difference that makes it difficult to do business at any civilized hour on the telephone between the two cities. This is something you will have to keep in mind if you open an account with one of Australia's brokers, a selection of whom are listed below. (Some of these, like Ord Minett, have offices in New York and London, but they are set up for big institutional business only.)

A.C. Goode & Co.
500 Bourke Street
Melbourne

Bain & Co.
6–10 O'Connell Street
Sydney

J.B. Were & Son
379 Collins Street
Melbourne

Ord Minett Ltd.
1 York Street
Sydney

Paul Morgan & Co.
410 Queen Street
Brisbane

Potter Partners
325 Collins Street
Melbourne

Rivkin Ltd.
20 Bond Street
Sydney

Names and addresses of other brokers, as well as further stock market information, may be obtained from the stock exchanges:

Australian Associated Stock Exchanges
388 George Street
Sydney

Stock Exchange of Adelaide
55 Exchange Place
Adelaide

Brisbane Stock Exchange
344 Queen Street
Brisbane

Hobart Stock Exchange
86 Collins Street
Hobart, Tasmania

Stock Exchange of Melbourne
351 Collins Street
Melbourne

Stock Exchange of Perth
68 St. George's Terrace
Perth

Sydney Stock Exchange
Exchange Centre
Bond Street
Sydney

Computer linkups permit all the exchanges to quote uniform prices. In 1984 the Melbourne Exchange established a Second Board market for new, smaller companies that did not yet qualify for regular exchange listing, an innovation that has since spread to the other exchanges. The minimum capital requirement for Second Board companies is A$200,000, which is not really all that much smaller than the A$300,000 required of AASE Official List companies. When its capital rises above A$20 million, a Second Board company is required to seek a regular listing.

The wave of innovation in the stock markets has spurred greater interest in stocks down under but only about 1 million Australians own stocks, about 10% of the adult population. The fact that Australia is a nation of homeowners—70% own their own homes—ties up a lot of family capital in housing that might otherwise flow into the stock market.

Perhaps stock brokerage commissions have something to do with it too. To retell an old, familiar story from other countries that deregulated their brokerage industries: when Australian brokerage fees were deregulated April 1, 1984, commissions went

down to about half the previous level for big institutional investors, but they stayed at about the same level as before for small
individual investors. Which is to say A$5 plus 2.5% on the first
A$5,000 invested, 2% on the next A$10,000, and 1.5% on the
next A$35,000 above that. These rates are for "marketable par-
cels" (round lots in U.S. parlance), which vary in size from 2,000
shares for penny stocks to fifty shares for stocks priced at A$10
or more. Most brokers have a minimum commission of A$25 to
A$50.

### Australian Stocks

Now that you have your salesmen, let us take a look at the wares.
At the time of writing, 1,053 companies are listed on the Australian Stock Exchange, plus forty-four investment trusts and
forty-four governmental or semigovernmental authorities, for a
total of 1,141 stocks. The list includes a handful of companies
from Papua–New Guinea and twenty-one companies from other
countries, including New Zealand, Britain, the United States,
and Fiji. If you always wanted to own a piece of the South Pacific
here is your chance to buy into Burns Philp (South Sea) Company
Ltd., which is based in Suva, Fiji. Does a gold mine or a plantation or an interisland shipping and trading company in Papua–
New Guinea appeal to you? Here are Bougainville Copper Ltd.,
Dylup Plantations, and Steamship Trading Co. Ltd.

Gold mines, incidentally, are the sector of the Australian
market that have aroused the greatest interest among foreign
investors. They have always been a big part of the investment
scene down under. Australia's first stockbroker, one Edmund
Barton, went into business in 1835, but stock market trading
only took off in a big way in the 1870s when the Australian gold
rush set off a frenzy of speculation in mining stocks. In our own
times, as South Africa's racial problems have mounted, investors
switched their attention to gold mines elsewhere, mainly Canada, the United States, and Australia. The Australian gold mines
moved up to price-earnings multiples of 20, 30, or 40, but were
still relative bargains since the PE ratios of Canadian and U.S.
mines were twice as high. Leading Australian gold stocks include

Central Norseman, Gold Mines of Kalgoorlie, and Placer Pacific.

As many Australian mines have operating costs ranging from $140 to $250 per Troy ounce, there is ample margin for profit with gold selling at around the $400 mark, as it did in 1987. From an annual rate of 18.4 tons in 1981, Australian gold production has risen to about 80 tons in 1987 and is expected to climb to 100 tons in 1988, which would be about 6.6% of world production, putting Australia in contention with the United States and Canada for third place behind South Africa and the Soviet Union, the two biggest producers.

## Market Indexes

U.S. and British financial publications such as *Barron's* magazine and the *Financial Times* of London give you a quick reading of current Australian stock price levels in their tables of foreign stock market indexes. The All-Ordinaries Index, the one most generally published, comprises 281 stocks and has a base value of 500 as of January 1, 1980. It includes about one-third of all companies with ordinary shares listed in Australia, accounting between them for nearly 90% of the total market capitalization. The index ranged from a low of 240 in 1976 to a high of 2,305 in 1987.

This index is the ultimate in online information. It is recalculated instantly every time one of the component securities shows a price change. The overall index is subdivided into twenty-four industry subgroups, such as metals and mining, solid fuels, oil and gas, gold mines, light engineering, and heavy engineering companies. Only the metals and mining index appears in the *London Financial Times*. To get the other subgroup indexes you will have to consult the Australian financial publications listed further on.

Despite Australia's heavy reliance on raw materials, industrial stocks represent about 70% of the capital on the Australian stock market, natural resource stocks only 30%. About 93% of all trading on the Australian Stock Exchange is transacted in Sydney and Melbourne, which are closely integrated, members of one exchange being admitted to the floor of the other.

The bulk of all trading is in ordinary shares, but some types of shares are not found in the U.S. market—deferred shares, for example, in which a company raising capital for a new mine or other project that is unlikely to be profitable for some time postpones payment of a dividend up to a specified date in the future. There are also contributing shares in Australia, which are not fully paid up to their par value and on which the company may later require payment of the remaining amount.

Australian companies mostly pay dividends semiannually, and they are only required to produce semiannual reports, except for mining companies, which have to turn them in quarterly.

One major difference with U.S. practice is that margin trading is not allowed, curbing speculative plays available to congenital risk-takers.

If you are of a conservative turn of mind however, you will find a number of investment trusts listed on the exchange. Westpac Banking Corporation (66 Pitt Street, Sydney) could provide information on the trusts it manages.

## Currency and Bonds

The biggest and most fundamental difference between your U.S. and Australian investments, of course, is that your investments down under are denominated in the Australian dollar, a currency that has been in a steady decline against the American dollar since 1979, when it was worth US$1.16. It sank as low as 66.5 cents in 1984 and at the time of writing in 1987 stands at 68 U.S. cents.

This is a factor you have to weigh most particularly against the double-digit returns that have been available on Australian bonds in the past few years. They were obviously not a particularly good buy in 1979 at US$1.16 to the Australian dollar. But they might be an outstanding buy at 66.5 U.S. cents if that should prove to be the low point at which Australian inflation and interest rates start to come down and the Aussie dollar starts to go up. If you hit the low point, your Australian bond will then rise in price, it will be worth more in U.S. dollars, and you still keep your high interest rate.

Most trading in Australian bonds is conducted over the counter. The government bond market is in the hands of twenty-one "reporting dealers" approved by the Reserve Bank of Australia, who are the main market-makers and investors in Commonwealth Government bonds. There is usually no brokerage charge. The dealer makes his money on the spread between the bid and asked quotes. Semiannual interest coupons are the most common, but some quarterly, annual, and even zero coupon bonds are on the market. Commonwealth Government bonds may have maturities up to thirty-five years. They come mostly in registered form and there is an active trading market. The minimum initial purchase is A$5,000.

Corporate bonds come in three varieties: debentures, unsecured notes, and convertible notes. Debentures are secured with the assets of the issuing company and have an active secondary market. Commission rates are generally the same as for stocks and here too margin trading is forbidden.

Australian government treasury bills are issued weekly by the Reserve Bank, and are sold at a discount (as U.S. treasury bills are sold in the United States) rather than paying interest. Maturities range from thirteen to twenty-six weeks. The minimum denomination is A$10,000. In order to buy treasury bills you have to go through the formality of registering with the Reserve Bank.

### Futures

Australia claims to have had the world's first futures contract based on individual listed shares. It became available in September 1985 on the Australian Financial Futures Market of Melbourne, which is now part of the Australian Stock Exchange. The AFFM offers you two choices: individual stock contracts and portfolio contracts. The individual stocks currently include the most actively traded stocks on the Australian Stock Exchange: Broken Hill Proprietary Co. Ltd., CSR Ltd., Santos Ltd., Australia and New Zealand Banking Group, National Australia Bank, Westpac Banking Corp., G.J. Coles & Co. Ltd., and CRA Ltd. Each futures contract represents 10,000 shares.

The portfolio futures, called the Australian Leaders Portfolio, comprises shares of all these companies, with a value per contract of A$110,000 at the time of writing.

These contracts may seem to require some hefty investing, but actually all that is required is a deposit of a couple of thousand dollars. You then acquire all the profit potential and risk of loss that every highly leveraged futures contract offers. Profits and losses resulting from changes in the shares' market values are credited and debited every trading day. If your contract declines sharply you will have to put up more margin or be sold out by your broker.

The Sydney Futures Exchange also offers futures contracts on ninety-day bank accepted bills (which can be traded up to two years ahead): two-year Commonwealth treasury bonds (also up to two years ahead); ten-year Commonwealth treasury bonds (twelve months ahead); share price index futures (up to eighteen months); and United States dollars (up to twelve months ahead). This last would obviously have the most appeal to an American investor in view of its hedging potential against a possible decline in the currency value of his Australian investments.

Before buying a futures contract you are required to put up a deposit, usually of 5% to 10% of the value of the contract. More margin is required when the realized loss in the market exceeds 50% of your original deposit.

The Sydney Futures Exchange, if you are interested, also trades futures contracts in steers and wool.

### Options

If you want to limit your risks of loss on the above futures contracts you have the alternative of buying options instead on the bank accepted bills, U.S. dollar, and share price index futures.

In addition to these, the Australian Options Market trades gold and silver options on a worldwide linkup with the Vancouver, Montreal, and Amsterdam exchanges. As each exchange closes, trading activity moves to the market in the next time zone around the globe.

Stock options are also traded on the Sydney Stock Exchange in lots of 1,000 shares per contract, with a maximum duration of nine months. The underlying stocks are listed on the Australian Stock Exchange. According to Australian Options Market manager Bruce Donoghoe, all this may eventually develop into a global market in which "individual stock options will be traded from various world centers on a round-the-clock basis."

## Taxes

To end on an unpleasant note, Australian withholding tax is imposed on dividend and interest income paid to a nonresident of Australia. Interest on government bonds used to be completely exempt, but as of July 1, 1986, interest on bonds issued by Australian and state government authorities also became subject to withholding tax. On interest the withholding is 10%. Dividend income is hit with a 30% withholding tax, except for residents of countries, such as the United States, that have double-taxation agreements with Australia. In this case the withholding is reduced to 15%. The Australian government was planning to remove the withholding tax on dividends in 1988 so as to encourage more foreign investment. Capital gains, which previously were tax-free, have been taxed at income tax rates since September 19, 1985.

As regards the United States tax authorities, the 10% tax on Australian interest is not covered by the double-taxation treaty, but you can take a corresponding 10% credit off your American taxes. Interest payments on foreign-currency bonds are taxed as ordinary income in the same way as on United States bonds.

Eventually, when you have made your pile down under, you will want to take your money out. You can do so quite freely, but you may have to get clearance from the Australian Taxation Office if the ultimate destination of your loot is the Bahamas, Bermuda, the Channel Islands, the Virgin Islands, the Cayman Islands, Gibraltar, Grenada, Hong Kong, the Isle of Man, Liberia, Liechtenstein, Luxembourg, Nauru, the Netherlands Antilles, Panama, Switzerland, Tonga, or Vanuatu. What you have there is a roster of the world's foremost tax havens, and the

Australian Taxation Office evidently takes a dim view of all of them.

## Information

The Sydney Stock Exchange is a gold mine of printed and electronic information on Australian stocks. Its publications include reports on individual companies, their operations and history, and a seven-year analysis of their financial statements; a daily diary of stock market developments; a weekly diary; a weekly summary; a daily list of stock market prices; a handbook on the fifty biggest companies; share price information on floppy disks with up to twenty years of data if you own an IBM or MacIntosh personal computer; a monthly analysis of the market indexes; and much more.

Radio Australia broadcasts daily stock market reports beamed at North America at 11:27 P.M. Greenwich Mean Time (6:27 A.M. Eastern Standard Time) on the 31-meter band if you own a shortwave radio and like to get up early.

Other sources of information include the *Australian Financial Review*, a daily; the *National Times* and the *Bulletin*, both weeklies; and *Personal Investment*, a monthly.

## · NEW ZEALAND ·

New Zealand, Australia's little brother down under, has had one of the world's hottest little stock markets in the early part of the 1980s, with an average price advance of more than 40% a year up to 1985. In that year the Labour government, applying the same distinctly nonsocialist policies as its Australian counterpart, began freeing the economy of a lot of restrictions, and the stock market boomed even further in 1986. Trading volume more than doubled from the 1985 level to NZ$4.8 billion and the total value of all listed stocks rose 142% to NZ$42.4 billion. The system almost broke down under the boom. Securities industry staff doubled; lack of trained personnel and exploding volume led to paperwork jams that the exchange was hoping to cure in

1987 with a new computerized trading system.

Then came the crash. All the factors that devastated the Australian stock market in October 1987 struck the overheated New Zealand market with equal force, and stock prices dropped about 40% in a matter of weeks.

A member of the British Commonwealth, with a population of 3 million European settlers and 300,000 Polynesian Maoris, New Zealand is a major supplier of meat, wool, and dairy products to world markets. These products compose 50% of New Zealand's exports, and the country started running into trouble when Britain, its major market, ended New Zealand's preferred Commonwealth status on entering the European Common Market. The soaring oil prices of the 1970s added another crushing blow. In the 1980s the Labour government decided that the only way out was a market-oriented economy open to world competition. Prices, wages, rents, and interest rates were decontrolled. Foreign exchange and other financial restrictions were removed. The New Zealand dollar, floating freely, began to recoup its lost value.

### Stock Markets

The New Zealand stock market started up with the gold rush of the 1870s, and gold mining stocks were the first mainstay of the market. Since then New Zealand has developed one of the world's most technologically advanced agricultural systems and a well-developed industrial base. Forestry, manufacturing, meat processing, and agricultural stocks have relegated gold mining to a minor role.

The stock market is small but broadly based, with a proportionately large number of individual stockholders. The New Zealand Stock Exchange, comprising regional exchanges at Wellington, Auckland, Christchurch/Invercargill, and Dunedin, lists 273 New Zealand companies and 130 foreign companies. A second board was set up in 1986 to accommodate smaller companies.

The most actively traded stocks are Brierley Investments, Fletcher Challenge, NZI Corp., Chase Corp., Emco Corp., NZ Forest Products, Equiticorp Holdings, Feltex New Zealand, Lion Corp., and Winstone.

The major market indexes are Barclays Industrial Index of forty major New Zealand companies, with a base of 100 as of January 31, 1957; the New Zealand Reserve Bank Index, comprising sixty-one companies and excluding mines; Barclays Mining Index, with a base of 100 as of August 31, 1981; and the New Zealand Stock Exchange Index, published since January 1987 with a base of 1,000 as of July 1, 1986. Unfortunately the indexes are inaccessible unless you read the New Zealand financial press or the *Financial Times* of London.

## Problems

There are other problems besides the lack of available information. The New Zealand dollar has been on a mainly downhill course since 1978, when it was worth US$1.06. By 1984 it was down to 46 U.S. cents, largely nullifying the effect of the stock market advance for American investors. After being set free from government intervention on a free float it surged upward again to 58 cents in 1986 and 60 cents in 1987. Despite this, its prospects do not look too bright at the time of writing as New Zealand flounders under a 12% inflation rate and a mounting foreign debt.

The stock market advance was notable too for its takeover fever. No less than thirty-two companies were taken over in 1986, many by dubious financial maneuvers. High-flying speculative stocks issued new shares to buy up other companies, revalued the victim's assets, and passed the revaluation into earnings, thus pushing the raider's stock yet higher for another takeover.

The New Zealand stock market is also conspicuously lacking in any specific legal prohibitions against insider trading, which has become a major activity. Company directors are not allowed to profit personally from their position of trust, but directors' wives and cousins are closely watched for their stock purchases at critical moments. Steve M. Spelman, manager of Acorn Group Trust, an investment concern, even founded Insider Trading Hotlines, a service to retail insider trading information to the public. According to the *Wall Street Journal*, informers were paid according to the price rise after their tips—as much as NZ$50,000 if the stock rose by 2,000%.

In its January 1987 report for 1986, the New Zealand Stock Exchange noted growing public demand for surveillance of insider trading, but said its options "are limited to the power of persuasion and publicity when possible cases come to its attention."

### Investing in New Zealand

Caution is the first word that comes to mind in circumstances like these, and a broad-based investment trust would appear to be the safest bet. Which brings us to Ronald Brierley, New Zealand's star investor. Brierley, who apparently ranks with the best that Wall Street has produced, runs three interlocking trusts that control a total of more than US$3 billion in assets: Brierley Investments Ltd. in New Zealand; Industrial Equity Ltd. in Australia; and Industrial Equity Pacific in Hong Kong. These trusts have their investments spread over companies ranging from auto distribution and brewing to cemeteries, real estate, and tourism. All three are listed in New Zealand, besides listings in London, Australia, and Hong Kong.

Brierley Investments is the giant of the New Zealand stock market. More than 3% of the entire population of the country are stockholders. The Wellington town hall is the only locale big enough for the shareholder meetings. Brierley dines regularly with the New Zealand finance minister and has been appointed chairman of the Bank of New Zealand.

For investors who are not U.S. residents, The New Zealand Fund offers another broadly based investment in the New Zealand market. It is the first New Zealand mutual fund offered to overseas investors, but has not registered with the SEC and so is not available to U.S.-based investors. Registered in the Cayman Islands, it is listed in Hong Kong. The sales commission is 5%, and there is a pretty big 2% annual management fee. Initial investment minimum is US$1,000.

Bank of New Zealand (1 Willis Street, Wellington) is the country's leading financial institution, holding about 20% of the assets of New Zealand's financial sector. Among its services it includes investment management and safe custody facilities.

New Zealand brokers include:

Finch Webster & Nathan
P.O. Box 2790
Wellington

Francis Allison Symes and Co.
P.O. Box 398
Wellington

Jarden & Co.
P.O. Box 3394
Wellington

Renouf Partners
P.O. Box 3648
Wellington

For independent advice, Leadenhall Investment Managers (Leadenhall House, 69–71 Boulcott Street, Wellington) claims to be New Zealand's largest independent investment company with no conflicting financial or merchant bank interests.

Dividends paid to nonresidents are subject to 30% withholding tax, but this is reduced by the double-taxation treaty with the United States.

Information is scant outside the New Zealand press, which includes the *New Zealand Herald*, the *Dominion*, the *Auckland Star*, all dailies; *National Business Review*, a weekly; and *New Zealand Financial Review*, a monthly.

The New Zealand Stock Exchange (Caltex Tower, 286–292 Lambton Quay, Wellington) publishes an annual report, and brokerage firms provide research on the market and individual companies.

# CHAPTER
# 13

## HONG KONG,
## SINGAPORE,
## AND MALAYSIA

## · HONG KONG ·

Imagine that you are faced with the following situation. You are in charge of a coastal enclave of just over 400 square miles—about one-third the size of Rhode Island—jammed with 5.5 million human beings. The majority of these people are refugees who have been pouring in, mostly penniless, from a giant communist neighbor, for the past forty years. This huge communist neighbor in fact lays claim to the territory you are trying to govern and may take it over at any moment; there is no adequate force available to prevent that. With a population density of 1,350 per square mile your territory has no natural resources at all except one deepwater harbor. Even some of your water supply comes from that threatening communist power on the other side of your defenseless border.

This has been precisely the situation of Hong Kong, a British colony on the coast of China, since World War II.

Your first reaction perhaps would be to apply for U.S. foreign aid, then to request interest-free loans from the World Bank, ask for help from the United Nations, the International Red Cross, and emergency food supplies from any other available source of help. Numberless countries have done just that.

Hong Kong, however, has followed a different course. Without asking anyone's help, without even running a budget deficit, it has become Asia's leading financial center, third in the world after New York and London. Hong Kong is Asia's largest gold-trading center, the world's biggest exporter of clothing, toys, and plastic products, of watches, clocks, and radios. Hong Kong in fact ranks eighteenth among the world's leading trading nations. Its container port is the third busiest in the world, after Rotterdam and New York. It has the world's biggest air-cargo terminal and is the world's third-largest diamond-trading center after New York and Antwerp. Forty-four of the world's top fifty banking groups find it necessary to have an office in Hong Kong. More than 2,000 foreign companies do business in the colony. Last but not least, together with Singapore it has achieved the highest living standard in Asia after Japan. The average daily wage for all Hong Kong workers is about $14 a day.

There is even money left over to help the needy. Social security benefits are all noncontributory, and the Hong Kong Social Welfare Department provides public assistance to more than 60,000 at the rate of $60 a month for single persons and considerably more for family groups. Hong Kong has even been able to care for thousands of refugee boat people from communist Vietnam in addition to its own refugees from Communist China who swelled the population tenfold from half a million in the 1940s.

The explanation for this implausible success story is simple. Hong Kong is run on a system that stresses a minimum of government interference in the marketplace and the right of everyone to take risks, work, make a profit, and keep the money they make. In short, laissez-faire capitalism. The Hong Kong government describes its policy as one of "minimal government involvement in the private sector, while ensuring an adequate base for monetary policy, the promotion of sound business practices and appropriate protection for depositors and investors." The late governor, Sir Edward Youde, told the London Stock Exchange in 1985 that his government would regulate "only when the orderly conduct of business, fair treatment of the work force and the good name of Hong Kong so required." Functioning on this basic premise, the Hong Kong economy has grown at an average rate of 10% a year since 1966.

The Hong Kong stock market, in the estimation of the *GT Guide to World Equity Markets*, "based entirely on the principles of a free market economy, is the freest investment market in the world. It has no exchange controls and no distinction is made between resident and non-resident investors."

The international accounting firm Peat, Marwick, Mitchell & Co. notes that "there are no laws on repatriation of profits; there are no value added or sales taxes; there are no foreign investment restrictions; and there is no cumbersome bureaucracy. Except in the very broadest sense, the Hong Kong government does not practice economic planning."

Hong Kong does not even have a central bank. Its money is issued by a couple of commercial banks: the Hong Kong & Shanghai Banking Corporation, and Standard Chartered Bank. As the government runs a consistently balanced budget it has practically no debt.

In this welcoming atmosphere and with the additional advantage of having English as an official language, Hong Kong has attracted about 800 American companies, which have invested $700 million in Hong Kong manufacturing enterprises. More than 16,000 Americans live in Hong Kong, and the United States takes more than 40% of the colony's exports.

There are also fifty-eight American banks, which compete with hundreds of other foreign banks in Hong Kong in foreign-currency trading. The entrepreneurial spirit of its Chinese population, the finest harbor in Asia, and the government's hands-off policy have made Hong Kong a worldwide trading power, but it is the foreign exchange market that has turned it into a leading financial center. Currency dealers exchange billions of dollars, pounds, marks, yen, lire, and francs every day. Some of this money is involved in international trade, but most of it is simply money roaming the world in search of the highest available rate of return. Money trading goes on around the globe around the clock, and Hong Kong is fortunately placed in a time zone where it is just starting its business day when one rival, London, is deep in midnight sleep. It is ending the day's work just as the London dealers go to work. A few hours after that, dinner time in Hong Kong, traders in the other rival center in New York begin their working day.

### Stock Market

However, our main interest as investors is the Hong Kong stock market, and we might well amend that word "investors" right now to "speculators." As the GT *Guide* notes, "The laissez-faire nature of the Hong Kong market is reflected in dealings on the stock exchange. Price rises and falls of 50% or more within a year are not unknown, and Hong Kong has been the scene of several spectacular corporate insolvencies." The volatility of the Hong Kong market is largely due to the colony's high degree of sensitivity to world trade conditions. It is aggravated by the penchant of local investors for operating on margin.

To the average Hong Kong citizen the stock market is a passion. Many banks and even some retail stores display the latest prices on video screens for their customers, together with financial information, interest rates, and currency fluctuations. Newspapers, radio, and television also provide extensive coverage of financial news. If you are not right there on the spot you can miss a lot of the action, and the action can be phenomenal. In some stock market booms, companies such as Hong Kong Land, a leading real estate company, have traded at 300 times earnings.

One memorable stock market frenzy took place in 1973. Trading volume soared so high that, one stock exchange proving insufficient, another three were founded, and there were plans afoot for a fifth, sixth, and seventh. As Ray Astin, Hong Kong commissioner for securities and commodities, recalls it: "By early 1973 trading was frenetic, gambling fever was rampant and affected all, from the taipans down to the humblest amah. Everyone was busy wheeling and dealing. The government issued orders to all civil servants forbidding them to use office telephones for private business. All lines were continually engaged with their calls to brokers. And then came the inevitable. The bubble burst."

By December 1973, the market's Hang Seng Index, which

had reached 1,775 points early that year, had collapsed to 400. By December 1974 it was down to 150 points. By this time the government decided that laissez-faire had its limits and set up a Securities Commission. Nevertheless this is not a market for the faint of heart even now. Despite the Commission's efforts it has proved difficult to restrain the capitalist enthusiasm of the colony's residents. In 1973 there were four Hong Kong mutual funds. By 1984 there were 100, and by 1987 more than 200. In proportion to the population this would be equivalent to 10,000 mutual funds in the United States instead of the current 2,000.

The Hong Kong Brokers Association, a stuffy, British, colonial sort of affair formed in 1891, gave the Exchange its formal start. By 1986 the Chinese entrepreneurs had got into the act and there were four rival exchanges—Hong Kong, Far East, Kam Ngan, and Kowloon. Under government prodding these were merged into one new, unified, technologically updated stock exchange that went into business in April 1986. Brokers, who used to shout, scream, and wave wildly to make deals, now sat sedately at computer terminals, and began to do a lot more business. Trading volume increased nearly sevenfold between 1986 and 1987, to the point where Hong Kong has become one of the world's most active markets. Yearly trading comes to about three-quarters of the exchange's total capitalization, a relatively huge turnover of 75% a year. While local speculators trade heavily, a lot of this activity has been due to foreign investors. According to Astin, orders from New York account for up to 15% of all Hong Kong stock market trading, with some brokers handling up to $40 million in U.S. orders in a single day.

As a result of some scandals in the 1980s, notably what became known as "the Carrian affair," Mr. Astin and his regulators were threatening in 1987 to impose tighter disclosure requirements on the freewheeling stock market. With regulation lax and in any case largely left to voluntary compliance, the authorities concluded that the odds tended to favor the big stockholders somewhat too heavily for the little guy's health. However, secrecy is precisely the attraction of Hong Kong for many investors in South-east Asia who have to slip their money through foreign exchange and investment restrictions in their own countries. The question was whether, with more American and European investors coming into the market, there was more advantage in tightening up the regulations for a more staid clientele.

All the foregoing may serve as background to what happened on October 19, 1987, and the following days. On that Black Monday the Hong Kong market's Hang Seng index dropped 11.1% in frantic trading; brokers were overwhelmed by an avalanche of sell orders and Hong Kong Stock Exchange chairman Ronald Li panicked. Throwing laissez-faire free market principles to the wind, he closed down the Exchange for the rest of the week. Hong Kong was the only major stock exchange in the world to close its doors during the crisis, and the closure merely postponed the crash for a few days. The following Monday, when the Exchange reopened, the Hang Seng index plunged another 33% in a single day.

The Hong Kong government then stepped in to form a Securities Review Committee to inspect the damage and recommend remedial measures. It also joined up with the Exchange and international banks to set up a HK$4 billion (US$500 million) rescue package to prop up the Hong Kong Futures Exchange, which had been reduced to a state of paralysis by the crisis. More than forty futures brokerage firms who had defaulted on their obligations were suspended and taken over. The crowning irony was that the Communist government in Peking directed its state banks to contribute to the bailout—a fact that was not lost on apprehensive capitalists seeking clues to China's future plans for the territory.

Mr. Li came under criticism for closing the Exchange, thus depriving investors of the opportunity to get out of the market and weakening the credibility of Hong Kong as a financial center— as well as favoring his fellow-brokers with the four-day respite. His defense was that the market would have ground to a halt under the selling blitz anyway.

There are 340 stocks listed on the Hong Kong Exchange, among which real estate companies have a disproportionate share of the market. They account for about 40% of the total market capitalization. Banks are another important sector. The colony's leading bank, Hong Kong and Shanghai Banking Corporation, is one of the world's twenty largest commercial banks. Many other companies are involved in trading and shipping. Manufacturing companies are a small part of the market, about 5%, due to the fact that most local industries are labor-intensive and seldom need to raise large amounts of capital.

All this is reflected in the market's main indicator, the Hang Seng index, which is composed of thirty-two stocks and which became the focus of the Black Monday debacle. The index is weighted by each company's capitalization and largely reflects the moves of such banking and real estate giants as Hong Kong Bank, Hang Seng Bank, Hong Kong Land, and Cheung Kong. The Index started from a base of 100 on July 31, 1964, and reached its lowest point at 58.61 in August 1967. It hit 500 for the first time in July 1972 and reached 1,000 in February 1973. It hit its all-time high of 3,949 just before the crash of October 1, 1987.

The Hang Seng Index became a market in its own right in the form of a futures contract launched in 1986. In one short year it became even more active than the stock market it derived from. The Hang Seng Index futures contract became the world's most active stock index futures contract outside of the United States. The price of the contract is the value of the Hang Seng Index multiplied by HK$50. As many as 25,000 contracts were traded daily in early 1987, and average trading volume came to HK$5 billion a day. This was approximately twice as much as the turnover on the Hong Kong stock market itself. Apparently almost all of this activity was generated by local investors.

After Black Monday all this came to a screeching halt on the Hong Kong Futures Exchange. A third of the Exchange's 127 members were suspended for defaulting on $230 million in stock index futures. By November, trading in futures was practically nonexistent, and the surviving brokers spent their days reading newspapers on a still and empty trading floor. What activity remained was concentrated in the Hong Kong Futures Exchange's gold, sugar and soybean contracts. The Exchange also has a cotton futures market, which has been dormant for some years.

Hong Kong is also a major player in the world gold market through the Chinese Gold and Silver Exchange Society, which plays a leading part in setting the world gold price. This is a thoroughly native market. Trading is conducted in the Cantonese dialect by the 193 Society members, deals are made in Hong Kong dollars, and the trading unit is the tael, a Chinese weight measure equal to 1.33 troy ounces. This is the third-largest gold market in the world, but it is not the only one in Hong Kong. A market known curiously as Loco-London provides a facility where international bullion traders and major banks are the main participants. Prices here are quoted in U.S. dollars, and delivery of the gold is made in London.

### Stocks and Stockbrokers

If you really want to take a flier on the Hong Kong stock market, shares are traded in board lots of 1,000 shares each. Odd lots are traded separately at a small discount. Brokerage fees come to about 1%, and both buyers and sellers also pay a 0.3% stamp duty. The minimum brokerage charge is HK$25. Ordinary, preferred, and convertible stocks are listed, but the bulk of trading is in ordinary stocks, and although companies are allowed to issue bearer shares, registered shares are the rule. Corporate bonds are a rarity in Hong Kong. The fact that the government runs on a practically debt-free basis has hampered the development of the kind of large-scale bond market that a chronic debtor like the U.S. government tends to foment.

The largest listed companies in Hong Kong are Hong Kong and Shanghai Banking Corp., Hong Kong Telephone, Hong Kong Land, China Light & Power, Hutchison Whampoa, Hang Seng Bank, Swire Pacific, Hong Kong & Kowloon Wharf, Hong Kong Electric, and Cheung Kong. It might be noted that the large number of land and utility companies on this list have no way of removing their assets from Hong Kong when the colony is taken over by Communist China.

Regional mutual funds, as noted above, proliferate. Most of them invest in Hong Kong stocks, although some invest also in Singapore and Malaysia, a few in the Philippines and Thailand.

These funds include Jardine Fleming's JF South East Asia Trust, Wardley's Wardley Nikko Asia Fund, and GT Management's GT South China Fund.

Brokers include:

Cazenove & Co. (Overseas)
Hutchison House
10 Harcourt Road
Hong Kong

De Zoete & Bevan (Far East)
New Henry House
10 Ice House Street
Hong Kong

Hoare Govett (Far East) Ltd.
Edinburgh Tower
The Landmark
Central, Hong Kong

James Capel (Far East) Ltd.
39th floor
Exchange Square
Hong Kong

Jardine Fleming Ltd.
Connaught Centre
Central, Hong Kong

Vickers da Costa & Co. (HK) Ltd.
1 Exchange Square
8 Connaught Place
Hong Kong

W.I. Carr, Sons & Co. (Overseas) Ltd.
St. George's Building
2 Ice House Street
Hong Kong

The Stock Exchange Compensation Fund has a relatively small HK$50 million to indemnify investors who lose money if their broker should go belly-up. There is a claim limit of HK$1 million per client, so it could accommodate fifty big investors.

Among brokerage houses, Carr, Vickers da Costa, de Zoete, and Hoare Govett are considered outstanding for their research reports.

The Hong Kong Bank, Hang Seng Bank, and Standard Chartered Bank also produce research on the Hong Kong economy. Newspapers carrying financial news in English include the *South China Morning Post*, the *Hong Kong Standard*, and the *Asian Wall Street Journal*, as well as the weekly *Far Eastern Economic Review*.

The Stock Exchange of Hong Kong Ltd. (Exchange Square, Hong Kong) offers a variety of publications, including a daily quotation sheet (US$72 a month), the *Securities Bulletin Monthly* ($40 a year), the *Weekly Report* ($235 a year), and its *Annual Fact Book* ($25).

## Taxes

Citicorp of New York notes that Hong Kong's rate of taxation is the lowest in Asia. There are taxes on company profits and on interest payments, but there are no taxes on dividends, royalties, sales, or capital gains. There is a withholding tax on interest charged at a standard 16.5% rate. There are no special taxes on foreign stockholders, who can freely take their capital, interest, and dividends out of Hong Kong without restriction. Hong Kong has no double-taxation treaties with other countries and does not tax income derived from other countries. The Hong Kong government does not consider the colony a tax haven, but merely an area with a low tax structure. And low taxation in Citicorp's estimation is "one of the fundamental tenets ensuring the continued strength of the Hong Kong economy."

## The Future

Unfortunately that future is rather problematical, particularly after July 1, 1997, when Hong Kong is due to become a part of Communist China under a Sino-British agreement signed in 1984. The days of this little jewel of laissez-faire capitalism are thus apparently numbered. China's claims to the territory had been causing bouts of nervousness for years, particularly in the early 1980s, when an incipient panic caused a run on the Hong Kong dollar. In one of its rare departures from free market economics, the Hong Kong government then moved in to peg its currency at a fixed rate of HK$7.80 per U.S. dollar.

Paradoxically, the signing of the agreement with China lifted a cloud of uncertainty and despondency from the colony, and local markets boomed. Under the agreement with the British, by which Hong Kong will become a Special Administrative Region of China, the Chinese government undertook to preserve Hong Kong's social, economic, legal, and generally capitalistic system for fifty years after 1997.

Members of the Hong Kong establishment insist that all is well for the future. Sir Michael Sandberg, retired chairman of the Hong Kong Bank, affirmed in February 1987 that "the territory will continue to gain stature as a business and financial center well into the next century." However, Jardine Matheson, Hong Kong's oldest trading firm, caused quite a to-do in 1984 when it moved its legal domicile to Bermuda.

Already there are straws in the wind. When Chinese Communist Party leader Hu Yaobang was suddenly removed from his post in January 1987 the Hang Seng Index dropped more than 3% in one day. Some remember too that until the Communist takeover in China in 1949, Shanghai was the region's business and financial center, and the Chinese Communists made all kinds of promises then about maintaining its facilities intact. The emergence of Hong Kong in its place was due in large measure to the fact that those promises were never kept.

But it is not only a matter of goodwill. It is a question of having the capacity to run a free market economy. As Hong Kong Stock Exchange chairman Ronald Li observed, "We have had Chinese delegations coming through here for four years, but they still need to understand exactly what a stock exchange is."

There is a theory though that the incoming Chinese Communist authorities will be on their best behavior in Hong Kong, which they will try to hold up as an example to Taiwan in the hope of enticing the Chinese Nationalist government on that renegade island to rejoin the Middle Kingdom.

Hong Kong has survived and flourished against all the odds so far. Perhaps it will continue to survive and flourish, particularly as the Chinese Communists have already begun to flirt with capitalism themselves. If not, then the primary beneficiary is likely to be Singapore.

## · SINGAPORE AND KUALA LUMPUR ·

Singapore is in many respects Hong Kong's twin in the Far East. It is a city-state, it is populated mainly by Chinese, it shares the same British colonial origin, it has survived and flourished on a system of economic laissez-faire and free trade. But destiny has favored it over Hong Kong in one vital respect: Singapore is an independent nation, albeit a midget one that covers an area somewhat smaller than New York City. Nevertheless, whereas Hong Kong's problem is imminent ingurgitation by Communist China, Singapore's is to disentangle itself from Malaysia, a nation whose history and economy it has been rather messily entwined with.

Originally an obscure Malay fishing village on an island at the tip of the Malay Peninsula, Singapore entered history in 1819 when Sir Stamford Raffles set up a trade depot there for the British East India Company. The British soon realized it also commanded a strategic chokepoint in the Straits of Malacca and made the colony their main naval base in the Far East. They also took over the Malay Peninsula, which later became Malaysia, a nation with which Singapore has had an on-again, off-again relationship since independence in 1959.

Similar unions and separations have marked the course of the stock exchanges at Singapore and Kuala Lumpur, the Malaysian capital. In 1963 Singapore joined the Malaysian federation, and the two exchanges joined up to form the single Stock Exchange of Malaya and Singapore. In 1965 Singapore seceded to form an independent republic, and in 1973 the two exchanges separated again.

However, many of their stocks are dually listed, and in December 1985 they were joined together again by a common disaster when Pan-Electric Industries Ltd.—a Singapore-based hotel, real estate, and marine salvage company—collapsed with $200 million in unpayable debts. Local brokers were holding $300 million worth of Pan-Electric stock, and when matters were finally sorted out seven of the twenty-five members of the Singapore Stock Exchange had gone under. Both the Singapore and Kuala Lumpur exchanges closed for three days, a scandal from which they have yet to recover fully. Twenty other stocks connected with Pan-Electric were still suspended from trading a year later. Shocked international traders found they were stuck as the exchanges closed, unable to sell out at any price. They began to make big block trades off the market while local brokers had great difficulty executing big orders due to lack of liquidity.

Seeing the writing on the wall, Singapore has taken vigorous measures. Its stock market is closely watched now by the Singapore Monetary Authority, which drastically curtailed brokers' ability to operate on margin. The Stock Exchange has also initiated a plan to internationalize its operations and make a niche for itself on the global market. International brokers were encouraged to buy into local brokerage firms. Hoare Govett of London took a controlling interest in Summit Securities. New markets were opened. You can now short the overheated Japanese stock market in Singapore, for example, by trading in the Nikkei 225 Stock Index futures contract, which the Singapore Exchange inaugurated in September 1986. (Trading in index futures is banned in Japan itself.) In 1987 the Singapore Exchange also began quoting fifty American over-the-counter stocks through an arrangement with the U.S. National Association of Securities Dealers.

However, when Singapore proposed to increase its competitiveness by deregulating brokerage commissions, the old relationship with Malaysia intruded once again: Malaysian brokers in Kuala Lumpur urged withdrawal of all Malaysian stocks from the Singapore Exchange. As 183 of the 317 stocks listed in Singapore are Malaysian companies, this was no idle threat.

Beset by internal problems, Malaysia is in much poorer shape than Singapore as an international stock market competitor. About two-fifths of the population are overseas Chinese, who have a dominant role on the Malaysian business scene; two-fifths are native Malays, who dominate the political stage. The outcome of this has been the government's New Economic Policy, designed to favor stock ownership by native Malays, or Bumiputras, as they are called. Part of each new share offering has to be set aside for Bumiputras at a reduced price. There are also restrictions on foreign ownership of Malaysian companies.

Until the Singapore stock market frees itself of its Malaysian entanglements, it seems unlikely to emerge as a serious global contender, although Singapore does rival Hong Kong in areas such as foreign exchange trading.

Singapore also weathered the Black October storm much better than Hong Kong did. Thanks perhaps to the experience acquired in the Pan-Electric Industries affair, the Singapore Exchange did not close down during the crisis, no brokers defaulted, and the market smoothly handled a huge increase in volume. Singapore even managed to accommodate the traders in Hong Kong who switched to the Singapore market during the week the Hong Kong Exchange closed down. The Singapore Exchange was also able to absorb a huge offering of seven million Singapore International Airline shares, which were all snapped up on October 20, Black Tuesday. However, when the dust settled, between late October and early November the average Singapore stock prices sank to about half their former level.

### Singapore Stock Market

Singapore and Kuala Lumpur, with their interlisted companies, account for a little more than 0.5% of world stock market capitalization between them. The rubber boom of 1910, when rubber plantations were all the rage, gave stock trading its first major boost in Singapore, followed by the flotation of new tin mines

in Malaysia. Nowadays the Singapore market offers a wide selection of industrial and commercial companies, as well as plantations and mines, but trading activity is low. Many companies
are family-owned or -controlled. Others have Temasek Holdings,
the state investment holding company, as their main, and quies-
cent, stockholder. Most active investors are individuals, with a
small amount of trading by insurance companies and mutual
funds. The latter include Singapore Growth Fund and a number
of Hong Kong–based funds.

The Singapore market has two sections, one for big board
stocks and the other for smaller companies. Big board listing
requirements are not all that stringent: a minimum capital of
S$5 million and at least 500 shareholders. Blue chips on the big
board include Overseas-Chinese Banking Corporation, Singapore Airlines, Fraser & Neave, and Singapore Press Holdings.
Other actively traded stocks include Development Bank of Singapore, United Overseas Bank, Overseas Union Enterprises,
Highland & Lowlands, Straits Trading, and a number of companies incorporated in Malaysia that are mentioned further on
in connection with the Kuala Lumpur market.

There are two kinds of trades: cash, with delivery in two
business days; and settlement, with payment deferred to the end
of each calendar month. Brokerage fees range from 1% to 1.5%.

The main market indicators are the Straits Times Index, comprising thirty stocks, and the Singapore Stock Exchange Index,
both of which include Malaysian as well as Singapore stocks.
The Stock Exchange Index, in addition to its all-share index,
has subindexes of industrials, finance, hotels, property companies, plantations, and mines. They can all register some pretty
violent swings. As a sequel to the Pan-Electric affair, the Straits
Times Index plunged to a ten-year low of 563.24 in April 1986.
By August 1987 it had tripled to 1,505, and even after Black
October it stood at the 900 level in November, about where it
had been a year earlier.

The Singapore dollar has been stable enough, ranging from
S$2.04 to S$2.18 per U.S. dollar since 1981, and capital gains
are tax-free on stocks held for more than three months. But

Singapore has a whopping 40% withholding tax on dividends, and another disincentive for foreign investors is that there is no double-taxation relief.

Brokers in Singapore include:

Alliance Securities
05-04 Far East Bank Building
156 Cecil Street
Singapore 0106

Cathay Securities Ltd.
2 Shenton Way
ICB Building
Singapore 0106

J.M. Sassoon & Co. Ltd.
1 Bonham Street
United Overseas Bank Building
Singapore 0104

Summit Securities
79 Robinson Road
Central Provident Fund Building
Singapore 0106

Sassoon is outstanding for its market and stock reports. The Singapore Stock Exchange (16 Raffles Quay, 16-03 Hong-Leong Building, Singapore 0104) provides Statex Service, a weekly update of financial reports from listed companies. Its book, *Securities Market in Singapore*, gives a comprehensive account of the stock market.

### Kuala Lumpur Stock Market

Many shares listed on the Kuala Lumpur Stock Exchange can also be bought and sold in Singapore, some in London and Hong Kong as well. Historically, Britons were the biggest stockholders, but local investors have been increasing their holdings, particularly in London-based plantations and tin companies that moved their incorporation to Malaysia as the colonial era of Somerset

Maugham planter types, gin and tonics on the veranda, and a spot of tiffin came to an end. Transactions are settled in Malaysian ringgits instead of Singapore dollars. About 300 stocks are listed and they provide a good cross-section of the Malaysian economy. Industrials, including shoes, food, textiles, and cement, predominate. Tin mines and rubber and oil plantations are also numerous, followed by financials, real estate companies, and hotels. Overseas-Chinese Banking Corporation and Sime Darby between them account for about 10% of the entire market value. As many of the largest companies are linked in some way to world commodity markets, they are highly sensitive to world trading conditions. Price swings can also be violent. In the first day of trading after the Pan-Electric closure, the Kuala Lumpur Industrial Share Price Index lost one-sixth of its value in one session.

Some of the major Malaysian companies are Harrisons Malaysian Plantations, Malayan Banking, Genting, Consolidated Plantations, Malaysian Tobacco Co., Malayan Airlines System, Kuala Lumpur Kepong, Malayan United Industries, and Multi-Purpose Holdings.

The Malaysian currency has held reasonably steady at between 2.24 and 2.42 ringgits per U.S. dollar since 1981, but investors here too get socked with a 40% tax on dividends. Profits, dividends, and capital can be freely repatriated, and nonresidents can buy shares without restriction—except citizens of Israel and South Africa, who are excluded apparently for political reasons.

The main Malaysian business newspaper is *Business News*. The *New Straits Times* and the *Star* also carry financial news. The Kuala Lumpur Stock Exchange (Block C, Damansara Centre, 50490 Kuala Lumpur) publishes *Investors Digest* monthly and other material.

Brokers include:

Ariffin & Low Securities
Menara Promet
Jalan Sultan Ismail
Kuala Lumpur

Charles Bradbourne & Co.
President House
Jalan Sultan Ismail
Kuala Lumpur

G.P. Securities
Jalan Raja Chulan
Kuala Lumpur

Seagroatt & Campbell
1 Leboh Ampang
Kuala Lumpur

The bottom line, however, is that for anyone who doesn't have much time to devote to this market, the easiest way to participate is to buy Malaysia Fund, a closed-end fund listed on the New York Stock Exchange. This is a relatively trouble-free way of betting on the future of a developing, resource-rich country that covers 128,000 square miles of mostly tropical forest and is the world's main supplier of tin and rubber, as well as a producer of oil, copper, and gold. It is largely a tax-free way too. The Malaysian government has exempted Malaysia Fund from the 40% withholding tax on dividends.

# CHAPTER 14

## JAPAN

In 1987 Japan became number one in one of the most crucial attributes of a capitalist power. It displaced the United States as the world's biggest stock market—a startling development that may be viewed with some skepticism and considerable misgiving. In April 1987, the combined value of all stocks quoted in Japan climbed to $2.69 trillion, edging the $2.67 trillion invested in all U.S. stock markets, according to the calculations of Morgan Stanley Capital International. Japan thus boosted its share of the total value of all the world's stock markets from 13.5% to 36.3% in ten years. The United States share, meanwhile, dropped precipitously to 36.% from the commanding 60.8% of the world total that it held in 1977.

Two factors boosted Japan's meteoric rise: a consistently huge yearly foreign trade surplus that left the country awash in cash, and the soaring value of the yen against the American dollar. The ocean of liquidity fed a wave of speculation that sent Japanese stock prices to unbelievable price-earnings ratios, creating what in the opinion of some hardheaded observers was a speculative mania reminiscent of the South Sea Bubble in eighteenth-century England. With this as cause for skepticism, there was ample reason for misgiving in that a reduced trade surplus might give the stock market bubble its fatal prick. Meanwhile, however, Japanese investors were stoking one of the great bull markets of all time, with prices, trading volume—and price-earnings ratios—setting almost daily records through 1986 and 1987.

The Tokyo Stock Exchange surpassed the New York Stock

Exchange in trading volume, and with the second-biggest economy in the world after the United States, Japan was moving into first place in all financial areas. The four biggest banks in Japan are also the four biggest banks in the world. Japan's number-one securities company, Nomura, employs 11,000 people in 155 offices and has about 4 million customers whose $230 billion in holdings are greater than the deposits of any bank in the world. Modeled consciously on Merrill Lynch as a purveyor of stocks to the masses, Nomura is also a major player in the United States government securities market, sometimes buying as much as 10% of some multibillion-dollar U.S. treasury issues in New York.

Thanks in large part to the gigantic sales efforts of Nomura, Daiwa, Nikko, and Yamaichi, the Big Four Japanese brokers, in mid-1987 the average Japanese stock was trading at a hyperbullish seventy-five times anticipated earnings for the coming year. More than 100 Japanese stocks were trading with prospective PEs of over 1,000. By comparison, the average stock in the United States had a lowly PE of 15.

As Takuya Iwasaki, president of Nikko Securities, saw it: "Financial assets in Japan now total about $4 trillion. Japan has also emerged as the world's leading creditor nation. At the end of 1986 Japan's external assets amounted to an estimated $200 billion. By 1991 we believe this total will rise to $500 billion. With this momentum behind it, and with continuing deregulation, the Tokyo market is expected to move out in front as one of the world's three leading money and capital markets."

However, this was not the only aspect of the great Japanese bull market. Prices of some properties in Tokyo doubled between 1986 and 1987. Commercial space in the Japanese capital rented for twice the New York rate. By some calculations, the total value of all the land in Japan was greater than the value of all the land in the United States, a country twenty-five times its size. Here too, skeptical observers saw signs of a speculative bubble, with prices squeezed into the stratosphere by the fact that the market is immobilized by such high taxes on land sales that only about 5% of Japanese land ever comes up for sale.

By some estimates, more than half the stock market too is largely frozen in place by owners who never sell their stock. As a traditional way of cementing a stable, friendly, and long-term relationship with each other, big Japanese corporations hold big blocks of stock in companies with which they do business. These stocks are hardly ever sold and are thus effectively out of the market. Even if relations ever did become unfriendly, they could not be sold anyway, for tax reasons. Carried for years on corporate accounts at book value, these shares would incur capital gains taxes of more than 50% if they were ever dumped on the market. According to some estimates about 40% of the Japanese stock market is immobilized by these intercompany arrangements, according to others as much as 60% or 70%. As bank relationships are particularly valuable, some banks may have up to 80% of their stock frozen in this way. Bank stock prices tripled between 1986 and 1987.

The meteoric rise of Japanese stocks was thus propelled by the fact that huge amounts of money were competing for a relatively small amount of shares actually available for trading. It was magnified too by the peculiarities of Japanese accounting methods. The price-earnings ratio on Japanese stocks has usually been calculated only on the parent company earnings. For many big Japanese corporations, earnings would be considerably higher if their subsidiaries' profits were consolidated. The PE ratio would thus actually be much lower if U.S. accounting procedures were followed. A real estate company carrying its Tokyo properties at their measly purchase prices thirty years ago would also have a ludicrous misrepresentation of their current bloated values on its books.

According to Paul H. Aron, vice-chairman of Daiwa Securities America Inc., "When a common accounting standard is used, Japanese corporations still earn less profits per unit of market value than their American counterparts. However, when these Japanese earnings, adjusted to conform to U.S. generally accepted accounting practices, are capitalized on the same basis as U.S. earnings, the average Japanese price-earnings ratio on

March 31, 1987, was 17.4 times—exactly the same as the U.S. price-earnings ratio as reported by Morgan Stanley Capital International."

The rise of Japanese stocks has also been inflated for Americans and other foreigners by the rise of the yen. In September 1985 Japan agreed with the United States, Germany, France, and Britain that the U.S. dollar should fall against the yen and other currencies as a way of reducing U.S. imports and boosting U.S. exports so as to reduce the huge American trade deficit. Despite this agreement and a huge rise in the yen from 240 to 140 per dollar, the U.S. trade deficit with Japan rose to a record $58.6 billion in 1986 and persisted almost undiminished in 1987. Nevertheless, the surge in the yen's foreign exchange value caused a painful bout of economic stagnation as the Japanese economy reduced its traditional emphasis on exports. While ominous, this signal did not deter Japanese investors, who had not seen a really bad bear market for more than twenty years—since 1965, when Yamaichi Securities nearly went under and had to be bailed out by the Bank of Japan as the stock market shriveled.

The rising yen had another effect. Japanese companies holding their export-generated profits abroad began to suffer big losses, particularly those that had put their money into such shrinking assets as U.S. treasury bonds. They began to bring the money home, adding more monetary fuel for the stock and real estate boom. The Japanese stock market favors bulls anyway, as short selling of individual stocks is forbidden. Meanwhile soaring stock prices were beginning to tempt small first-time investors. Stock exchange trading has always had a rather disreputable aura in Japan, but Japanese government bonds were yielding a miserable 3.5% in 1987, and the government controls interest rates on small bank deposits. Many small-time investors were thus sorely tempted to remove their money from that crummy 1% bank savings account and try something more exciting. Some of them doubled their money in less than two months in Nippon Telephone & Telegraph stock, a giant corporation where their interests coincided with the government's urgent need to deal with a budget deficit by selling off assets. The deficit was as big proportionately and as worrisome as the U.S. government's sea of red ink.

With a soaring stock market and a shortage of saleable stock, the Japanese government saw a great opportunity to sell off a few government-owned corporations and raise some ready cash. Japanese National Railways, a troublesome enterprise with a debt of $172 billion (nearly as much as the foreign debt of Brazil and Mexico combined) was split up into eleven parcels and scheduled for privatization. The government also prepared to dump the state tobacco monopoly and to sell its remaining shares in Japan Airlines. But the crown jewel was Nippon Telephone & Telegraph, which the government decided to sell by stages through 1989. The first 12.5% of the company, 1.65 million shares, went by lottery to 1.65 million lucky individual Japanese investors at 1.2 million yen per share (about $7,800 at the time). When these newly issued NTT shares hit the market in February 1987 they doubled in price in about a month. As their initial capital gains were not taxed, the original investors were well satisfied with the minuscule 0.2% (taxable) dividend yield.

The price rise boosted the company's total value to more than $300 billion. That made it the world's biggest company, bigger in market value than IBM, AT&T, Exxon, General Motors, and General Electric put together, bigger than the valuation of the entire West German stock market, more than 12% of the total value of all Tokyo Stock Exchange stocks.

Such a frenzied overvaluation set alarm bells ringing in a lot of minds. As *Forbes* magazine commented in May 1987, "What has happened recently in Tokyo bears more than a few resemblances to past manias like the Dutch tulip bulb craze. The Tokyo market is more like the U.S. market 60 years ago, when what we today call stock rigging, insider dealing, painting the tape, buying pools, market manipulation called the tune. Only in Japan part of the rigging is done as government policy."

Others too feared that Japan's skyrocketing stocks and soaring land boom could be heading for a crash that might shake the entire world financial system and send other markets tumbling around the globe. To some the situation looked like the U.S.

stock market in 1929—speculation feeding on itself and creating yet more speculation. In this cycle, stock speculators buy into the market, take their profits, and then with nothing else worth buying (bank deposits and bond yield being too paltry) go back into the market again, pushing prices up even higher than before. Such a house of cards could plausibly come tumbling down if the Japanese foreign trade surplus should shrink or the yen should decline against the dollar. The most efficient instrument to prick the bubble would be a strongly protectionist U.S. foreign trade bill to eliminate the trade gap with Japan. And congressional sentiment for such a bill was boiling up in Washington through 1987.

Nevertheless, it was in New York, and not in Tokyo, that financial panic struck first in October 1987. Prices on the Tokyo Stock Exchange dropped 15% on Monday, October 19. This followed the Dow Jones 100-point drop in New York the previous Friday, and came just before the Dow Jones 508-point free fall on Black Monday. The decline in Tokyo was checked initially by stock exchange rules limiting how much any stock price can fall in one day. Then the government stepped in quickly to stop the rout. On Tuesday a Japanese Finance Ministry official met with top executives of the four big Japanese brokers and hinted that the government would not be averse to a rise in stock prices—the Japanese equivalent of a pep talk. All four firms immediately mounted aggressive campaigns urging investors to buy. A few days later a Finance Ministry official was meeting with executives of Japan's three leading banks and three major insurance companies. They too had the distinct impression that the government would like stock prices to rise, and they started buying aggressively.

As the Wall Street Journal commented, "Rumors of meetings between the government and financial institutions had a reassuring effect: Many Japanese investors seemed convinced that Tokyo share prices remained safe from the spasms of selling by anxious foreigners because financial authorities were using their considerable power to manipulate the market." The impression in Japan was that most of the selling in Tokyo was being done by panic-stricken foreigners. Anyway, the incident provides a good illustration of how problems are solved in Japan Inc.

## · THE TOKYO EXCHANGE ·

The Tokyo Stock Exchange, the main forum for what has become the world's biggest securities market, has been in business since 1878 and now handles about 80% of all Japanese trading. Osaka, the second-largest market, and six other exchanges complete the picture. The eight exchanges have somewhat less than 2,000 companies listed and another 150 or so small and medium-sized companies are traded over the counter by the Japan Over-the-Counter Trading Co., which runs an automated quotations system similar to NASDAQ in the United States and accounts for about one-fifteenth of all Japanese stock transactions. The Tokyo Stock Exchange is divided into two sections. The first section, listing more than 1,000 issues, includes the larger corporations and represents about 95% of the market's total share value. The second section, with more than 400 stocks, includes smaller companies.

Transactions on the TSE were computerized when the Exchange moved into new quarters in 1985, but the 250 most active stocks are still traded manually by traders in identical blue blazers who gesticulate wildly to identify the stocks they are buying or selling: a hand held to the nose signifies Mitsubishi Gas Chemical Co., and a two-handed V indicates Victor Co. of Japan.

The Japanese securities market operates under post–World War II laws patterned after the two 1930s laws that still govern U.S. stock markets. Thus there is a strict separation between banks and brokerage firms, as in the United States.

A round lot on the TSE is 1,000 shares of stock with a par value of 50 yen and 100 shares of stock with 500-yen par value. Brokerage commissions on stock are fixed and amount to 1.25% of the transaction up to 1 million yen, and decline progressively from there on to 0.25% on trades of 1 billion yen or more. Commissions on bonds run from 0.8% to 0.25%. There is also a transfer tax of 0.55% of the gross amount of the transaction.

Bonds on the market include government bonds with maturities ranging from two months to ten years; government-guaranteed bonds issued by public corporations such as Japan National Railways; the municipal bonds of Tokyo, Osaka, and other cities; the corporate bonds of major industrial and utility companies; financial debentures of the Industrial Bank of Japan and other official financial institutions; and bonds issued by foreign borrowers such as the World Bank or the Kingdom of Denmark denominated in Japanese yen.

There are two main stock market indicators. The Nikkei Average of 250 Stocks has a base of 100 as of January 4, 1968. It does not give greater weighting to the larger component stocks and so tends to reflect the volatile fluctuations of smaller companies. The Tokyo Stock Exchange Index, also with a base of 100 as of January 4, 1968, is a weighted average that was created to give a truer picture of the overall market.

Japanese companies are open to foreign investors except for restrictions in some areas, such as nuclear power, oil refining, and other industries considered of national interest. NTT is off-limits to foreigners. Foreign trading accounts for about 15% of the activity on the TSE and has gone as high as $40 billion a month.

Japanese companies pay dividends annually, some semiannually, and foreign investors receive them with some delay, up to three or four months after the dividend is declared.

There is a foreign angle to futures trading too. The TSE began government bond futures trading in October 1985 with a contract based on the 6% ten-year Japanese government bond with a face value of 100 million yen per contract. The minimum margin is 3% of the total value. In July 1987 the London Financial Futures Exchange also began trading Japanese government bond futures, and the Chicago Board of Trade had plans to follow suit with an interchangeable contract in 1988. Index futures trading is not allowed in Japan but the Singapore Exchange offered a way around this with its Nikkei 225 Stock Index contract. The value of the Singapore contract is 500 times the Index in yen. If the Index stands at 25,000, one contract is then worth 12.5 million yen (about $90,000 at current exchange rates), but you have to deposit only about $4,000 up front. The contract is settled for cash in Singapore, where a broker's commission comes to about $25 to buy or sell. Meanwhile the Osaka Exchange found a way around the Japanese ban on index futures in June 1987 by offering a contract consisting of a basket of 50 stocks in lieu of an index. The 50 stocks represent about a quarter of the total valuation of the Tokyo Stock Exchange stocks.

## · TRADING IN TOKYO ·

The Big Four brokers handle about 70% of all trading volume and have enough clout to move the market with their sales recommendations. When Nomura is bullish, the whole market is bullish. These are enormous enterprises, with worldwide operations. Even Yamaichi, the fourth-largest, has offices around the globe from Montreal and Seoul to Bahrein. Nomura reported net profits of $1.46 billion in 1986, Nikko $607 million, Yamaichi $548 million.

These four big brokers are the obvious recommendations if you want to trade in Tokyo, but there is really very little need or incentive for an individual American investor to trade in Japan, and there are considerable difficulties. As noted in Chapter 6, there are more than 100 Japanese stocks available in the United States in the form of American Depository Receipts, which remove all the hassle involved in dealing with a broker abroad as well as eliminating global time-zone problems such as the fourteen- to seventeen-hour difference between Japan and the United States. American brokers are not much use unless you do business with a big international firm that has a seat on the TSE, such as Merrill Lynch, Morgan Stanley, or Goldman Sachs.

Japanese brokerage subsidiaries in the United States are mainly interested in institutional clients and are reluctant to take on individual American investors. As mentioned in Chapter 7, Nikko Securities welcomes "high net worth" American investors at its

U.S. offices, and in addition offers its services for trading American securities, as well as investments in the stock markets of Australia, Singapore, and Hong Kong. Nikko (140 Broadway, New York, NY 10005) appears to be the most eager to deal with individual Americans. Its booklet *A Practical Guide to Investing in Japanese Securities* is an excellent introduction to the practical aspects of opening a securities account in Japan, giving you a step-by-step explanation of what is involved, plus a copy of the power of attorney form you would have to sign for a Japanese broker to act as your broker in Tokyo. Nikko would in fact be your broker, proxy, and custodian for your shares.

To open a securities account in Japan, you have to appoint a securities company as your standing proxy. This is a government requirement, since foreigners are not allowed to vote their own stock. The proxy fee is 2,000 yen for each issue you hold plus 0.20 yen per share, with a minimum of 20,000 yen (currently about $160). Share and bond certificates are not ordinarily sent out of Japan, and you are thus stuck with a minimum expense of $160 a year for every stock you own, so you might as well forget about dealing in Japan unless you are a substantial investor. The only really practical alternative is to trade in ADRs in the United States or the Japan Fund and the U.S.-based mutual funds mentioned in Chapter 4, unless you can reach a satisfactory arrangement with one of the American brokers that operate in Tokyo.

## · INFORMATION ·

The big four Japanese brokers all turn out extensive stock market and individual company research reports in English. Their addresses in the United States are:

Daiwa Securities America
1 Liberty Plaza
New York, NY 10006

Nikko Securities Co. International
140 Broadway
New York, NY 10005

Nomura Securities International
180 Maiden Lane
New York, NY 10038

Yamaichi International
2 World Trade Center
New York, NY 10048

The Tokyo Stock Exchange (2-1-1, Nishombashi-Kayaba-cho, Chuo-ku, Tokyo 103) publishes a yearly *Fact Book*, an *Annual Statistics Report*, a *Monthly Statistics Report*, and other literature in English. The Osaka Securities Exchange (2-1, Kitahama, Higashi-ku, Osaka 541) also has some material in English. The *Japan Times* (C.P.O Box 144, Tokyo 100-91) carries general and business news from Japan as well as Tokyo stock quotations in its daily airmail edition ($486 a year) and weekly airmail edition ($70 a year). Other useful periodicals include the *Asian Wall Street Journal* daily and weekly editions; the *Japan Economic Journal*, the *Japan Stock Journal*, the *Oriental Economist*, and the *Far Eastern Economic Review*, all weeklies.

Nihon Keizai Shimbun (1221 Avenue of the Americas, New York, NY 10020), Japan's leading purveyor of financial information, can provide you with more Japanese stock market and economic information than you will ever need. Its services include a computer database available through your home computer, with stock price reports updated ten times a day, business data on 16,000 companies, news items, and other computerized information; *Nikkei Business*, a biweekly, and other periodicals; newsletters on the high-tech, biotechnology, artificial intelligence, and other fields; annual corporation reports; business books, including a *Guide Book* to 2,030 Japanese companies; there is even a telephone service for business data. It all depends on how much you want to spend. Some of it comes pretty expensive.

## · TAXATION ·

For foreigners there is a 10% Japanese withholding tax on interest, 20% on dividends, all of which can be claimed on your U.S. tax return. (If you buy Japanese ADRs, taxes and proxy matters are all taken care of for you.) There is no capital gains tax, and there are no limitations on the repatriation of capital and earnings.

## · THE YEN ·

The crux of your Japanese investment program is of course the exchange rate of the yen against the dollar. The fluctuations have been so extreme in recent years that they can easily outweigh any other consideration. The dollar has done extremely badly for the past few years, but it will not continue sinking forever, and when it strengthens, the United States will once again be the biggest stock market in the world. The American economy is twice the size of the Japanese economy, and American stockholders outnumber Japanese stockholders by about ten to one.

# CHAPTER 15

## GERMANY

Individual Germans are the most reluctant stock market investors among the citizens of all the world's major capitalist powers. They appear to have a positive aversion to stocks and stick their money relentlessly into bank savings accounts, bonds—anything with a fixed, guaranteed rate of interest. This is a curious mindset for a nation that experienced two financial calamities in this century. One generation's savings were wiped out by sextuple-digit inflation after World War I. The next generation's entire monetary wealth was totally expunged by a stroke of the pen after World War II when the government simply abolished the old Reichsmark and gave every person in the country 40 new Deutschmarks to start life anew in 1948.

The German public does indeed have a fear of inflation that verges on paranoia, but it also has a government in the Federal Republic of Germany that knows this and will risk a recession or perhaps even a depression rather than let inflation rear its head. The average West German citizen evidently has confidence in that government's antiinflationary resolve. The typical West German family saves 13% of its income—more than three times the American family's average savings rate—and then socks nearly all of it in the bank. There are about 4 million individual shareholders in Germany, one-tenth the U.S. total. The result is a relatively anemic stock market in which the total value of the shares on all German stock exchanges amounts to about one-sixth of the nation's yearly gross national product. Stocks on the New York Stock Exchange are valued at about half the American

GNP. German mutual funds that invest in common stocks have a paltry $15 billion in assets, while bond funds double that with their $30 billion. In fact, stock funds significantly outperformed the bond funds with a 13.8% average return in the first half of the 1980s, but the individual German investor refused to be tempted. The stock funds experienced net redemptions nearly every year.

The worldwide stock plunge of October 1987 did not spare the German stock exchanges—stock prices lost about a quarter of their value in a few weeks—but most Germans were only mildly interested. The market crash "is a curiosity for most Germans," one Frankfurt stockbroker commented. The average citizen was mainly concerned about his savings account, and it gave him great satisfaction that the government had been raising interest rates in the previous few months, and keeping up the good fight against inflation. In the United States, some blamed the Wall Street debacle on those very interest rate hikes by the German government, but the Federal Republic of Germany itself, "the country that may have helped bring on the crash, is a relative isle of tranquility," the Wall Street Journal observed.

One big German bank chided the citizenry's "excessive preoccupation with fixed interest instruments which often yield less than stocks," but to no avail. Individual Germans consider the stock market risky, and their ownership of German stocks fell from 27.7% of total stock market value in 1970 to considerably less than 20% in the 1980s. Banks are big players, but other large financial institutions shun the stock market. Insurance companies own only about 5% of the available stock supply. Traditionally, German banks and founding families have held the majority of shares in German companies, and these holdings hardly ever came on the market, so that in some cases only 10% or so of a corporation's shares were actually available for trading. This made for a torpid stock market. As the Dusseldorf Stock Exchange remarked in its yearly report, "The share issuing sector has tended to vegetate."

Despite all this, the German stock market is one of the biggest in the world. In 1985 $75 billion worth of stocks were traded on German stock exchanges, more than doubling the 1984 total, surpassing London and ranking third in the world behind New York and Tokyo. In 1986 the trading volume soared to more than $100 billion. The driving force behind this surge of activity was the flood of money from foreign investors, who poured 58 billion marks into the market in 1985 and helped push the price level up more than 70%, the best one-year advance since the 80% surge recorded in 1951. In 1986 foreign investment rose to 91 billion marks, but the price level rose only 5% (although this translated into much larger percentages for foreign investors who reckoned their holdings in dollars or other currencies). The foreign investors accounted for nearly a third of all trading in 1985, one-sixth in 1986, and have accounted for as much as 40% in other recent years.

As most German shares are anonymously held bearer certificates, precise figures on share ownership are hard to come by, but it is estimated that foreigners hold nearly 30% of all German listed shares.

The structure of the German stock market reflects all this faithfully in the number of issues listed. There are 490 stocks of German companies on the Frankfurt Stock Exchange and 180 foreign corporations. Meanwhile there are 6,000 bonds listed. Only 690 of these are foreign issues, accounting for a mere 15% of total bond trading.

It must be said that if inflation is anathema to most Germans, they do not have particularly encouraging experiences with the stock market either, which probably accounts for their lack of interest in stocks. The Frankfurt market was forced to close for a time in 1931 during the Depression, foreign exchange trading dried up under the currency controls of the Nazi regime, the Exchange's trading floor was almost totally destroyed in a 1944 air raid, and Berlin, the country's former number-one exchange, was swallowed up inside communist East Germany.

All in all, Tokyo's wild stock market boom has aroused some envy in Germany. As Deutsche Bank, Germany's biggest bank, commented in its publication *Atlantic Weekly* in April 1987, "With Japan's Nikkei index tripling to 24,000 in under five years, price-earnings ratios and yields have reached levels that are clearly alien to the valuation standards prevailing elsewhere. This relative insensitivity to foreign influence may be symbolic of the country's ascendancy to top rank in the international investing horizon. This stands in contrast to Germany's securities markets, which continue to be heavily impacted by actual or anticipated activity of foreigners from East or West."

In Commerzbank's opinion, "West Germany's development as a financial center has been hampered above all by its authorities' apparent reluctance to adopt financial innovations." Novelties like bond options cannot be expected to become a hot issue "as long as some of those who would be most interested in making use of them, namely insurance companies and investment trust funds, remain barred by law from making use of them."

And yet, said Commerzbank, Germany's third-biggest commercial bank, "The tendency of the German financial markets to be innovation-shy may not be so regrettable after all. It might indeed indicate a laudable preference for sound longer-term principles."

The authorities themselves had no doubts on the matter. Karl Otto Poehl, president of Bundesbank, the German central bank, affirmed that "Germany has the best possible prerequisites for holding and consolidating an appropriate position among the competing major financial centers. For almost 30 years the mark has been a fully convertible currency which is second only to the dollar among world currencies. We have offered freedom from interest rate controls and from restrictions on capital movements; free access to the market for all financial institutions. These conditions are unrivalled in many countries even today."

And Rudiger von Rosen, vice-chairman of the Association of German Stock Exchanges, noted that "Germany has achieved an impressive position worldwide as a financial center without it having been necessary for it to imitate every new idea. Germany has a qualitative lead as a financial center in the competition between international financial markets."

Let the above suffice to make this point: Germany offers a psychologically stable, institutionally conservative, relatively inflation-free market that has attracted a lot of foreign investors even if Germans themselves do not have much personal interest in it.

In contrast to the triple-digit price-earnings ratios to be found in Tokyo, in the sedate atmosphere of the German market PEs have been consistently modest, ranging from a lowly average 8.5 in 1981 to a reasonable 16.7 in 1985.

However, it is a market as dependent on foreigners as the German economy is. A major trading nation, West Germany accounts for 10% of world trade. Export industries employ every fourth German worker and represent one-third of gross national product. By contrast, exports are a mere 17% of GNP in Japan and only 7% in the United States.

## · GERMAN STOCK MARKETS ·

The German stock market, with its eight separate exchanges, constitutes one of the top half-dozen securities markets in the world. The Frankfurt Exchange accounts for about 50% of all trading, Dusseldorf for another 25%. Hamburg, Munich, Berlin, Bremen, Hanover, and Stuttgart share the rest. With the isolation of Berlin deep in East Germany in 1945, the leading role was taken over by the Frankfurt Exchange, a venerable institution which celebrated its 400th anniversary in 1985. Frankfurt is also West Germany's banking center. The city has 350 banks, 220 of them from abroad, including almost all of the world's fifty biggest. Seventeen major currencies are traded on the Frankfurt foreign currency market, and since 1968 the city has been one of the world's major gold-trading centers. Frankfurt has always had an international orientation: it was into the business of issuing coins and trading foreign currencies more than 800 years ago, back in 1180.

Fragmented and lacking one unchallenged financial center to rival London, New York, or Tokyo, the German stock exchanges banded together in February 1987 to form the Association of German Stock Exchanges. The chief aim of this organization is to link the exchanges into a unified system that will enable them to compete with the growing strength of London after the Big Bang. The Association now reports overall trading on all German exchanges, including off-exchange dealing, and coordinates interexchange policies. Both London and the Association, incidentally, count both buying and selling volume, thus doubling the figures as reported by New York, which counts only one side of any transaction. The German exchanges also have a highly efficient computerized system in which stock transactions are settled by book entry through central securities depositories. Holdings are simply transferred by the numbers from one account to another, avoiding a lot of certificate shuffling.

Actual trading is notably different from U.S. practice. German banks act as brokers. Banks in fact are the only brokers allowed on German exchanges. Floor brokers—in U.S. practice, specialists who deal with certain specified stocks on the floor of the exchange—are known as *Kursmakler*, and they are state officials appointed by the provincial governments. It is the *Kursmakler*'s duty to run an order book, match up buy and sell orders, and set daily official prices according to supply and demand at some middle level where trading will be maximized. For most stocks there is thus a single price quotation set by the *Kursmakler* for each daily session and which stands as the standard price for the day. The larger and more active stocks, however, are quoted continuously from noon onward and trade at fluctuating prices in lots of fifty shares. Big block transactions are usually made off the exchange so as not to disrupt the market. The official quotations are published in the *Amtliches Kursblatt* (the official daily quotation list). This is the only complete list, as the German press usually lists only selected companies.

This official market (Amtliche Notierung) is strictly regulated by the government, but it is only part of the picture. The official market is supplemented by a semiofficial market known as Geregelter Freiverkehr for companies that have small trading volume or are not on the official list because they are listed on some other exchange. The regulations here are less severe and cheaper to comply with, and trading is in the hands of *Freimakler*, the unofficial counterparts to the *Kursmakler*. The *Freimakler* perform the same functions but are not allowed to fix prices for the bigger, officially quoted securities.

In addition to these two markets there is also off-exchange trading known as Telefonhandel, in which banks, institutions, and private investors deal with each other by telephone. Only banks are allowed to accept orders on this over-the-counter market, so whatever you do, a bank is going to have a hand in your trading activity. However, the bank is obliged by law to execute your order on a regular stock exchange unless you specifically request otherwise.

Nevertheless most trading is transacted before or after the brief two-hour official sessions of the German exchanges, whose reports of daily volume thus understate actual trading by half or more.

There are no restrictions or regulations affecting stock investments by foreigners in Germany, nor are there any foreign exchange controls. All transactions are on a cash basis and must be settled within two days. You pay a commission to the bank that acts as your broker (about 0.5%, with a minimum of 10 marks), a brokerage fee to the *Makler* (0.1%), and a 0.25% turnover tax. About 10% of shares traded in Germany are preferred stock, the rest are ordinary shares, which are issued in bearer form, registered shares being a rarity except in the case of insurance companies. All German shares are required to have a par value, normally 50 marks, with some at 100 marks.

The most actively traded stocks are Daimler-Benz, Deutsche Bank, Siemens, Volkswagen, Bayer, Dresdner Bank, Commerzbank, Hoechst, BASF, Allianz, AEG, Mercedes Automobil, VEBA Bayerische Motoren Werke (BMW), and Continental Gummi.

The German bond market is now third in the world after the United States and Japan, with 1 trillion marks' worth outstanding. Industrial corporation bonds having practically disappeared, German banks and the government are the main borrowers. Foreign investors seeking to gain from the appreciation of the German mark against other currencies have become a major factor in the bond market, particularly since the abolition of the bond coupon tax in 1984. In fact the federal government sells nearly all its bonds to foreigners, who are willing to accept a yield lower by 1% or so than bank bonds because of their supposedly greater creditworthiness. However, Friedel Neuber, chairman of the Westdeutsche Landesbank, affirms that bank bonds backed by loans to public authorities are just as good as the government issues. In a grudging gesture to innovation, the authorities allowed the introduction of zero coupon bonds and floating rate bonds in 1985.

You can buy options on the stocks of about fifty German companies and more than a dozen foreign companies on German exchanges. Frankfurt is the main market with about 90% of all option trading. The options are available for terms up to nine months, and they are of the U.S.-style variety that you can trade before expiration. Contracts are for fifty shares.

The most widely watched stock market index in Germany is the FAZ Index of 100 actively traded stocks published by the *Frankfurter Allgemeine* newspaper. Its base is 100 as of December 31, 1958. The main Index is divided up into fourteen subindexes which cover market sections from automobile stocks to utilities, but these subindexes are generally inaccessible unless you read the *Frankfurter Allgemeine* or the German financial press.

For an investor who wants to play the averages there are no closed-end investment funds in Germany, but there is a choice of about 150 mutual funds, about half of which invest in German stocks, fifty in German bonds, the rest in international stock-and-bond portfolios. There are also eight real estate funds. The standard sales commission is 5%. Many of the funds do not issue their reports or literature in English, concentrating their sales efforts on the 1.6 million German families that hold mutual fund shares. A few that do cater to English-speaking investors include the following:

ADIG-Investment (Mainer Landstrasse 5, D-6000, Frankfurt) runs ten mutual funds, among them Adifonds (portfolio of sixty German companies, seeking income and growth); Aditec (German and foreign high-tech companies); Fondak (German growth fund); Fondirent (international fixed-interest); Adirenta (German fixed-interest).

Deutsche Bank's mutual fund management company DWS (Gruneburgweg 113-115, D-6000 Frankfurt) runs a stable of funds with total assets of about $8 billion. It sells funds that include Investa (high-quality German stocks), Inrenta (German bonds), and Inter-Renta (international bonds).

Dresdner Bank's stable of funds includes Concentra and Internationaler Rentenfonds, which issue trilingual reports in German, English, and French.

Getting adequate information in English is usually a problem if you invest in individual German companies. Only the bigger internationally oriented corporations publish their yearly reports in English. Language is not the only problem, however. Companies outside the United States and not subject to strict SEC reporting requirements generally provide much less information to their shareholders than American corporations do. British laws require fairly detailed financial reporting, but laws in continental European countries are skimpy and laxly applied, and Germany is no exception to this rule. Siemens AG, for example, Germany's biggest engineering firm, listed a $3.5 billion item under unspecified "other costs" in its 1986 balance sheet. This unexplained amount was four times its profits and three times its tax bill. German companies publish yearly reports, some of the bigger companies half-yearly and even quarterly reports, but they can be pretty slow in coming. Krupp publishes its yearly results in June for a fiscal year that ends in December.

General information on the German stock market is available in English from the Frankfurt Stock Exchange (Frankfurter Wertpapierborse, Borsenplatz 6, Postfach 10 08 11, 6000 Frankfurt 1), from the Dusseldorf Exchange (Rheinisch-Westfalische Borse zu Dusseldorf, Ernst Schneider Platz 1, 4000 Dusseldorf 1), or from the Association of German Stock Exchanges (Deutsche Delegation der Arbeitsgemeinschaft der Deutschen Wertpapierborsen, 2000 Hamburg 11). If you are able to read German, in addition to the *Frankfurter Allgemeine* you have in Frankfurt two business dailies, *Handelsblatt* and *Borsen Zeitung*, and a weekly, *Wirtschaftswoche*.

The three big banks, Deutsche, Dresdner, and Commerzbank, provide abundant research and company reports. Westdeutsche Landesbank Girozentrale (450 Park Avenue, New York, NY 10022) offers an investment service which provides foreign investors with individual company research as well as general financial and economic information in English. Its asset-estate-trust management service is restricted to high-income individuals. The minimum amount for management is $250,000, and the annual fee is $500 to $800.

## · GERMAN BANKS ·

Since a bank will necessarily be your broker if you decide to trade in German stocks, there is no getting around the German banking system. There are about 250 commercial banks in Germany, with about 6,000 offices around the country and 170,000 employees. They field about 25,000 investment consultants, who naturally tend to steer customers into the bank's other products as well as stocks. The banks are into portfolio management as well as investment counseling. They collect dividends, exercise subscription rights, and monitor bond drawings for their customers. They vote for you at shareholder meetings, and they have a leading role in issuing new stocks.

There is an inherent conservatism about German banking. The big three go back to the last century. They were split up by the victorious allies after World War II but soon put themselves together again. They now have 200,000 shareholders among them, a large number of whom are the banks' own employees. Their addresses are:

Commerzbank AG
Neue Mainzer Strasse 32-36
6000 Frankfurt 1

Deutsche Bank AG
Taunusanlage 12
6000 Frankfurt 1

Dresdner Bank AG
Jurgen Ponto Platz 1
6000 Frankfurt 1

The banks are not aggressive marketers in the United States. Dresdner Bank, for example, does not solicit individual American accounts for its 950 branches in Germany, but it is equipped to deal with English-speaking clients. The bank publishes a stock exchange report every two weeks with its view of the current German stock and bond market, as well as information on individual stocks. It also has periodical publications in English on German economic trends and statistics.

## · TAXES ·

Nonresidents pay a flat 25% withholding tax on dividends. There is no taxation of the interest on straight bonds, but convertible bonds are subject to the 25% withholding. To get a tax reduction under double-taxation agreements, you have to ask the German tax authorities for a 10% refund. The remaining 15% can be credited against your U.S. income tax. There is no capital gains tax for nonresidents and no withholding tax on income from German mutual funds. The 0.5% stock-transfer tax has come under fire for discouraging interest in German stocks, and its abolition has been under consideration.

## · THE MARK ·

Together with the Japanese yen and the Swiss franc, the German mark has been recognized for years as one of the world's hardest currencies, thanks largely to the German government's persistently hard line against inflation. This has to be one of the main factors in considering any German investment. German government bonds might be yielding 3% less than U.S. government bonds when you are considering a fixed-interest investment, but the joker in the pack is that the dollar lost about half its value against the mark between 1985 and 1987. In 1986 the FAZ Index gained a measly 3.4%, but American investors still would have ended up with a 31.4% gain for the year, thanks to the appreciation of the mark against the dollar. Since 1974 the exchange rate has fluctuated between 1.67 and 3.15 marks per dollar. If you had foreknowledge of what it is going to do in the future, you could forget about the trivial interest-rate differential and make your fortune on changes in the exchange rate.

## · GERMAN BANKS AS INVESTMENTS ·

Although there are no closed-end investment trusts in Germany, the big-three German banks might be considered as reasonable substitutes. The German commercial banks not only play a dominant part in the nation's financial markets, they also own huge chunks of West German industry. They hold 25% or more of the shares of many of the country's biggest companies, plus similar holdings in scores of smaller companies. Besides direct ownership, they control additional blocks of shares as trustees, investment managers, and dealers. According to one estimate, the big-three banks control about one-third of the stock of the country's seventy-five biggest corporations. Deutsche Bank and Commerzbank between them own more than half of Karlstadt, the Federal Republic's biggest retailer. The big banks, led by Dresdner, rescued AEG, a failing electrical giant, in the early 1980s, ended up with more than half the shares, and then sold the company to Daimler-Benz. Deutsche Bank owns more than 25% of Daimler-Benz, an auto company with 300,000 employees, which accounts for 3.5% of West Germany's GNP. An investment in the big banks is thus an investment in interlocking sections of the West

German economy. It also presents the possibility of even further advantages.

The banks' huge economic power has provoked rising criticism, and the German Monopolies Commission has proposed limiting banks' investments in other companies to 5% of their stock. A particular target of criticism is number-one Deutsche Bank, which owns a quarter each of nine big industrial corporations. It also has a stake of 25% to 75% in eight holding companies, each of which in turn owns big chunks of other large German corporations. Dresdner has three similar holding companies.

As we noted in an earlier chapter, closed-end investment trusts offer big opportunities if they are liquidated when they are selling at a discount. Like closed-ends, the German banks' industrial portfolios could be liquidated if their critics ever force them to disgorge their holdings. And many of these holdings probably figure on their books far below their current value. Profits from their sale might leave the banks awash in money, and in their capacity as brokers the banks could make further profits on the actual sales.

Pure conjecture, of course, and the authorities would have to ensure that such massive bank disinvestment did not collapse the stock market. But an interesting possibility to consider. The big-three banks' stocks are all publicly traded. In fact, foreign investors own 30% of Commerzbank and 33% of Dresdner Bank. It is a remarkable feature of Germany's current economic liberalism that such extensive foreign ownership of institutions that control so much of the country's economy apparently causes little concern to anyone in the Federal Republic.

# CHAPTER
# 16

## FRANCE

When investing in France do as the French do: keep a jaundiced eye on what the government is up to. Government actions are likely to weigh far more heavily and impact far more drastically on your investment than any stock market developments or individual company news. State control of the French economy, known as *dirigisme*, has been a dominant fact of French economic life at least since the time of Jean-Baptiste Colbert, finance minister to Louis XIV in the seventeenth century, and not even the French Revolution had any appreciable effect on it. No matter what the party in power, under the Bourbons, both Napoleons, the Empire, the Republic, the Vichy regime, and all the post–World War II governments, *dirigisme* has always been there. It was a major element in the conservative government of General Charles de Gaulle, and it only took on a somewhat more extreme form in the nationalization campaign of President Francois Mitterrand's socialist government, which came to power in the early 1980s.

The effect of French government policy on the stock market is overwhelming. A French presidential election has a lot more stock market significance than the electoral struggle between Republicans and Democrats for the White House. The French Socialist government's nationalization program of 1981 and 1982 removed five major industrial corporations, thirty-seven banks, and two other financial companies from the stock market—25% of the market value of all stocks traded on the Paris Stock Exchange. And the violent swings in government policy are no less disconcerting. In 1986—one French election later and with President Mitterrand deprived of his socialist majority in parliament—the conservative administration of Prime Minister Jacques Chirac launched a denationalization campaign in which he undertook to sell back to private investors sixty-five major state-owned companies and banks.

It is decades of political ups and downs like these, plus a series of major wars and resulting bouts of inflation, that have given most French citizens a cynical view of French financial investments. Land, real estate, gold coins, and bank accounts in Switzerland have always seemed much safer.

In spite of all this turmoil, the French stock market has enjoyed seven fat years in the 1980s. Prices have quadrupled, trading volume in stocks and bonds has multiplied more than thirtyfold from under $9 billion in 1976 to more than $300 billion worth in 1987, and the number of individual French stockholders has grown dramatically.

Ironically it was the socialist government's nationalization program in 1981 that led to the stock market boom. The removal of 25% of the stock market's inventory created a shortage of stock. The socialist government clamped down on real estate investments, making investment in that area unappetizing. It reinforced controls on sending money abroad. New regulations forced buyers of gold to identify themselves, an obligation that violated their sense of privacy and decency. Consequently, a lot of French money had no place to go but the stock market.

When the conservative government got in, it fed the boom even more fuel by cutting corporate taxes, selling off sixty-five state concerns at bargain prices, and undertaking a deliberate campaign to spread share ownership so broadly among the French population that the companies once privatized could never be renationalized again. It aimed at creating a share-owning entrepreneurial society able to compete with Japan, the United States, or any other major industrial power. Finance Minister Edouard Balladur embarked on a shrewd marketing strategy. The privatization campaign was launched with the greatest investor-relations media blitz ever seen in France, with television commercials, newspaper advertisements, and even road shows.

The first companies to be sold were deliberately underpriced. The state oil company, Elf-Aquitaine, was sold at what the socialist opposition denounced as a giveaway price. The issue was oversubscribed six times over, attracting 400,000 buyers of small ten-share lots. The neophyte investors in St. Gobain, a glass and construction materials company that was one of the first to go on the market, had a 50% gain on their stock within six months. To keep them happy, and keep them invested, Balladur offered investors in the privatized stocks one free share for every ten they bought, provided they held their shares for at least eighteen months. French investors snapped up the new issues with the most un-French avidity. Some stocks were oversubscribed by as much as sixty-five times, and bidders received only a fraction of the amount they put in for.

Some financial analysts said 1987 seemed to mark a fundamental change in the French investment scene, the creation for the first time of a broadly based stock market, the birth of popular capitalism in France. The number of individual stockholders doubled in the first few months of the French privatization program to more than 4 million, plus 5 million investors in mutual funds. The government put on the block $50 billion worth of stock in its five-year privatization program, four times the value of the British state enterprises denationalized by the vigorous Mrs. Thatcher in her first five years of hacking at British state monopolies.

However, in France as in England, the October 1987 crash did serious damage to the privatization campaign directed by conservative Prime Minister Jacques Chirac. French stocks shed a third of their value on average between October and November. Three million small French investors who had rushed in to buy Banque Paribas shares from the government at the "bargain" price of 405 francs a share suddenly found their new stock had dropped from a high of 460 francs down to 375 francs on the Paris Exchange. For millions of French citizens it was the first realization that stocks can go down as well as up, and political pundits began to doubt whether popular capitalism was such a sure bet in the political arena after all. Meanwhile, the government postponed the sale of Union des Assurances de Paris, a large state insurance company, and delayed the planned sale of other government-owned companies.

But even if Mrs. Thatcher and M. Chirac do succeed in their efforts to create nations of stockholders, an investor in French securities might well keep in mind the secular persistence of *dirigisme* under French governments of the left and of the right. French government intervention in economic affairs has produced violent stock market swings in this past decade, and it would be rash to assume that it will not do so in the next decade.

Government control has also straitjacketed for many decades the instrument that is supposed to bring about the new stockholding democracy—the French stock exchange. There are forty-five stockbrokers in Paris, sixteen on provincial exchanges; they are known as *agents de change*, and all of them are appointed by the French finance minister. Napoleon I gave the brokers a nice little monopoly nearly two centuries ago, in 1807, and laws dating back to Napoleon have made it almost impossible to found a new brokerage firm since then. Since the last century the stock exchanges have met in brief daily two-hour sessions and the brokers have fiercely defended their privileges, including the right to fixed commissions.

Meanwhile the Paris market lagged far behind other world stock markets. Even with the boom in 1986, the market value of French shares was only a fraction of the capitalization of New York, Tokyo, or London at $160 billion. Competition from abroad, especially Swiss, German, and British brokers, was siphoning off business from the Paris Bourse. It was estimated that London alone, where six big brokers make a market in French stocks, was taking a 15% share of the Paris Exchange's daily volume.

Struggling to maintain control of trading in its own wares, the Paris market organized its own "*Petit Bang.*" Commissions on larger block trades were made negotiable. A morning session was added for the most active stocks. The Bourse leased the

Toronto Exchange's computer stock trading system in June 1986, computerized trading in the top fifty stocks, and planned to put another 200 into the system. A new second market for smaller companies was opened. And—the ultimate sacrilege for the *agents de change*—the government planned to end the two-centuries-old brokers' monopoly. By 1989 outsiders will be able to buy 49% of any French stock brokerage firm, by 1990 100%, and by 1992 the monopoly will be completely gone when, in the most daring innovation of all, outside investors will actually be permitted to found new brokerage firms.

The battle for control of the stock market has been a battle between the brokers and the French banks, with the brokers defending their ancient prerogatives and the banks trying to break in. The banks gained a major foothold when they went into partnership with the stockbrokers in 1986 to launch the European continent's first financial futures market. In a few months futures trading volume exceeded by far the traditional stock and bond markets combined, climbing to 10 billion francs a day. When Matif (Marche a Terme des Instruments Financiers) went into operation in February 1986, the banks gained the right to trade directly in financial futures. The banks used this as a wedge to become market-makers in bonds and in the options markets that opened up in 1987.

However, the brokerage community was still holding on to its most precious perk, fixed stock commissions. Xavier Dupont, chairman of the French Stock Exchange, insisted that the spate of reforms did not mean an end to fixed commission rates for small French investors or for foreign investors. Banks provide about 75% of the stock brokerage business from individuals, but the brokers pointed out that dealing directly with a broker produces the lowest commission rates even if they did give the banks some concessions on block trades. Brokers' commissions for private investors range from 0.65% on the first 600,000 francs in a stock transaction to 0.215% on investments of more than 1.1 million francs. Make a deal of more than 2 million francs and you can negotiate your commission. Commission rates on bond trades range from 0.5% to 0.165%. Buy 10 million francs worth at a time and negotiate your own commission. For nonresidents there is a 25% withholding tax on dividends but interest on government bonds is tax-free.

Although there are seven stock exchanges in France, the only significant market is the Paris Bourse, which handles more than 95% of the business. The entire market is supervised by the Commission des Operations de Bourse, the equivalent of the American SEC. The Paris market divides up into three sectors: the official list, the second market, and the over-the-counter market. The official list comprises the biggest French and foreign companies. Trading on the official list is either for cash or for settlement at the end of the month. The second market, set up in February 1983, includes more than 100 medium-sized and small companies, some of them very small and very thinly traded as they can come on the market with only 10% of their stock, the remainder being in the hands of founding families who maintain close control of the company. The over-the-counter market, even less enticing for the foreign investor, is a catchall for any companies that don't make it onto the official list or the second market. These OTC stocks are under no obligation even to publish a prospectus or to provide any information to stockholders beyond the minimum rudimentary disclosures required of all French publicly owned companies. The number of French companies on the official list declined from 743 in 1981 to less than 700 in 1987, losing some stocks to the second market, where the listing requirements are less onerous.

The most actively traded French stocks include Michelin, Thomson CSF, BSN, Peugeot, Ciel du Midi, Moet-Hennessy, La Farge Coppee, Carrefour, Air Liquide, Elf-Aquitaine, Total, and Club Mediterranée.

The main market indicator is the CAC Index, an average of 250 stocks compiled by the Compagnie des Agents de Change, the stockbrokers' association. It is broken down into eight categories, such as construction, services, and finance; and these in turn into thirty-one subgroups such as chemicals, aeronautics, and banks.

The Paris Stock Exchange (Palais de la Bourse, 4 Place de la

Bourse, 75080 Paris) provides French-language information, including biweekly charts of price and trading volume figures of stocks on the official list, and monthly statistics on market activity, prices, and index fluctuations.

Brokers include:

Cheuvreux-de Virieux
2 Rue de Choiseul
Paris 75002

Courcoux-Bouvet
5 Rue Gaillon
Paris 75002

De Lavandeyra
17 Rue de la Michodiere
Paris 75002

Meeschaert-Rousselle
16 Blvd. Montmartre
Paris 75009

These four are noted for their outstanding research on the general market and individual stocks. But the research is not always available in English.

Banque Paribas (55 East 52 Street, New York, NY 10055) publishes *Conjoncture*, a monthly English-language survey of French and international economic developments, and also *STATECO*, a weekly statistical analysis of the economies of France, the United States, and other countries. *Conjoncture* is free; *STATECO* costs $500 a year.

## · PROBLEMS ·

With the French stock market we come to the point where the problems and hazards involved in investing abroad by an American investor appear to outweigh any possible advantage. The reasonable thing to do is to limit yourself to whatever French

ADRs are available in the United States or to buy the France Fund on the New York Stock Exchange.

France is a country where politics and government policy bear down more heavily at times than market developments; where one government can nationalize a quarter of the stock market one year, while the next administration may denationalize all that and more a few years later. It is a country where controls are frequently imposed on foreign exchange transactions, and where such regulations may change frequently and suddenly; where brokers are required to segregate the accounts of nonresidents into special accounts; and where the general assumption is that civilized people use the French language in preference to English. Paris is a financial center where only two American brokers, Merrill Lynch and Smith Barney, maintain offices at the time of writing—with skeleton staffs due to French protectionism in the financial market. It is a market where there are no ratings systems like Moody's to evaluate the bonds you buy, and where financial information in English is hard to come by. It is a market where even prices come under Exchange regulation, with a maximum permitted daily fluctuation of 5% on the forward market and 8% on the cash market, so that, just as on the U.S. commodity exchanges, you might be stuck with your position until the officially sanctioned price comes back in line with the real market price.

And last, but by no means least, you have the hazard involved in any foreign investment: currency fluctuations. This can be an opportunity rather than a danger in a market where economic factors are dominant, and subject to reasonably logical analysis. In the case of France, where politics and government policy usually tend to take precedence, the problem is to predict wildly gyrating government policies. Largely as a result of these policies, the franc ranged from 5.70 to 9.64 francs per dollar between 1981 and 1987.

# CHAPTER
## 17

# THE NETHERLANDS, BELGIUM, AND LUXEMBOURG

## · THE NETHERLANDS ·

Up to World War II the Netherlands had in Amsterdam the third-biggest stock market in the world after New York and London, a remarkable achievement for a nation that even now has only 14.4 million people. And yet more remarkable when you realize that the country is so small in size, resource-poor, and overcrowded—its population density is exceeded only by poverty-stricken Bangladesh. And more remarkable still when you consider that one-third of the Netherlands' meager 15,900 square miles of territory is below sea level and would not exist at all without Dutch technological ingenuity. A country that has twenty times more people per square mile than the United States has to survive on ingenuity, and the Dutch have done very well on their native wits. Their merchant ships dominated intercontinental trade back in the 1600s and early 1700s (until the British displaced them as the world's premier naval power), producing a tide of wealth that made the Dutch the bankers of Europe (and also major financiers of the American Revolution against their British rivals). Nowadays the Dutch survive on their over-crowded, semisubmersible habitat mainly as an industrial nation, as producers of chemicals, heavy machinery, foodstuffs, and electronics, a nation that has attracted 4,500 foreign firms—1,000 of them American—to invest in Dutch industrial operations.

The Dutch ushered in the modern capitalist era when the United East India Company became the first corporation in the world to seek financing through public subscription to shares issued through a stock exchange. In business since 1611, Amsterdam is the world's oldest continuously functioning stock market.

Amsterdam did not really begin to recover its pre–World War II prominence as a stock market until 1982, when the government started deregulating financial markets, cutting corporate taxes, and taking other measures to liberalize the economy. Its rise was boosted by foreign investment—mainly from Britain, the United States, and Switzerland—which has accounted for more than half of all trading in Amsterdam since 1982. There are many non-Dutch stocks on the Amsterdam market, and about half the Amsterdam trading volume is in these securities. A handful of Dutch multinationals like Philips, Unilever, and Royal Dutch Petroleum represent a huge chunk of the purely Dutch share market. So what you really have in Amsterdam is a large international tail wagging a small Dutch dog. If you are going to invest here it is most likely to be at the international rather than the purely Dutch level, and you will find big Dutch banks who are as willing and as competent as the Swiss banks to help you do this, as we shall see further on.

The situation now is that Amsterdam is struggling to hold its niche in world stock trading against powerful rivals like London. The Dutch government revamped its securities laws in 1986, but to some observers the Netherlands' efforts to modernize its financial markets have seemed slow and hesitant compared to London's revolutionary Big Bang. Nevertheless, the Dutch have got an options market going that is five times the size of London's. The Amsterdam Stock Exchange has made a pitch for smaller international investors with a Eurobond market for odd-lot traders ("odd-lot" meaning in this case lots of less than $100,000). It has also made a play for the business of the big boys with its new Amsterdam Interprofessional Market, where huge financial institutions trade bonds in $50 million lots with each other at minimum brokerage commission rates. And the Dutch have even gone into competition with the New York Stock Exchange in American stock dealing.

Dutch stocks did not escape the worldwide October 1987 massacre, shedding about a third of their total value in a period of three weeks or so. But this should be viewed in an appropriate time frame. Like many other stock markets in the preceding worldwide equity boom, the level of Dutch share prices had risen so far in the first ten months of 1987 that even after the crash it was still about 4% higher in November 1987 than it had been in November 1986.

Overall Amsterdam trading volume has risen more than sevenfold in the last decade, from 30 billion guilders in 1976 to more than 250 billion in 1987. And stock trading has grown even faster than bond trading, which rose from 13 billion to more than 100 billion guilders in this period. Stocks account for more than 150 billion guilders in trading volume.

Guilders, incidentally, are the same thing as florins, and are in fact usually abbreviated Hfl. In English the name Holland is also habitually used interchangeably with the country's official name, the Netherlands, a fact that displeases the Dutch since Holland is only one of the country's provinces.

### Amsterdam Stock Market

More than 2,000 securities are traded in Amsterdam, including about 1,300 Dutch government and corporate bonds and 150 foreign bonds, plus more than 200 Dutch stocks and nearly 300 foreign stocks.

The purely Dutch component in the field of common stocks is thus rather small, and it is in any event dominated by a handful of the country's biggest corporations. Royal Dutch Petroleum alone has a market value representing nearly 30% of the value of all Dutch shares. This is reflected in the main stock indicator, the ANP-CBS Index of 100 stocks published by the Dutch news agency ANP. With a base of 100 in 1970, this Index largely tracks the moves of the top five stocks (Royal Dutch, Philips, Unilever, Nationale Nederlanden, and Robeco), which together compose 48% of the weighted ANP-CBS Index. Other actively traded stocks include Akzo, KLM, ABN Bank, Amro Bank, Aegon, and Heineken. The government's central bureau of statistics also publishes an index of bond prices known as the CBS Index.

In addition to the official market, Amsterdam has a Parallel Market, set up in 1982 to accommodate medium-sized and smaller stocks that do not qualify for the official list. The minimum capital required for listing here is 2.5 million guilders compared with 4 million guilders on the main list. There are less than 100 stocks in this group, and the market for them is rather thin, but they are quoted daily on the Exchange's Daily Official List even if there is no trading. At a further level below this you have the unlisted market, containing hundreds of stocks, where trading may be even more sporadic, and where quotes are not published unless there have been some actual transactions. For a foreigner, the lack of market information and the paucity of trading volume are two good reasons to stay out of the Parallel Market. One further reason is that a company listed here may have only 10% of its stock on the market, the remainder being in the hands of a probably closemouthed founding family.

One other area to stay away from is any Dutch broker who operates internationally without the sanction of the Amsterdam Stock Exchange. These boiler-room operators bilked investors around the world of more than $300 million in recent years, according to police estimates. Amsterdam, according to *Barron's* magazine in November 1986, "is the stock fraud capital of Europe." Hard-sell swindlers used the mail and the telephone to peddle worthless American, Canadian, and European stocks, as well as semilegitimate stocks and mutual funds and even legitimate stocks at inflated prices, promising short-term gains of 30% or more. These swindlers were attracted to Amsterdam, according to *Barron's*, by "a regulatory environment that was lax even by European standards." Unlike the Amsterdam Stock Exchange brokers, who are closely watched by the authorities, the international operations of these off-exchange hucksters were unregulated. In 1986 the Dutch Finance Ministry introduced legislation requiring them to get a broker's license before doing any business.

The legitimate brokers charge commissions on bond trading ranging from 0.36% to 0.15% depending on the size of the trade. Fixed commissions on big block trades were abolished in 1986. Commissions on small-size stock trades are higher at 1.5%. Every transaction carries a 7.50 Hfl handling fee, and there is also a stamp duty of 0.12%. There is a 25% tax on dividend income, none on bond interest. Dividends are paid semiannually. There are no controls on repatriation of capital or income. For margin traders the bad news is that Dutch law forbids buying securities with borrowed money.

In its efforts to make an international niche for itself, Amsterdam began trading American stocks through a system known as the American Shares Amsterdam System. It works much like the ADR system in the United States, the actual certificates being held in New York and trading in Amsterdam being carried out with depository receipts and a book entry system. This is the biggest market for American stocks outside the United States, with more than seventy corporations listed. In 1984 the ASAS system was extended to include British stocks and later Australian, Canadian, and Japanese securities. While it offers European investors an easy way to invest in the United States, ASAS would also permit an American to invest in U.S. stocks at prices that are seldom more than 25 cents off the NYSE quotation.

Amsterdam has achieved one of its most successful innovations with its European Options Exchange (Optiebeurs, Dam 21, 1012 JS Amsterdam), where volume has been five times the London options level in recent years. Consciously modeled on the Chicago Board Options Exchange, the EOE deals in American-style traded puts and calls. Options are available on fifteen Dutch stocks, one Belgian stock, eight Dutch government bonds, six different currencies, and gold and silver. The precious-metals options are quoted in U.S. dollars and traded almost around the clock through a linkup with Sydney, Vancouver, and Montreal. The silver option is for 250 troy ounces, the gold option for 10 troy ounces.

Besides speculating in gold and silver, a U.S. dollar option allows you to protect yourself at little cost whenever you think the dollar is in for a prolonged sinking spell, as it was in 1986 and 1987. You can then buy a guilder put option with a face value of US$10,000 for, say, $150 and later cash in a sizable profit if the dollar declined as you anticipated. The leverage is such that it is not impossible to make a 100% profit on your premium in six to nine months without ever risking the loss of more than your $150 per option. Even if you had no other foreign investments at all, this would be a way of protecting the real value of your net worth in dollars whenever the dollar heads south in foreign exchange markets.

The stock options too have maximum expirations of nine months and trade in 100-share lots, but you can also buy five-year options on Akzo, Royal Dutch, Philips, and Unilever. Profits on options, incidentally, are not taxable in the Netherlands. American members of the EOE are Merrill Lynch and Prudential-Bache.

Dutch brokers include:

Algemene Bank Nederland
Vijzelstraat 32
1017 HL Amsterdam

Amsterdam-Rotterdam Bank
Herengracht 595
1017 CE Amsterdam

Nederlandsche Middenstandsbank
Eduard van Beinumstrasse 2
1077 XT Amsterdam

Pierson, Heldring & Pierson
Herengracht 206-124
1016 BS Amsterdam

This group includes the three largest Dutch banks, and Pierson is a subsidiary of Amsterdam-Rotterdam Bank. They are all considered outstanding for their research reports.

## Investing in the Netherlands

The Netherlands is one of the most politically stable countries in the world. Its three main parties, all middle-of-the-road groups, have dominated coalition governments in different combinations since World War II. The country is vulnerable to slumps in world trade since international trading dominates the Dutch economy. The total of Dutch exports and imports at times exceeds the gross national product, thanks to the international trade that passes to central Europe through Rotterdam, the world's largest port. The country depends heavily too on natural gas fields, where production will decline sharply by the 1990s, but the Dutch economy functions on ingenuity rather than resources and it is well run. The country achieved a practically zero inflation rate in the past two years. Interest rates have thus been low—a mere 6% on long-term government bonds in 1987—and the Dutch currency is one of the strongest in the world. As West Germany is its largest trading partner, with 30% of the total, the Netherlands aligns its currency with the West German mark, maintaining Dutch interest rates at a small premium. Dutch bonds thus tend to have slightly better yields than German bonds.

The Netherlands, as we mentioned earlier, might be considered as an alternative to Switzerland as a base for international investing. The big Dutch banks have international capabilities and offer additional advantages compared to Switzerland: no withholding tax on interest, higher interest rates, sometimes lower bank-service charges. As in Switzerland, there are no capital gains taxes or death duties for nonresidents in the Netherlands.

Amro (Amsterdam-Rotterdam) Bank maintains a Private Client Department (47 Rembrandtplein, P.O. Box 1220, 1000 EH Amsterdam), which offers international investment facilities and welcomes foreign customers. The bank has branches all over the world, from Dubai to Singapore. There is no charge for keeping an Amro private account. The only charge is for postage for forwarding your investment mail or a fee for holding your correspondence. The bank says, "It is our practice to use plain envelopes without the name of Amro being printed on them." Clients in some countries might get unwelcome attention from their tax authorities if they openly receive mail from foreign banks.

You can also open a numbered account or an account under a code name without any extra charge, although you would have to be a substantial client to qualify for this. You can also open a checking account in guilders or any major currency you prefer, a savings account in guilders, or a time deposit account. The bank also undertakes to buy or sell securities for you in any part of the world. It is a member of the Amsterdam Stock Exchange, and outside Holland it deals through local brokers. Amro also manages a stable of mutual funds and offers gold and silver accounts through which you can buy precious metals in amounts as little as 200 guilders. There is no value-added tax or custody fee.

As for secrecy, the bank says that under Dutch law "banks are not permitted to give information on their clients to third parties unless compelled to do so by court order. For foreign clients this means a criminal offense" or an investigation by Dutch authorities of suspected Dutch tax evasion. You can even rent a safety deposit box for $15 a year and apply for overdraft and loan facilities.

One investment that should not go unmentioned is Robeco, an investment company that manages more than $13 billion in assets and is the world's biggest investment group outside the United States. It controls assets greater than the combined value of the top twenty British investment trusts put together. Robeco has investments in more than 300 companies in twenty different countries, and its own stock is quoted on nineteen stock exchanges around the world. Robeco is a curious hybrid between an open-end mutual fund and a closed-end fund. Like the mutual fund, its shares trade at net asset value, but like the closed-end fund it is a company owned by its stockholders and not run by a separate fund management company. Robeco itself constantly buys and sells its own shares so as to keep the stock market price in line with the net asset value. The outstanding quality of

Robeco is its inexpensive management. Annual operating costs are a remarkably low 0.3% of assets under management per year. The Robeco fund invests in a portfolio of international blue chip equities, seeking income and growth. Its other funds are Rolinco, which emphasizes international growth stocks; Rorento, international fixed-interest securities; and Rodamco, which invests in worldwide commercial property, such as shopping centers and office buildings.

Robeco has such an international mix of investors that it publishes its annual reports in English, French, German, and Japanese as well as Dutch, and its international board of directors uses English as a lingua franca. Trading in the four Robeco funds sometimes accounts for one-fifth of the total activity on the Amsterdam Exchange, Robeco's main market. For American investors there is a snag. Robeco's funds have not been registered with the SEC, and being punctiliously Dutch, Robeco will not even send its sales literature to American investors. It is hard to see, however, how Robeco could prevent an American from buying its shares on the London or Zurich stock exchanges through a British broker or Swiss bank.

## · BELGIUM ·

The Belgian stock market was one of the sleepiest in Europe until 1981, when the government passed tax reforms aimed at encouraging investment. Stock prices tripled in the next few years.

The most widely watched index is the Brussels Stock Exchange's Belgian General Return Index, which has a base of 1,000 as of October 1, 1980. The index comprises all Belgian shares and hit an all-time high of 5,412 in August 1987. After the October crash it dropped back to the 4,300 level in a month-long plunge, but even then it was still about 20% higher than its November 1986 reading.

There are stock exchanges at Antwerp, Ghent, and Liege, but the Brussels Exchange (Bourse de Bruxelles, 1000 Brussels) has 90% of the trading. More than 330 companies are listed there, of which nearly 150 are foreign. This is a market dominated by a few huge companies—the top ten account for more than half the market value of all stocks on the exchange.

Brokers include:

Banque Bruxelles Lambert
Avenue Marnix 24
B-1050
Brussels

Peterbroeck, van Campenhout
Place Sainte Gudule 19
1000 Brussels

Peterbroeck turns out a monthly bulletin in French, Dutch, and English. The Stock Exchange produces an *Annual Report* in the same three languages. Otherwise there is not much information available in English. This is a small and rather parochial market that does not provide anything much else in the way of information for the English-speaking investor. The complicated trading system includes a cash market, a forward market (where big institutions predominate and most of the action is), and a dealer market for blocks of more than 10 million Belgian francs that operates before and after official Stock Exchange hours.

Perhaps the best way to invest in it is through Belgian Growth Fund (Dumenil Unit Trust Management, 54 St. James's Street, London SW1A 1JT, England), which is oriented toward English-speaking investors and whose yearly reports could give you some clues on interesting prospects among individual Belgian companies.

The ten biggest Belgian stocks are Petrofina (an oil company that represents 11% of the value of the entire market), Intercom, Ebes, Generale de Belgique, Cockerill Sambre, Generale de Banque, Groupe Bruxelles-Lambert, Solvay, Unerg, and Krediet-bank.

## · LUXEMBOURG ·

The grand duchy of Luxembourg completes the trio of countries known as the Benelux group. Despite being considerably smaller than neighboring Belgium—its population is only 360,000 and it covers less than 1,000 square miles—Luxembourg is much more interesting as a financial center since it has the second-largest Eurobond market in the world after London. In fact the Luxembourg Stock Exchange has one of the biggest trading lists in the world, with about 5,000 stocks and bonds quoted, about one issue for every seventy inhabitants. More than 4,000 of these are bonds issued by 1,800 institutions from fifty-five different countries. They are denominated in currencies ranging from American and Canadian dollars to Kuwaiti dinars, New Zealand and Australian dollars, European Currency Units, Italian lire, and French, Belgian, Swiss, and Luxembourg francs. The bonds are issued by such eminently trustworthy borrowers as the Kingdom of Denmark, the European Investment Bank, the French Railroads, the Province of Quebec, and the City of Tokyo. A large number of them get a triple-A rating on a par with U.S. government securities.

All these are Eurobonds, securities listed outside their country of origin and sometimes in a different currency. The Danish government might have a bond issue denominated in Canadian dollars or Japanese yen, for example. Luxembourg can be credited with giving birth to the first Eurobond in 1961, an international loan managed by a local Luxembourg bank, and it can give thanks for the giant business that grew out of that to President John F. Kennedy, who in 1963 slapped his Foreign Interest Equalization Tax on foreign borrowers who were taking advantage of lower American interest rates to raise money in the United States. To avoid the tax the borrowers merely sought their dollars in Luxembourg. Later on, the idea spread to other currencies.

Luxembourg is also home to about 300 international mutual funds, which together with the bonds put the total amount of funds invested in or through Luxembourg at an astounding $160 billion. A lot of this is money seeking a tax haven and secrecy. The only way to crack Luxembourg's bank secrecy safeguards is through a court order. And the advantage over Switzerland is that Luxembourg does not tax interest, dividends, or capital gains. Also, unlike Switzerland, Luxembourg does not have two different classes of stock for foreigners and natives. As the Luxembourg Exchange stated in reply to a query: "There are no special rules for foreign investors. Most of the investors (and most of the companies) are foreigners."

Some of the companies with listed common stock, indeed, are extremely exotic. Among them you will find Plantations des Terres Rouges of Vanuatu and several dozen companies from Bermuda, the Cayman Islands, and the Bahamas.

The Luxembourg Stock Exchange (Societe de la Bourse de Luxembourg, 11 Avenue de la Ponte Neuve, BP 165 L-2011 Luxembourg) publishes a daily *Official Price List* (in French, but with an easily understood English explanatory brochure), as well as other literature in English. Brokers include:

Asset Investment Management SA
87 Grand-rue
L-1661 Luxembourg

Banque Generale du Luxembourg
27 Avenue Monterey
L-2163 Luxembourg

Kredietbank Luxembourgeoise
15 Avenue du Bois
L-1251 Luxembourg

As there are more than 120 banks in Luxembourg, including almost all the world's largest, any of the Swiss, British, or other banks mentioned in other chapters of this book could be of use as a broker.

Luxembourg provides a wide open market in which you may even use any number of foreign currencies, settling each deal in whatever is the currency denomination of the bond you are buying. However, for the American investor there are some restrictions. Because of SEC regulations, foreign bonds are not available to Americans during the initial offering period by the underwriters. They may only be bought by Americans ninety days after they commence trading on the open market, which in fact opens up practically the whole caboodle of 4,000 bonds on the Luxembourg Exchange list.

Standard & Poor's Corporation publishes ratings of most of these Eurobonds in its monthly publication *International Credit Week* (but unfortunately no prices).

The ratings are a useful guide because the choice you face is bewildering—between, for example, a yen bond issued by a Norwegian corporation and a Swiss-franc bond issued by a Japanese city, or the German-mark bond of an American company and the French-franc bond of a German bank. In addition, you have bonds with specialized features—they may be linked to the price of gold like some French government bonds, for instance, or tied to the price of oil like some Mexican issues. Some new types of bond are worth mentioning.

*Dual-currency bonds.* You buy this kind of bond in Swiss francs, for example, and collect your interest in Swiss francs, but the principal is repayable in American or Canadian dollars. The advantage is that you get a somewhat higher rate of interest than you would on a purely Swiss-franc bond. An example of this type is IC Industries Finance Corporation's 7 ½% 1983–1993 bond. Another variation is a bond with a Swiss-franc face value on which the interest is payable in dollars. The coupon is adjusted yearly on the basis of the yield of ten-year U.S. treasury obligations. Your investment is thus in strong Swiss francs and your income is at high U.S. interest rates. An example of this is Pepsico's 7 ½% foreign interest payment security. And then you have multiple-currency bonds. You are given the choice of two or more currencies when your principal is repaid. You choose, of course, whichever is strongest at the time you cash in.

*European Currency Unit bonds.* These are denominated in the currency of the European Monetary System. The ECU is a synthetic currency—no banknotes or coins are ever issued—composed of a basket of European national currencies. Since the purchase price, the interest payments, and the principal repayments are all figured out in ECUs, you assure yourself of the European average return on capital and do especially well if the American dollar plunges. (Note that the Swiss franc is not a part of this basket.)

*SDR bonds.* The SDR, or Special Drawing Right, is the synthetic currency unit of the Washington-based International Monetary Fund and is composed of a basket of five major currencies (American dollar, German mark, Japanese yen, French franc, and British pound). One example is the 1975 Alusuisse SDR bond. The advantage of ECU and SDR bonds is a greater stability than any one national currency can provide as the fluctuations of the component currencies tend to cancel each other out.

You have other intriguing bonds known as minimum-rate floaters, capped floaters, mini-max floaters, mismatch floaters, and drop-lock bonds, for which we unfortunately have insufficient space for discussion, but which may be found in Credit Suisse's booklet *Swiss Capital Market.*

# CHAPTER
# 18

## SCANDINAVIA

The Nordic countries appear to form a closely knit group. Their citizens can move and work freely in each others' nations without passports or work permits, and they enjoy full social welfare rights throughout the region. But there are considerable differences. Finland lives in the shadow of the Soviet Union and has given the word "finlandization" to international affairs as a description of enforced neutrality. Sweden is also neutral, its ports plagued by the clandestine intrusions of mysterious and presumably Soviet submarines, while Norway and Denmark are members of NATO. In matters of investment the similarity is that all four countries have small stock markets which are not particularly receptive to foreigners. The dissimilarities are noted below.

## · SWEDEN ·

Sweden has the biggest stock market in Scandinavia, but less than 200 companies are listed on the country's only stock exchange, at Stockholm. Apart from the small market there are other problems. An overgrown welfare state has damaged Sweden's competitiveness on international markets. Since 1920 the government has had restrictions in place on foreign stock ownership. Even so, the stock market boomed for several years after 1980 when the government created special tax incentives for investors in Swedish mutual funds.

There is a fair amount of stock market information in English, including literature from the Stock Exchange (Stockholms Fond-bors, Kallargrand 2, P.O. Box 1256, S-111 82 Stockholm). Big Swedish banks and brokers turn out research material on the Swedish economy and stock market and on individual compa-nies. Svenska Handelsbanken publishes a weekly newsletter with data on the twenty leading companies. The Stockholm news-papers *Svenska Dagbladet* and *Dagens Industri* publish English-language issues on Swedish business, and the business weekly *Affarsvarlden* publishes an English-language *Sweden Business Re-port* biweekly (Affarsvarlden, Skeppsbron 52, Box 1234, 111 82 Stockholm).

Brokers include:

Carnegie Fondkommission
Box 160 80
S-103 22 Stockholm

Skandinaviska Enskilda Banken
S-106 40 Stockholm

Svenska Handelsbanken
S-103 28 Stockholm

The most actively traded stocks are Volvo, Electrolux, Erics-son, Fermenta, Pharmacia, Saab-Scania, SKF, ASEA, Astra, and Skanska.

Company stocks are divided into A shares and B shares. Only B shares may be bought by nonresidents, and they often trade at a substantial premium above the A shares because of their limited supply. The Swedish government has undertaken a cam-paign to liberalize Sweden's financial markets, but at the time of writing was still balking at the abolition of exchange controls.

There is a 30% withholding tax on dividends. Margin trading is forbidden to foreign investors, and domestic Swedish bonds may not be sold to foreigners. There is a small, unofficial—and recently scandal-plagued—market for options. One relatively bright spot is that brokerage commissions are a flat 0.3% on all trades.

If you want to keep an eye on this rather unwelcoming market, a small investment in Sweden Innovation Fund (Skandifond AB, Jakobsbergsgatan 17, Stockholm) might prove useful. This mutual fund was specially designed for foreign investors; its reports come in English and could keep you abreast of Swedish stock market developments as well as possible companies to invest in.

A number of companies (including SKF, Nobel Industries, Procordia, Flakt, Swedish Match, Perstorp, Carnegie, and Euroc) turn out annual reports in English. The Swedish Institute of Authorized Public Accountants (Foreningen Auktoriserade Revisorer, Norrtullsgatan 6, Box 6417, 113 82 Stockholm) also offers an eight-page English-language *Key to Understanding Swedish Financial Statements*.

## · DENMARK ·

Denmark has only one stock market, at Copenhagen, and it does hardly any business. About 90% of all trading takes place off the exchange. A major point of interest for foreigners is the Danish bond market. The government has been running up big budget deficits since the 1970s and has issued huge amounts of bonds to pay for them. In 1982 the yield on long-term Danish government bonds rose to 21%, and at the time of writing in 1987 they are yielding nearly 12%. Not only is this five points better than a comparable U.S. government bond, but the Danish kroner also appreciated by 40% against the American dollar from 1985 to 1987. Furthermore, there is no Danish withholding tax on interest and no capital gains tax. The bonds come in denominations of 1,000 kroner and the market for them is highly liquid. It is also highly efficient. Denmark is the first country in the world to abolish the bond certificate and move completely over to computerized trading.

Information in English on the Danish securities market is available from the Stock Exchange (Kopenhavns Fondsbors, 6 Nikolaj Plads, P.O. Box 1040, DK-1007 Copenhagen K). About

250 companies are listed, the most actively traded of which are Superfos, Novo Industri, Handelsbanken, Den Danske Bank, Ostasiatiske Kompagni, Danske Sukkerfabrikker, Privatbanken, Sophus Berendsen, and Jyske Bank.

Brokers include:

Benzon & Benzon
Ved Stranden 20
1061 K Copenhagen

Lannung & Co.
Kronprinsessegade 2
1306 K Copenhagen

Thestrup & Thestrup
Frederiksborggade 4 1360 K
Copenhagen

As the only Scandinavian country in the European Economic Community, Denmark has been liberalizing its financial markets for a number of years and is now the most open of the four Nordic nations to the international financial scene.

Nevertheless, for substantial investors, restrictions remain. If you open an account with a Danish bank (for instance Copenhagen Handelsbank, 2 Holmens Kanal, DK-1091, Copenhagen K), you cannot raise your balance above 1 million kroner (about $140,000) without getting special permission from the Danish Central Bank. The minimum deposit at Handelsbank is 100,000 kroner. Handelsbank does accept unlimited deposits from foreign investors in other convertible currencies, however. It also provides advisory services, reports, and recommendations on Danish securities in English, and its stock brokerage subsidiary, COCO Securities Borsmaeglerselskab, handles stock market transactions. It might be noted that Danish banks are required by law to give information to the Danish tax authorities. Handelsbank observes that at its branch in Luxembourg "bank secrecy standards are higher."

## · FINLAND ·

Living in the giant shadow of the Soviet Union, Finland has fought two wars against the Russians in the last half-century, and, being a small nation of 5 million people, lost them both with extreme heroism. Nevertheless, their scrappy resistance enabled them to keep their independence, their democratic form of government, and their strongly free enterprise economy. The neighboring Baltic countries—Latvia, Lithuania, and Estonia— were not so fortunate; they were swallowed alive and incorporated into the Soviet Union—a fact the Finns are well aware of in their dealings with the Kremlin. Finland treads warily in matters that might annoy the Soviets.

Less than 100 stocks are traded in Helsinki. This includes the official list traded on the country's only stock exchange, a separate Broker's List for smaller companies, and a minute over-the-counter market. The most actively traded stocks are Pohjola Insurance, Nokia Corp., Farmos Group Ltd., Bank of Helsinki, Kesko Oy, Union Bank of Finland, Finnish Sugar Co., Rauma Repola Corp., Kansallis-Osake-Pankki, and United Paper Mills Ltd. Information on the stock market in English is available from the Stock Exchange (Helsingin Arvopaperiporssi, Fabianinkatu 14, 00100 Helsinki).

Foreign shareholding in Finnish companies is restricted by Finnish law. In most companies foreign ownership is limited to 40% of the share capital. Due to the limited supply of these nonrestricted shares available to foreigners, they trade at a premium over the restricted shares. All Finnish domestic bonds were placed off-limits to foreigners in 1985, but the Central Bank eased the restrictions to make some government bonds available to foreign investors in 1987.

Finnish securities may be bought through an authorized foreign exchange bank, one of which, Kansallis-Osake-Pankki (Aleksanterinkatu 42, P.O. Box 10, SF-00101 Helsinki), has a brochure in English for the guidance of foreign investors. This bank offers advisory services on taxation and foreign exchange regulations, and brokerage and custodial services. Another stock brokerage firm oriented toward a foreign clientele is Unitas Ltd., Mannerheimintie 2, 00100 Helsinki. Unitas produces market research on Finnish companies from the overseas investor's viewpoint.

Margin trading is prohibited to foreign investors in Finland, brokerage commissions are a flat 1% on all trades, and there is a 25% withholding tax on dividends.

## · NORWAY ·

About 150 stocks and 800 bond issues are quoted on the Oslo Stock Exchange, Norway's only stock market. Except for a few internationally traded issues, the domestic Norwegian bonds are entirely out of bounds for foreign investors. The Oslo Exchange says that "foreign investors are welcomed to the Norwegian stock market." It has, however, been a rather grudging welcome. Up to the late 1970s foreigners were limited to investments of 50,000 Norwegian kroner each (about $7,500). In the 1980s the per capita limit was raised and then abolished. Foreign investors still may not own more than 10% of Norwegian banks, 20% of industrial and insurance firms, or 40% of shipping companies. The most actively traded companies are Norsk Hydro, Elkem, Scanvest-Ring, Dyno Industrier, Media Vision, Elektrisk Bureau, Kosmos, Saga Petroleum, Aker Mek Verksted, and DNL.

Information in English on the stock market and individual companies may be obtained from the Oslo Exchange (Oslo Bors, P.O. Box 460—Sentrum, 0105 Oslo 1).

Banks (who also act as brokers) also provide market research reports. They include:

Den Norske Creditbank
Postboks 1171 Sentrum
Kirkegt 24, Oslo 1

Sparebanken ABC [Union Bank of Norway]
Postboks 1172 Sentrum
Kirkegt 14/18, Oslo 1

The Norwegian Stockbrokers Association (Norges Fondsme-glerforbund, Tollbugaten 2, Oslo 1) can also provide statistical market data.

The four Scandinavian markets are so small and are hedged about with such restrictions for foreigners that an investment fund wrapping up the whole region in one hassle-free package would appear to be the easiest solution. The easiest of all is the Scandinavia Fund, a closed-end trust quoted on the New York Stock Exchange. Among other possibilities (neither of which has been registered with the SEC but is open to non-U.S.-resident investors):

Skandifond Bond Fund
(Westbourne, The Grange, St. Peter Port, Guernsey, Channel Islands)

Hellerup Scandinavian Fund
(Tyndall House, Kensington Road, Douglas, Isle of Man)

The stock markets of all four Scandinavian countries suffered declines of between 10% and 30% in the October 1987 crash, but even so all four were still above their November 1986 levels in November 1987.

# CHAPTER
# 19

## AUSTRIA, ITALY, AND SPAIN

## · AUSTRIA ·

Austria, the heartland of a great, polyglot empire in central Europe and the Balkans up to World War I, is now a small neutral German-speaking nation of less than 8 million people that models itself on Switzerland. The pattern of imitation includes bank secrecy laws that outdo the Swiss in their protection of anonymity.

The Austrian secrecy laws allow foreigners to open bank accounts and buy and sell securities absolutely incognito. If you want a secret account, the Austrian bank is required to verify only that you are in fact a foreigner by looking at your passport or some similar identification. It does not record your name, and therefore could not divulge it even if it wanted to.

You then use this account to make investments in Austria— or elsewhere in the world if you like. The Oesterreichischer Landerbank (am Hof 2, 1010 Vienna), for instance, one of the biggest Austrian banks, asserts in its sales literature that "nonresidents of Austria may purchase domestic and foreign stocks and bonds without disclosing their identity to the bank. The protection afforded by the bank secrecy law also extends to the conduct of their accounts in Austrian schillings and foreign currency. Banks in Austria are pledged to secrecy regarding their customers' affairs. The law is very severe in this matter and any disclosure of information to third parties would render banks liable to fines and damages. In Austria it is also possible to open safe custody accounts without proper identification." An Austrian bank employee is in fact liable to one year in jail for violating a customer's bank secrecy.

Now this obviously outdoes the Swiss if you should be worried that bank confidentiality is becoming rather porous in Switzerland. But there are evident problems with this kind of account. If you are run over by a taxi in Vienna or fatally mugged in New York, your heirs are likely to have major problems proving their right to the money in an account whose owner is not even known to the bank.

You do not really have to go to that extreme. (It is difficult to imagine who would, except a Soviet or Bulgarian trade official trying to do private capitalist deals on the side, or an international drug smuggler, or some other character with a really pressing need for privacy.) Another major bank, Creditanstalt Bankverein (Schottengasse 6-8, 1010 Vienna) offers a numbered account in which your identity is known only to a handful of the bank's senior officials. This is for private individuals only (no business accounts), and you will need a minimum of 1 million Austrian schillings (about $75,000) to open it. You may "operate your account yourself, personally or by letter, or authorize a nonresident or an Austrian lawyer, notary public or chartered accountant. The authorized person may operate the account without any formalities, also personally or by letter."

A Creditanstalt spokesman in New York said this type of account "would only make sense with a large amount of money and in special circumstances. We don't advertise it." Of course you can also open a plain old bank account in your own name in Vienna and use it to buy stocks, bonds, and precious metals anywhere in the world. Creditanstalt, one of the 100 biggest banks in the world, has branches in London and New York and offices in other countries from Argentina to the United Arab Emirates. It can deal with you in English and has an interesting English-language brochure, *Investment in Austria*.

Creditanstalt handles about a quarter of all the securities trading in Vienna. This is not really saying all that much, however. The Austrian Stock Exchange is a small—and, until recently, somnolent—market on which a mere ninety-eight companies are listed, of which thirty-one are foreign and only sixty-seven Austrian. The major activity is in the bond market, where 1,848 issues are quoted.

Austrian stocks were long ignored because of tax laws that hit them specially hard. However the stock market came to life in 1985 when the government deliberately set out to stimulate investments in industrial firms. Dividend taxation was reduced, and Austrian investors in industrial companies were allowed to offset 40,000 schillings of investments in new shares against their income taxes. The resulting boom catapulted Vienna to first place among the world's stock exchanges with a gain of 130% that year. Trading multiplied sixfold, and foreign investors flocked into the market.

The most active Austrian stocks, which include a disproportionate number of insurance companies and breweries, are Anglo-Elementar Versicherungs, AKG Holding, Brauerei Schwechat, Bruder Reininghaus Brauerei, Creditanstalt Bankverein, Erste Allgemeine Versicherungs, Donau Chemie, Gosser Brauerei, Internationale Unfall und Schaden Versicherung, and Jungbunzlauer.

The main brokers include the two banks mentioned above and the Girozentrale und Bank der Oesterreichischen Sparkassen, Schubertring 5, 1010 Vienna. These three produce some English-language research on the stock market and local companies. The Stock Exchange (Wiener Borsekammer, Wipplingerstrasse 34, A-1011 Vienna) also provides some material in English. The Exchange actually plays a relatively minor role in trading activity. Most transactions take place between banks, and only the volume that cannot be handled by a bank ever gets to the Stock Exchange floor. Stocks and bonds used to be quoted not in actual monetary terms but as a percentage of par value, a cause of confusion since Austrian shares have different par values of 100, 500, or 1,000 schillings. However, common stocks are now quoted in schillings. Brokerage commissions and taxes come to 1.25% of each transaction.

In the competition with Switzerland, Austria seems to rank

a distinct second-best as a neutral haven for your money. The country has become the seat of major United Nations and other international organizations, but its status as a recognized neutral is nowhere near as solid as Switzerland's. Taken over by Hitler's Third Reich in 1938 and occupied by the Allies after World War II, the country was partially controlled by Soviet troops up to 1955. Austria has nowhere near the military muscle of Switzerland's citizen army to defend its newly declared neutrality.

It has, however, a well-run economy with one of the lowest average annual inflation rates of any nation over the past decade, and the Austrian schilling has become one of the most stable currencies in the world. The exchange rate has risen from 26 to 13 schillings per dollar since 1970.

## · ITALY ·

There are two sides to the Italian economy: the official and the unofficial. Officially, Italy has one of the world's highest budget deficits—totaling 13% of gross national product—a high unemployment rate, and a stifling bureaucracy. The interest on government debt amounts to 10% of the gross national product and is a crippling hindrance to economic growth. Another 6% of GNP goes to pay for current government deficits. This, however, has nothing much to do with the "unofficial" or "black" economy that operates out of sight of officialdom, avoids bureaucratic hindrances, pays no taxes, and keeps Italy going from day to day in the area of small business. This underground economy represents a precisely incalculable but very large part of the country's economic activity. Unfortunately, investing in it is beyond the scope of this book.

On the "official side," a single state-owned conglomerate, Istituto per la Ricostruzione Industriale (IRI), employs 3% of all Italian workers, loses $2 billion a year, and has a debt of $24 billion—topping the debts of most Third World nations. This astonishing collection of 1,000 companies has been described as a "garbage pail" for unprofitable Italian companies that faced bankruptcy at various times since Benito Mussolini founded IRI in 1933 during the Depression. They were then swept into the IRI trash receptacle to be managed by political appointees and government bureaucrats.

However, in 1987 IRI began a turnaround that may be symptomatic for the entire Italian economy. Under Romano Prodi, an energetic university professor, IRI began to sell off some of its businesses and started to turn a profit. Prodi sold more than twenty companies to private investors, including Alfa Romeo, the racing-car manufacturer, and chunks of Alitalia, the Italian airline, and SIP, the state telephone company. Private investors now hold about 20% of IRI's assets.

Italy has a long way to go to match the drastic privatization campaigns launched by Britain and France. "Between 1983 and 1987," Prodi noted, "26 enterprises of different size, from Alfa Romeo to small Ducati, from banks to glasses and washing machine producers, have been divested. In broad terms there is good reason to be optimistic about the future of IRI in particular and of Italy in general."

The IRI companies were being sold into a long-straitjacketed financial market that has also been liberalized in a modest way since 1984. One major step was the abolition in 1984 of a long-standing Italian ban on mutual funds. Italians rushed to buy these newfangled inventions and set off a stock market boom that in 1985 was exceeded only by Austria in the whole world. This development initiated an era of what some describe as the birth of *capitalismo di massa* (people's capitalism) in Italy. Italians rank with the Japanese as the world's most compulsive savers—they regularly squirrel away 20% of their disposable income in savings accounts—but until 1984 they had never shown any great interest in the stock market. The newly authorized mutual funds soaked up about $50 billion worth of investments, and trading volume quadrupled on the Milan Stock Exchange.

The battle now is for control of the stock market as the financial liberalization plan advances, the stock brokers defending their traditional monopoly, and the banks trying to break into the market. One bank, Banca Nazionale del Lavoro, actually started round-the-clock trading in 1987, bypassing the Stock Exchange altogether. Legislation to allow the banks onto the Exchange floor seemed likely to take somewhat longer.

The battleground is a surprisingly small one, considering that Italy is a major industrial country. Less than 200 companies are listed on the Milan Stock Exchange. Milan has 80% of the business, the rest being spread out among the stock exchanges of Rome, Turin, Genoa, Bologna, Florence, Naples, Palermo, Trieste, and Venice. Trading, furthermore, is concentrated heavily on a few major companies. Assicurazione Generali, Fiat, and Montedison among them account for more than 20% of all trading. Other heavily traded stocks are Cigahotels, Olivetti, SME, Snia, RAS, and IFI. Information on these companies in English is hard to come by. The Milan Stock Exchange (Borsa Valori di Milano, Piazza degli Affari 6, 20123 Milan) has some market material in English, including a *Stock Exchange Monthly Report.*

Banks and brokers include:

Banca Nazionale del Lavoro
Piazza San Sedele 3
20100 Milan

Credito Italiano
Piazza Cordusio 2
20123 Milan

Euromobiliare
Largo Donegani 1
20121 Milan

Istituto Mobiliare Italiano
Piazza San Fedele 2
20121 Milan

Studio Albertini
Via Borromei 5
20121 Milan

However the Italian stock market is less than enticing to a foreigner who knows no Italian, and the ordinary American investor would be well advised to play the Italian market from his own home base by buying Italy Fund on the New York Stock Exchange or one of the Italian ADRs.

## · SPAIN ·

The major economic legacy of Fascist regimes like Benito Mussolini's in Italy and Francisco Franco's in Spain includes giant grab bags of failed capitalist enterprises. The Spanish equivalent of Italy's IRI is the Instituto Nacional de Industria (INI), which holds a sizable chunk of Spanish industrial companies and reports losses approaching $1 billion a year. The Spanish state conglomerate is in even worse shape than its Italian counterpart since the more profitable companies, specializing in petrochemicals, gas, and oil, were spun off in the late 1970s to form a separate state holding company, the Instituto Nacional de Hidrocarburos. INI was left with a bunch of loss-making steel, coal, capital goods, and shipbuilding companies. It has managed to sell some, including Maropeche, a fishing company; Pamesa, a paper manufacturer; and Entursa, a chain of luxury hotels. It also sold SEAT, Spain's leading auto manufacturer, and Tarazona, a carpet maker. However the state remains a major, and highly inefficient, player in the Spanish economy. The remainder of Spanish industry in private hands includes many companies in the leather, shoes, textile, clothing, and furniture trades that are small family-run businesses, short of capital and poorly managed.

As a recent member of the European Economic Community, Spain has until 1994 to shape up economically before trade restrictions between it and the rest of the Community are completely abolished for manufactured goods. The government has been making great efforts to make Spanish industry more competitive, and it has sworn off the old statist habit of taking over or bailing out private companies that get into difficulties. But many Spanish companies seem to have rather slim chances of surviving full-scale, unrestricted competition in the twelve-nation European Common Market. Nevertheless, Spain's entry into the European Community in the 1980s touched off a stock market boom as international investors suddenly saw Spanish stocks as European-class companies with attractively low price-earnings ratios.

If you are thinking of investing in one of these Spanish companies, the available pool has been shrinking rather fast. Nearly 500 companies were listed on the Madrid Stock Exchange in 1981, but the number is now down to less than 400. The shrinkage is due to the delisting of many smaller, marginal companies.

This is in any case a relatively illiquid market in which share ownership is concentrated in the hands of big Spanish banks. Banesto, for example, has stock holdings of 20% or more in each of 147 Spanish companies. The major companies, furthermore, account for practically all the trading. Telefonica, the Spanish telephone company, represents one-sixth of the market value of all stocks on the market, and the top ten companies account for nearly half the market value. They include Banco de Santander, Hidrola, Iberduero, Banesto, Banco Central, Endesa, Banco de Bilbao, Banco de Vizcaya, and Union Fenosa.

The government was planning to set up a new computerized market in 1988 (which would eventually supersede the existing exchanges at Madrid, Barcelona, Valencia, and Bilbao) as well as an Instituto Nacional de Valores—the Spanish equivalent to the SEC in the United States.

As an investor in Spain you would have to deal with a Spanish bank, which relays your order to a stockbroker. Spanish brokers have a monopoly on stock trading but are not allowed to provide other financial or advisory services to investors. You would also have to figure out Spanish stock prices, which are quoted as a percentage of their par value. The par value is usually, but not always, 500 pesetas.

There is hardly any research available on the stock market in English. Banks that turn out reports in Spanish include:

Banco Central
Alcala 49
28014 Madrid

Banco Hispano Americano
Plaza de Canalejas 1
28014 Madrid

Banco de Vizcaya
Paseo de la Castellana 110
28046 Madrid

The Madrid Stock Exchange (Bolsa de Madrid, Plaza de la Lealtad 1, 28014 Madrid) publishes a *Daily Official List*, a *Weekly Report*, a *Quarterly Information of Companies Listed*, and a *Yearly Summary*, among other publications. If you can read Spanish, that is.

For the investor who has no Spanish, more practical alternatives for investing in Spain would appear to be the Swiss mutual fund Espac, or Banco Nacional, which is quoted on the New York Stock Exchange. In view of Spanish banks' extensive holdings in Spanish industry, you might consider this bank as a surrogate Spanish mutual fund.

The October 1987 world stock market crash affected these three countries differently. Austria suffered relatively minor damage, and in December 1987 was slightly above its December 1986 level. Italy dropped about 30% in the crash and by December was down about 23% from December 1986. Spain plunged about 20% in the October massacre, but thanks to the preceding bull market by December 1987 still stood a good 30% higher than in December 1986.

# CHAPTER
## 20

ISRAEL, KOREA,
SOUTH AFRICA,
AND OTHER
INTERESTING
MARKETS WITH
PROBLEMS

Our world tour now brings us to about two dozen countries where, for a variety of reasons, you are unlikely to have any great, sudden urge to invest your money under present circumstances, but which may present some interesting opportunities in the future. We include in this category a number of nations with outstanding economic potential and in some cases highly developed stock markets. This group includes Israel (surrounded by enemies, huge defense expenditures, crushing taxation, runaway inflation); South Africa (internal racial problems, international boycott); Taiwan and Korea (the government discourages foreign investors); the Philippines, Mexico, Brazil, and Argentina (a group of nations with huge foreign debts, economic mismanagement, uncontrolled inflation).

We include also a second group of countries that, in addition to economic and political problems, at present have relatively undeveloped stock markets, which at some time in the future may blossom into viable nurseries for profitable stock investments. This group comprises Greece, Portugal, Chile, Colombia, Ecuador, Egypt, Indonesia, Jamaica, Kenya, Morocco, Nigeria, Pakistan, Peru, and Sri Lanka.

## · ISRAEL ·

Israel's Tel Aviv Stock Exchange is the biggest and most sophisticated financial center in the Middle East, its 270 listed companies having a total market value of about $8 billion. This market also presents a number of problems, however, that might make any but the most enthusiastic supporter of Israel hesitant about investing in it. Israel is surrounded by a sea of hostile Arab states and contains a large and hostile Arab minority of 1.4 million within its borders. This minority may become the majority within two decades if high Arab birth rates and low Jewish birth rates continue. The country is heavily dependent on American financial and military aid. Israel's 4 million people face a foreign national debt of $24 billion, the highest per capita debt in the world. The tax rate may well be the world's highest, and taxation transfers nearly 60% of national production to the government, which still runs at a deficit. The national government employs one-third of the population, while local governments and state bodies employ another third. This leaves the remaining third to support the first two. The inflation rate rose to 1,000% a year in 1984, and even though it was cut back to 20% in 1987, the Israeli currency declined in value from 15.6 shekels per dollar in 1981 to 1,600 in 1987.

The stock market is dominated by a few big bank stocks, fourteen of which represent about 70% of the market's total value. More than 40% of this is concentrated in only two stocks, Bank Hapoalim and Bank Leumi. Corporate profits are taxed at 61%, a burden that has contributed to a spluttering economy and a slow growth rate. There is also a 25% withholding tax on dividends and interest for nonresidents.

The government's efforts to contain the runaway inflation hit Israeli private industry with particular severity. However, the government has undertaken a program to reduce the state role in the economy and boost private enterprise. Israeli minister of industry and trade Ariel Sharon noted in 1987 that "we own about 200 companies, including communications, electronics, aircraft, refineries and a chemical conglomerate, and they are all for sale."

These companies would join a private sector in which high-technology companies give Israel international significance in products ranging from fiber-optic communications to surgical and industrial lasers, and solar-generated electricity. These industries, plus free trade agreements with the European Economic Community and the United States, have made Israel the biggest exporter in the world on a per capita basis.

Investing in Israel means dealing with a bank. Foreign investors have to pay for their investments through banks registered as foreign exchange dealers. They include:

American-Israel Bank
28a Rothschild Street
Tel Aviv

Bank Hapoalim
52 Yehuda Halevy Street
Tel Aviv

Bank Leumi Le-Israel
35 Halevy Street
Tel Aviv

United Mizrahi Bank
113 Allenby Street
Tel Aviv

Brokerage commissions are high on small trades, ranging from 3% of a $500 purchase to 1.5% on a $10,000 trade.

The most active stocks are Bank Hapoalim, Bank Leumi, IDB Bank Holding, United Mizrahi Bank, Israel Discount Bank, Dead Sea Works, Discount Investment Co., IDB Development Co., Clal Electronic Industries, and Clal Industries.

Bank Hapoalim offers deposits linked to the Israeli consumer price index. As a result of the raging inflation, Israel was a pioneer some years ago in the introduction of inflation-indexed bonds. State of Israel bonds come in minimum denominations of $250 and maturities up to fifteen years. They pay interest annually, and the secondary market is not very liquid if you want to sell.

There is a fair amount of information available in English. The Stock Exchange (54 Ahad Ha'am Street, Tel Aviv) prints an official list of daily prices in Hebrew and English as well as other publications in English. The major banks also publish reports on the stock market. The English-language press includes the daily *Jerusalem Post* and the monthly *Israel Economist* (P.O. Box 7052, Jerusalem 91070, $88 a year airmail).

## · SOUTH AFRICA ·

South Africa produces about three-quarters of the noncommunist world's newly mined gold and is a treasure house of other mineral wealth, including diamonds, coal, platinum, and uranium. Its industrialized economy and its financial wealth are unequaled in Africa. Even South Africa's downtrodden blacks have a higher living standard than the citizens of many black southern African nations. Blacks immigrate voluntarily from neighboring countries such as Mozambique to work in South African gold mines, and like the United States, South Africa also has a substantial population of illegal immigrants from undeveloped neighboring countries. In Johannesburg the country has a highly developed stock exchange where nearly 600 companies are listed. All these positive factors are offset by the effects of the country's official policy of apartheid, set up to keep the races apart and to preserve political power in the hands of the white minority. In protest against this policy, American and other businesses have pulled out of South Africa, boycotted trade with the Republic, and refused it loans. There have even been intimations in Congress of a ban on ownership of South African securities by American citizens.

In this atmosphere, investment in South Africa is not particularly alluring. The Stock Exchange—which got its start in 1886 with the discovery of the world's greatest source of diamonds in Kimberley, and was then boosted again with the discovery of the world's most productive gold mines near Johannesburg a few years later—seems likely to function on its own internal power until foreign investors are attracted again by more promising political conditions. South Africans have been kept from sending money abroad by foreign exchange restrictions, and this has maintained the stock market's stability during all the recent racial turmoil.

The Johannesburg Stock Exchange (Diagonal Street, P.O. Box 1174, 2000 Johannesburg) offers an abundant supply of informative material in English, including a *Monthly Bulletin* and an *Annual Report*. Research is also available from stockbrokers, among them J.D. Anderson & Co.; Davis, Borkum, Hare & Co.; Ed Hern Rudolph Inc.; Ivor Jones, Roy & Co.; Martin & Co.; Mathison & Hollidge Inc.; Max Pollak & Freemantle. (All have the same address as the Stock Exchange.)

The most actively traded stocks are Vaal Reefs & Exploration, De Beers Consolidated Mines, Anglo American Corporation of South Africa, Western Deep Levels Ltd., and Driefontein Consolidated.

A number of these and other South African shares are traded as ADRs in the United States. ASA Ltd., listed on the New York Stock Exchange, is a closed-end fund that offers dozens of South African stocks in one parcel.

News on South African business is available in several English-language South African periodicals, including the *Business Day*, the *Financial Mail*, and *Finance Week*.

From the South African end, the most significant legal regulation for foreign investors is a 1985 foreign exchange law which channels investment funds in and out of the country through the Financial Rand, a variety of the South African national currency which trades at a discount to the Commercial Rand. It tends to make investment in South Africa more attractive. Restrictions on the remittance of dividends have also been applied in the past.

In current circumstances, the most interesting speculation on the South African situation appears to be ASA Ltd., which offers a cross-section of the Johannesburg market and generally sinks to a discount of as much as 50% from net asset value whenever the bouts of racial disorder flare up. The discount tends to narrow when the rioting subsides, providing an opportunity to sell at a profit.

## · TAIWAN ·

The most interesting fact about Taiwan from the investor's point of view is that Communist China lays claim to it. Of slightly less interest is the fact that Taiwan, with a population of 20 million and ruled by the former Nationalist government of China, lays claim to China and its population of 1 billion. As Taiwan has achieved remarkable success with a free enterprise economic system and Communist China has been flirting with capitalism, the two Chinas may yet surprise the world with a happy reunion in the years ahead. Chinese treatment of Hong Kong, the British colony to be regained by China in 1997—and the fulfillment or nonfulfillment of promises to preserve capitalism there—should be a good indication of Taiwan's future. A combination of Taiwanese capitalist drive and Chinese population could possibly put the economic rise of Japan in the shade in the decades to come.

However, for an investor in the here and now, all this is theoretical speculation. Direct foreign investment in listed Taiwan companies is not allowed. As a nonresident you are not even allowed to have a bank account in Taiwan. The only way to invest is through a couple of investment trusts: Taiwan Fund, a closed-end fund listed on the New York Stock Exchange, and the International Investment Trust Company Ltd. (Worldwide House, 685 Min Sheng East Road, Taipei, Taiwan). The IITC is the first mutual fund to be established in the Republic of China for investment by nonresidents. Intended for institutional investors, it is sold in the form of International Depository Receipts, which consist of 1,000 shares each. The price is quoted in the *Financial Times* of London. There are complications involved in trading, and the large sums involved will put most small individual investors off this fund.

The Taipei Stock Exchange, Taiwan's only stock market, is in any case viewed with some reserve by big institutional investors due to the lack of information on listed companies and a rather low level of accounting standards. It is regarded with some distrust even by local middle-class Taiwanese as a gambling house for speculators. Nevertheless, the number of companies listed has grown sharply from sixty-eight in 1975 to double that number in 1987. Plastic and chemical companies, textiles, banks, and cement producers predominate.

Most actively traded stocks: Hualon-Teijran, Chung Shing Textile, Yue Loong Motors, China General Plastics, Tatung, Chia Hsin Cement, Nan Ya Plastic, Cheng Loong, Taroko Textile, and Far East Textile.

The Taiwan Stock Exchange (1 Nan Hai Road, Taipei) has some English-language reports and statistical data available. Vickers da Costa (85 Jen Ai Road, Section 4, Taipei) has a research department in Taiwan.

Mainland China itself has reached a stage of capitalist-road backsliding that must have Mao Tse-tung turning in his grave: actual real-life stock markets in Shanghai and other mainland cities. The Shanghai market is small, with a total value of only 225 million yuan (about $60 million), but 1,480 enterprises are already listed and the value of their stocks and bonds could grow rapidly. Leading lights of the New York Stock Exchange were even invited to Beijing in 1986 to explain the workings of stock exchanges and other financial markets to the Communist bigwigs. The Shanghai market opened in October 1986, with two companies selling shares initially, and what might perhaps be described as a roaring Communist bull market immediately developed. Both issues were sold out the first day and trading in them then dried up entirely for several months as there were no sellers among the capitalist comrades.

There would indeed be no point in selling. The return on Chinese Communist common stocks is too attractive, 15% a year or more compared with 7% on bank deposits. But capitalist development in Red China has not yet opened the market to foreigners, although as a distinguished visitor to the Shanghai Exchange you might be allowed to buy one share as a souvenir.

## · KOREA ·

The Korean stock market is only just emerging from its Hermit Kingdom phase despite the country's startling success as an international trading nation. Foreign investors were excluded up to 1981, when the government established the first of a half-dozen investment trusts for the benefit of nonresidents. In 1985 Korea took the first limited step toward allowing direct investment by foreigners in individual Korean companies, but this was limited to a dozen companies that issue convertible bonds overseas. The overseas bonds can be exchanged for shares after an eighteen-month holding period, but even so, no individual foreigner may hold more than 3% of a Korean company. The government is planning further cautious moves toward liberalization and expects to have a completely open market by the 1990s.

In the meanwhile the perception of Korea as a rising industrial power, a second Japan in economic might and stock market potential, has led to a huge demand for Korean shares. Korea Fund, a closed-end trust listed on the New York Stock Exchange, has traded at times at more than twice its net asset value. This investor enthusiasm seems to pay little attention to some menacing political facts. South Korea faces a powerfully armed communist antagonist in North Korea. This aggressive rival invaded once in the 1950s, has murdered South Korean cabinet members in a series of terrorist incidents in the 1980s, and may possibly invade again. The Seoul Stock Exchange is within artillery range of the North Korean army 25 miles away. The authoritarian South Korean government has also faced increasing riots and disorders from dissatisfied elements of the southern population.

The easiest way to invest in Korea is through Korea Fund on the NYSE. The other funds are quoted in London and their prices will be found in the *Financial Times* of London in the section on Offshore Trusts. They include Korea International, Korea Trust, Korea Growth, Seoul International, and Seoul Trust. However, these latter funds are intended for big institutional investors, and trading procedures can be disconcerting for the individual investor. Contact Vickers da Costa in London, for example, about buying Korea International Trust, and you discover that the fund is traded only in the form of International Depository Receipts (each of which represents 1,000 shares and costs about $20,000). Furthermore, says Vickers da Costa, "Trade in the IDRs is not regular, and if you wish to invest in the fund we will place you on a waiting list so that we can contact you when any units become available."

Despite the SEC restrictions on foreign mutual funds, however, these IDR bearer certificates qualify as internationally traded stock market investments and are open to American investors under SEC regulations.

The Seoul Stock Exchange itself has grown dramatically from a mere twelve listed companies in 1956 to nearly 400 in 1987. The most actively traded stocks are Korea Oil Stock Holding, Sun Kyung, Hyundai Motor, Chin Heung International, Lucky Gold Star, Han Yang, Han Shin Construction, Lucky, Jung Woo Development, and Keung Nam Enterprise.

A monthly review and other information on the stock market in English is available from the Korea Stock Exchange (33 Yeo-ido-dong, Yeongdeungpo-ku, Seoul 150), and from the Korea Securities Dealers Association at the same address. Citizens Investment Trust Management Co. (112-1 Ineui-dong, Jongro-ku, Seoul 110) publishes a monthly English-language *Korean Investment Review*.

## · THAILAND ·

Thailand is a relatively new arrival on the international financial scene—its stock market only really got going in 1975, with a mere fourteen quoted securities—but it has attracted growing international interest. There are now about ninety companies listed in Bangkok with a total market value of about $3.5 billion, and foreign trading accounts for about 10% of total market activity. Except for Japanese occupation during World War II, Thailand has always managed to maintain its independence, even when neighboring countries were falling under Western colonial rule in the last century. It has also steered clear of the huge international debts that have burdened other Third World nations. The Thai stock market got off to a slow start due to the Vietnam War and the spread of communist regimes in neighboring lands. Attempted coups by disgruntled Thai generals have not helped either, but an improving Thai economy and official efforts to promote stock market investments contributed to a sharply rising market in 1986 and 1987.

The Thai market is small and divided into two groups of stocks: a handful of big companies with widely traded issues and a large number of smaller, family-owned companies that rarely change hands. The most active stocks are Siam Cement, Bangkok Bank, Siam City Cement, Thai Farmers Bank, Jalaprathan Cement, Mah Boonkrong, Siam Commercial Bank, Bank of Ayudhya, IFCT, and Bangkok Metropolitan Bank.

Nonresidents can open bank accounts and trade stocks in Thailand without restriction, except that some companies have limits on the extent of foreign ownership. There are exchange controls, however, that involve paperwork and delays when you take your money out of the country. Information on the stock exchange and listed companies in English is also scarce. The Securities Exchange of Thailand (Sinthon Building, 132 Wireless Road, Bangkok 10500 Metropolis) turns out a fact book and a yearly report. International brokers that take an interest in the Thai market include Merrill Lynch, Vickers da Costa, and Cazenove.

Thai brokers include:
Adkinson Securities Ltd.
Sinthon Building
132 Wireless Road
Bangkok 10500
Bangkok First Investment & Trust Ltd.
300 Silom Road
Bangkok 10500
Book Club Finance & Securities Ltd.
Siam Commercial Bank Building
1060 New Petchburi Road
Bangkok 10500
International Finance & Consultants Co. Ltd.
44 Sathorn Nua Road
Bangkok 10500

There are two internationally traded Thai funds for foreign investors, The Bangkok Fund (300 Silom Road, Bangkok 10500), launched by Merrill Lynch and Cazenove in 1985, and The Thailand Fund, launched in 1986 with the participation of the World Bank's International Finance Corporation and Vickers da Costa. Both are listed in London, and the latest prices are published in the *London Financial Times*.

With a market value of about $2 billion, the Thai stock market is a midget, a mere 0.2% of Japan's. But average price-earnings ratios of 8 for Thai stocks compared with PEs of 20 in Singapore and Malaysia began to attract the attention of big international investors in 1987.

## · THE PHILIPPINES ·

The Philippine stock market took off spectacularly after the fall of President Ferdinand Marcos in February 1986, but it is still a very small, and largely speculative, affair in which trading amounts to only $1 million or $2 million a day. In the Marcos years, trading had dwindled to as little as $2,000 a day. The country too has its share of problems, among them an armed communist insurgency, an armed Moslem insurgency, a crushing foreign debt of $28 billion, and an economy that stagnated for years in the hands of Marcos cronies and protégés.

There are two stock markets, the Manila Stock Exchange, founded in 1927, and the Makati Stock Exchange, established in 1965. The same 115 companies are listed on both. Much of the speculative action has traditionally been in small mining issues. There are only a score of big, solid companies on the market. The most actively traded stocks are Insular Bank of Asia & America, Philex Mining Corp., Globe Mackay Cable & Radio Corp., Ayala Corp., Overseas Drilling & Oil Development Corp., Philippine Long Distance Telephone Co., San Miguel Corp., Seafront Petroleum & Mineral Resources, and Benguet Corp. There are two classes of shares: A shares for Filipinos, and B shares for both Filipinos and foreigners.

Brokers include:

Barcelon-Roxas Securities
Far East Asia Building
303 Dasmarinas Street
Binondo, Metro Manila

Credit Manila Inc.
Bankmer Building
6756 Ayala Avenue
Makati, Metro Manila

Information in English is available from the Manila Stock Exchange (Prensa St. Cor Muelle de la Industria, Binondo, Manila) and the Makati Stock Exchange (Makati Stock Exchange Building, Ayala Avenue, Metro Manila). The Center for Research and Communications (Pearl Drive, Ortigas Commercial Complex, Pasig, Metro Manila) also turns out economic and financial information. Publications in English include *Business Day*, *Asia Week*, and *Far Eastern Economic Review*.

Philippine stocks available in the United States as ADRs include Philippine Long Distance and Benguet. If you plan to buy other stocks in Manila, insider trading is reportedly commonly practiced and has not been prosecuted within living memory, so the safest bet would probably be an investment fund. There are two available (to non–U.S. residents) in London or Hong Kong: Jardine Fleming Philippine Trust (G.P.O. Box 11448, Hong Kong), and Thornton Management Philippine Development Fund (16 Finsbury Circus, London EC2M 7DJ).

## · INDIA ·

No less than 3,883 companies are listed in India. There are thirteen stock exchanges and an estimated 18 million stock market investors. This may sound like a big market, but none of it is of any practical interest at the moment to non-Indians as the capital market is closed to foreign investors who are not of Indian origin. Rajiv Gandhi, who was elected prime minister in 1984, undertook a market liberalization process to accompany his policy swing from India's traditionally statist economy toward a market economy. He has a long way to go. Nonresident investors (expatriate Indians, that is) have a 25% to 50% tax on dividends and capital gains, and the more affluent ones also pay a "wealth tax" (capital levy). They have to get a holding license for their investments. Sale or transfer of shares requires the approval of the Reserve Bank of India. No individual abroad can hold more than 1% in any Indian company. Opening an Indian bank account requires Reserve Bank approval. Four of the stock exchanges, incidentally, are classified as "temporary" entities, until the government bureaucrats decide, in about four or five years, whether they should grant them permanent status.

There is one way for non-Indians to invest in India, if you should be interested. It is the India Fund (c/o Merrill Lynch, 119 Cannon Street, London EC4), run by Unit Trust of India, the only mutual fund in the country, which—as you might have guessed—is run by the government of India.

In case Mr. Gandhi should liberalize the markets to actually allow investors in, the biggest stock exchange, with 80% of the trading, is the Bombay Stock Exchange (Phiroze Jeejeebhoy Towers, Dalal Street, Bombay 400-023). Brokers include:

Bhupendra Champaklal
Bhupen Chambers
Dalal Street Fort
Bombay 400-021

D.S. Purbhoodas
1107 PJ Towers
Dalal Street Fort
Bombay 400-023

Jamnadas Morarjee
Stock Exchange Plaza
Dalal Street
Bombay 400-023

The most actively traded shares are Tata Steel, Associated Cement Companies, Reliance Industries, Southern Petrochemicals, Century Mills, Premier Automobiles, Tata Engineering, Orkay Silk Mills, Larsen & Toubro, and JK Synthetics.

## · MEXICO ·

For a poor Third World country with a crushing $100 billion foreign debt, soaring inflation, huge unemployment, and other assorted problems, the chances of a raging stock market boom might seem wildly improbable. But the Mexico City Stock Market racked up a 277% gain in 1986 and followed that with a further 243% advance in the first half of 1987. Not since 1978, when the petroleum-exporting country was riding high on the world oil boom and the Mexico City Bolsa was one of the top-performing stock exchanges in the world, had Mexican investors made so much money in so short a time. Inflation had driven the Mexican peso down from 26 per dollar in 1981 to 1,400 in 1987, but in 1986 alone, investors in Tamsa and Penoles, two Mexican steel companies, made gains of around 700%. And in the first few months of 1987 investors in other stocks saw their prices multiply tenfold and twelvefold. On January 7, 1987, the Mexico Stock Index gained nearly 10% in one day.

All this took place on a market where less than 200 stocks are listed. Their total market value rose from about $2 billion in 1986 to more than $9 billion in 1987. Analysts, noting that nothing fundamental in the nation's economic situation had changed, held their breath waiting for the crash.

In October it duly arrived. By this time the market was up 692% for the year. By November the Mexico Stock Exchange index (whose inflated figures are a vivid illustration of the effects of years of double-digit inflation) had plunged from a peak of 373,216.24 on October 6 to 145,116.83 three weeks later. The Mexican government then got together with major banks and brokerage firms to set up a $650 million fund to prop up the market.

The violent gyrations of the Mexican market are exaggerated by the small size of the market; even a $9 billion valuation on the nation's productive capital is pretty insignificant against a $100 billion debt to foreign banks. And the Mexican stock market is really small. Up to 1975 there were fewer than 5,000 active stock investors in the country and daily trading rarely went over $1 million a day. Even now there are probably less than 50,000. It is hard to get reliable figures since Mexico has its equivalent of Swiss bank secrecy in *el secreto bursátil*, which protects the privacy of major investors.

This is not only a small, secretive market; it also lacks published information in English, so that the easiest way to invest in it is simply to buy Mexico Fund, a closed-end fund listed on the New York Stock Exchange. FIMSA (Venustiano Carranza 51, Col. Centro, Cuauhtemoc 0600, Mexico DF) also runs a mutual fund, FIRME, that publishes reports in English. FIMSA also operates a brokerage business.

Two other brokerages that provide some market information are Casa de Bolsa Interamericana (Insurgentes Sur 1886, Col. Florida, Alvaro Obregon 01030, Mexico DF) and Estrategia Bursatil (Eje Central Lazaro Cardenas 13, Col. Centro, Cuauhtemoc 06050, Mexico DF). The Mexico City Stock Exchange (Bolsa Mexicana de Valores, Uruguay 68, Colonia Centro, Delegacion Cuauhtemoc, 0600 Mexico DF) offers some information in Spanish.

## · BRAZIL ·

Brazil is another country where double-digit and triple-digit inflation has been a way of life for decades, and it too has a $100 billion foreign debt. But the Brazilian stock market is one of the most innovative among the developing countries of the world, and Brazil itself is rapidly becoming a modern industrial power of the first rank. Securities on the market include futures and options on more than 100 stocks. There are stock exchanges in ten different Brazilian states, but the bulk of all trading is transacted in Sao Paulo and Rio de Janeiro, where more than 600 companies are listed, most of them dually. The total market value comes to about $50 billion. The cumulative inflation from 1980 to 1985 came to 10,000% but, incredibly, stock market values somehow managed to stay ahead by a comfortable margin.

The most actively traded stocks are Paranapanema SA, Petrobras, Vale do Rio Doce, Sharp SA Electronicos, Banco do Brasil, Banco Itau, SID Informatica, Banco Brasileiro de Descontos, Copene Petroquimica do Nordeste, and Semente Agroceres.

In an effort to attract foreign capital, the government passed a law in 1975 to stimulate special mutual funds for foreigners. There are a dozen of these Brazilian-incorporated funds, most of which issue their reports in English. One of them is Brasilvest S.A. (Unibanco, Rua Direita 250, 27 Andar, Sao Paulo).

Otherwise, market information in English is scarce, apart from some material from the Sao Paulo Exchange (Bolsa de Valores de Sao Paulo, Rua Alvares Penteado 151, Sao Paulo) and the Rio Stock Exchange (Praca 15 de Novembro 20, 20010 Rio de Janeiro).

If you can read Portuguese you will also benefit from *Bolsa Hoje*, the Rio Stock Exchange's daily report, and *Revista Bolsa*, the Sao Paulo Exchange's magazine. You will also be able to communicate with Brazilian brokers, who include:

Bozano Simonsen
Rua Boa Vista 88
Sao Paulo

Unibanco
Rua Libero Badaro 293
Sao Paulo

## · GREECE ·

Athens is one of the smallest stock exchanges in Europe, with 114 companies listed and a trading volume of about $100,000 a day. Many of the listed companies are small. Only about a quarter of the 200 biggest Greek companies are listed, the remainder being government-owned or family businesses. The biggest listed companies are National Bank of Greece, Aluminium of Greece, Commercial Bank, Bank of Greece, National Mortgage Bank, Lampsa Hotel, National Investment Co., Ionian & Popular Bank, Hellenic Investment Co., and Credit Bank. There are restrictions on foreign ownership of banks, and shipping and insurance companies. There are also exchange controls, and government approval is required to remit funds out of Greece.

Information from the Stock Exchange (Athens Stock Exchange, 10 Sophocleous Street, Athens 10559) includes a daily *Gazette of Stock Market Prices* and two annual publications. The National Investment Company (1 Skouleniu Street, Athens 10559) also provides some market information in English.

## · INDONESIA ·

Jakarta is the smallest of the Southeast Asian stock markets, with only twenty-four listed companies. The biggest are Unilever Indonesia, Pan Indonesia Bank, BAT Indonesia, Jakarta International Hotel, and Tificorp. None of them is available to foreigners as foreign investors are not allowed to own Indonesian stocks. The Exchange is run by a government agency, Badan Pelaksana Pasar Modal (Capital Market Executive Agency), and if the market should ever open up, its address is Jalan Medan Merdeka Selatan 13-14, P.O. Box 439, Jakarta.

## · CHILE ·

Under General Augusto Pinochet's military government, Chile has adopted a fiercely antisocialist and pro–free enterprise stance in the past decade. The Santiago stock market is small, with about 230 listed stocks, and probably has a promising future if the Pinochet regime should continue in power—a rather large if. Foreign investors are treated on an equal footing with Chilean investors, but investments over $5 million require the approval of the government. There are also exchange controls, and if you want to repatriate your capital eventually, as you presumably do, you must register your investment with the Foreign Investment Committee. The largest listed companies—a group that includes utilities, industrials, and mining companies—are Endesa, Cartones, CAP, Telefonos, Copec, CCT, Entel, Soquimich, Chilmetro, and Melon.

Market information (in Spanish) is available from the Stock Exchange (Bolsa de Comercio de Santiago, Calle la Bolsa 64, Casilla 123, Santiago), and from these brokerage firms, among others: Blanco y Cia. (La Bolsa 74, Santiago) and Ureta y Bianchi y Cia. (La Bolsa 76, Santiago).

## · PORTUGAL ·

The Lisbon Stock Exchange has been making something of a comeback in the last couple of years after being practically wiped out in a wave of nationalizations of Portuguese companies in the 1970s. The political balance has swung sharply to the right in the late 1980s after the leftist fervor and the nationalizations that followed the overthrow of the remnants of the rightist Antonio Salazar dictatorship in 1974. However, many of the leading companies nationalized by the leftists after 1974 remain nationalized now, and the stock market also has to recover from an orgy of illicit speculations that tarnished its reputation in the past decade before it can attract serious foreign investors. When the situation improves further, and the Stock Exchange is able to provide information in English, you may want its address: Bolsa de Valores de Lisboa, Praca do Comercio, Torreao Oriental, Lisbon.

## · ARGENTINA ·

Up to the 1940s Argentina stood at a general level of economic development and per capita income comparable with Canada's. And for largely the same reason: a huge influx of foreign private capital. After decades of mismanagement and government intervention in the economy, Argentina is now perhaps the most highly educated and technically competent nation in the underdeveloped Third World. It saw itself in the 1940s as a leading regional power, but has since lost the economic race with Brazil. It saw itself becoming the Colossus of the South, as the United States is the Colossus of the North, but after losing the Falklands war to the British in 1983 has had to recognize that it is no such thing. Argentina is a country where every dream has turned sour for nearly five decades, and that includes the stock market.

It was the first stock market in South America, too, founded in Buenos Aires in 1854. Nowadays it does hardly any business in stocks, although more than 200 companies are listed. Nearly all trading is in bonds, which are linked to the U.S. dollar or some other external prop because of the chronic inflation of the Argentine currency, which has at times approached 1,000% a year.

There is no sign of any foreign interest in Argentine stocks, but the government has restrictions on foreign investment anyway. Foreign investors are not allowed to own more than 20% of an Argentine company, and any individual foreigner's investment may not exceed $2 million. The Argentine Registry of Foreign Investments must be informed of the purchase of shares by foreigners and of any changes in shareholdings. There is a minimum investment period of three years before investments made after 1980 can be repatriated. And there are other restrictions.

We dwell on Argentina here because, like India, it is a country with tremendous potential and enormous resources. Unlike India, it is practically an empty land, with only 25 million people in a territory as big as the United States east of the Mississippi. When it gets back on the right track it will be worth investing in again.

For the present the only possible strategy is to make a small investment in the Templeton Emerging Markets Fund on the American Stock Exchange. If Argentine stocks start to show up on its portfolio, perhaps the investment picture there is starting to change and it might be worth investigating further (by writing, say, to the Stock Exchange, Mercado de Valores de Buenos Aires, 25 de mayo 367, 1002 Buenos Aires). That is perhaps the only practical strategy too for countries like Chile, Colombia, Nigeria, Indonesia, and others, including even Communist China, that have stock exchanges (ranging from rudimentary to fairly modern, but still functioning, stock exchanges) and that are yet languishing in poverty on a treasure trove of wealth. In almost every case they are languishing almost entirely because of their own misguided economic policies.

For the record, and in case the picture should brighten in any of them in the future, the following countries also have stock exchanges. These markets function at levels of efficiency, reliability, and sophistication that for the time being do not merit further comment as you are unlikely to be doing anything practical about them at this time.

*Colombia:*
Bolsa de Bogota
Carrera 8
13-82, Bogota

*Ecuador:*
Bolsa de Valores de Quito
Avenida Rio Amazonas 540
Apartado Postal 3772, Quito

*Egypt:*
Cairo Stock Exchange
4-A Cherifein Street
Cairo

*Jamaica:*
Jamaica Stock Exchange
Bank of Jamaica Tower
P.O. Box 621
Nethersole Place, Kingston

*Kenya:*
Nairobi Stock Exchange
Stanbank House

Moi Avenue
P.O. Box 43633
Nairobi

*Morocco:*
Bourse des Valeurs de Casablanca
98 Boulevard Mohammed V
Casablanca

*Nigeria:*
Nigerian Stock Exchange
NIDB House
63–71 Broad Street
P.O. Box 2457
Lagos

*Pakistan:*
Karachi Stock Exchange
Stock Exchange Road
Karachi 2

*Peru:*
Bolsa de Valores de Lima
Jiron Antonio Miro Quesada 265
Apartado 1538
Lima 100

*Sri Lanka:*
Colombo Brokers' Association
P.O. Box 101
59 Janadipathi Mawatha
Colombo 1

As circumstances in each country change with the passage of time you may want to update your information on the world's stock exchanges by purchasing the *GT Guide to World Equity Markets*, published annually by Euromoney Publications Ltd. (Nestor House, Playhouse Yard, London EC4, England) This book costs $95 and contains eight to ten pages of information on each of the world's major stock markets plus some, but not all, of the minor markets mentioned in this chapter.

# CHAPTER 21

## SUMMING UP

We have now come to the end of our world tour. The 20 foregoing chapters have piled up for you a mass of information on foreign stocks, bonds, and other more exotic investments and speculations available to you around the globe, as well as the names and addresses of stock exchanges, banks, brokers, trade associations, and others who can help you invest abroad.

The question now is what, if anything, to do about it all. As we have seen, the variety of ways to invest your money around the world verges on the mind-boggling. As Lloyds Bank of London observes, "For a person whose funds are freely transferable, there is a choice of over 50,000 securities available through 20 major stock exchanges throughout the world in 10 important currencies." If you include the lesser markets mentioned in this book you have 139 stock exchanges in 45 countries, and Lloyds Bank's figure is in fact a conservative estimate.

However, you might make a note of that phrase "For a person whose funds are freely transferable." It may possibly become an important phrase for Americans in coming years. At the present time an American resident can send his money anywhere he likes overseas without any restrictions—except a few minor regulations that are more of a nuisance than anything else. This is a freedom that few foreigners have enjoyed for any length of time in recent decades, except the residents of Switzerland, Hong Kong, and West Germany. Most other countries of the world restrict, regulate, and control the inflow and outflow of their citizens' money in one way or another.

Up to 1939, for example, British investors enjoyed about the same foreign investment freedoms as Americans do today, and they had millions of pounds invested in American industrial corporations, Argentine railroads, African mines, Brazilian meat-packing plants, and other enterprises overseas. When World War II broke out, however, the United Kingdom government required them to register all their foreign investments with the British authorities—and then bought them out in a forced sale. At depressed wartime prices. The foreign investments of private British subjects were needed to finance the war effort. The British government also imposed stringent foreign exchange controls that (like New York City rent controls) endured long after the war ended. It was not until four decades later that the redoubtable Mrs. Thatcher restored to Britons the unrestricted right to spend their money abroad on travel or investments without first asking the permission of the Little Old Lady of Threadneedle Street—the Bank of England.

If current U.S. foreign trade and federal government deficits persist over a number of years and the U.S. foreign debt keeps on growing, it is not inconceivable that Americans too may find one day that they need the permission of government bureaucrats in Washington to spend their money abroad.

You may then face approximately the moral choice that presented itself in the Revolutionary War period to Americans who invested in the new republic's "continental" currency. Financing the war against George III brought about such an inflation that "not worth a continental" became part of the American language. Individual Americans who trusted in the continental did indeed help the Revolution to a successful conclusion, but they faced personal ruin themselves. It boils down to a choice between patriotism and self-interest. The person who chooses self-interest might make his assets abroad as untraceable as possible, and fail to declare them if Uncle Sam ever requires him to do so. The patriot will do his duty, and probably lose a large part of his money. You might have to decide one day which course would give you the greater satisfaction.

However, these misfortunes have not yet befallen us, and perhaps never will. While we still have the freedom we enjoy today, the immediate question is what to do about investing in 50,000 foreign securities.

To take the minimalist alternative first: don't invest in any foreign stocks and bonds at all initially—you can still make money abroad simply by holding a foreign bank account. You may perhaps earn a higher rate of interest in a foreign currency than you can at home with a U.S. bank. You might possibly make some extra money if the foreign currency should rise in value against the U.S. dollar. And you don't need to worry about the ups and downs of foreign stock markets. It is no great problem to open a foreign bank account in most major convertible currencies. In preceding chapters we mentioned the names and addresses of a number of banks: Union Bank of Switzerland, Swiss Bank Corporation, Credit Suisse, and other banks in Switzerland; Barclays Bank, Lloyds Bank, and Bank of Scotland in the United Kingdom and its offshore tax havens; Royal Bank of Canada; Westdeutsche Landesbank in Germany; Amro Bank in the Netherlands; Handelsbank in Denmark; Bank of New Zealand; Hong Kong and Shanghai Banking Corp.

You can even open your foreign currency bank account right in the United States. Deak International (29 Broadway, New York, NY 10006), the country's biggest foreign exchange trading firm, offers term deposits in Swiss francs, German marks, Japanese yen, British pounds, Dutch guilders, and Canadian dollars. The term deposits are available for periods of three, six, nine, and twelve months. You open an account with Deak, which then arranges for the currency to be deposited in the bank and country of your choice. (Deak, incidentally, also offers precious-metals accounts through which you can invest in gold, silver, or platinum, with minimum $100 monthly, bimonthly, or quarterly payments.)

Another alternative is a money market fund that invests in foreign currencies. You may recall that Chapter 4 mentioned International Cash Portfolios, a fund in which you can switch your investment among short-term money market portfolios, one denominated in dollars, another in a basket of foreign currencies, and six more in individual foreign currencies.

Now, to take the maximalist approach. Once you decide to advance beyond foreign currency bank accounts and money market instruments to take the plunge into foreign stocks and bonds, your choice of investments expands to the full 50,000 or more securities available around the globe.

Obviously, you will have to set yourself limits. You will remember that Chapter 1 cited studies according to which fifteen to twenty disparate investments is about the outer limit of diversification you will ever need in order to limit your risks. Once you go beyond twenty you do not make any appreciable gain in risk reduction. So let us set the limit at twenty. Any larger number is likely to be unmanageable from a practical standpoint, and is theoretically unnecessary in any case.

At this point, remember, you have added one more dimension of risk and opportunity: the ups and downs of foreign stock markets in addition to the fluctuations of foreign currencies.

What are the most likely candidates for our Top Twenty?

Let us assume that you will consider the sixty American companies mentioned in Chapter 2 (those with extensive foreign operations) and the eighty mentioned in Chapter 3 (those quoted on stock markets abroad) as possible additions to your U.S. portfolio.

Let us then build up our foreign Top Twenty like a pyramid. One global fund or international fund mentioned in Chapter 4 would be a perfectly adequate base to cover all your worldwide investments.

A couple of regional funds, Europe or the Pacific Basin, would make up the second tier. The Japanese consider themselves the third pillar of the capitalist world, the other two being the United States and Western Europe.

For the third tier you have a choice of about a dozen mutual funds and closed-end funds to pinpoint specific countries: Canada, Japan, South Africa, Australia, France, Germany, Switzerland, Italy, Korea, Malaysia, Mexico, Taiwan, and Great Britain.

We are already up to sixteen, and have just about blanketed the whole capitalist world. If you want to go further you might start looking through the ADRs mentioned in Chapter 6, particularly the German and Spanish banks which make a pretty good substitute for investment funds, thanks to their extensive stock portfolios.

A flier on Templeton Emerging Markets Fund would extend your interests into the developing countries of the Third World, and together with Scandinavian Fund just about completes our quota of twenty diversified stocks.

As Chapter 1 remarked, international investment can offer you two things: first, safety through diversification into different markets, and second, potential profit by investing in markets that have consistently outperformed the U.S. stock market over the past decade or so. You also have the international and global bond funds listed in Chapters 4 and 5. These were the stars of the October 1987 stock market crash. Every one of them gained ground while equity markets were plunging around the world.

With a portfolio like the above—built up over time, whenever conditions seem propitious in each particular stock market—it would practically take a global depression or a world war to do you any serious financial damage. With an average of about fifty stocks in each closed-end fund or mutual fund, your money would be spread over about 1,000 of the 50,000 individual securities that constitute our universe. So much for safety. As for potential profit, our twenty investments provide a cross-section of just about every one of the foreign markets that have outperformed the U.S. market.

The investments mentioned in the remainder of the book you might consider the icing on the cake. Perhaps you can pick your own individual ADR stock and strike it lucky with a company that gains 580% in one year like Philippine Long Distance Telephone or 226% as Banco Central of Spain did in 1986. You may have compelling personal reasons to set up a tax-free trust on the Cayman Islands. Your company may transfer you to Europe, making a British or Dutch or Swiss bank a convenient base for your finances. If you work in the Middle East a tax haven like the Channel Islands or Luxembourg may come in useful.

Personal circumstances will be different for every reader of this book. However, the way the book is organized means that it becomes less and less likely that you will actually do anything practical about the markets described in the later chapters, since the book proceeds from the simple and easy investments available without leaving U.S. jurisdiction to the exotic and more difficult investments in unfamiliar lands where knowledge of a foreign language may be indispensable.

Nevertheless, the later chapters are important too. When you are considering a French company's ADR in the U.S. over-the-counter market you should really know something about the French stock market and the proclivities of successive French governments for nationalizing and denationalizing major French corporations. It doesn't hurt either to know about insider trading practices in New Zealand and the peculiarities and idiosyncracies of other markets overseas. Innocents abroad are more likely to be fleeced than to make a killing.

Indeed, the same warning is applicable to innocents at home. Let us suppose that you have no foreign investments at all, nor any thought of making any. However, you have had a good year in the U.S. stock market, and you reckon, shall we say, that your net assets have risen from $180,000 to $210,000 in the last twelve months. In U.S.-dollar terms, that is. Now, broaden your mind a little. Expressed in other terms that result might not look quite so satisfactory. If in those same twelve months the price of gold has risen from, say, $300 to $500 a troy ounce, then your net worth as reckoned in gold has actually declined from 600 ounces to 420 ounces. And if, in those twelve months, the Swiss franc has risen from 50 U.S. cents to 80 U.S. cents, then your net worth in Swiss francs has fallen from 360,000 to 265,000 francs. By thinking in purely dollar terms and by holding all your investment eggs in a dollar basket you may actually have lost financial ground when you thought you were gaining.

Even if you do not make any of the investments suggested so far in this book, it is still possible to avoid this unhappy result by buying foreign-currency options. Such options do not necessarily involve much money (a few hundred dollars will do), and they can also protect you against loss when your foreign-currency holdings go down against the dollar.

Foreign-currency options are available on the Philadelphia Stock Exchange (1900 Market Street, Philadelphia, PA 19103) in British pounds, Australian and Canadian dollars, West German marks, Japanese yen, and French and Swiss francs. Two kinds of option are listed, American-style and European-style. The American-style options can be exercised at any time up to the expiration date, while the European-style options may be exercised on the expiration date only. Because of their greater flexibility, the American-style options are more expensive to buy. The exchange has explanatory booklets on the various aspects of option trading.

You can of course buy options as pure speculations, but what we want to do here is to hedge our net worth in dollars with foreign-currency options. When you reach a certain level of investment—let us say 12,500 British pounds (about $19,000 at the time of writing)—in your British bank account, you can protect yourself against loss by buying one option on the Philadelphia Exchange. Each option contract is for 12,500 pounds. Since you are worried in this case that your pounds may decline in value against the dollar, you buy a pound put option (for a premium that may cost $200, or more, or less, depending on your striking price). If the pound does decline, your profit on the option contract would counterbalance the loss on your British bank account. A person who has all his investment eggs in the U.S. dollar might profitably buy a call option on the Swiss franc to hedge against a falling greenback. Swiss franc options in Philadelphia are for 62,500 francs. The other option contracts are for 62,500 German marks, 6,250,000 Japanese yen, 125,000 French francs, and 50,000 Canadian or Australian dollars. In all cases the maximum term runs nine months into the future.

You can quite easily lose every cent you put into an option

contract if the market goes the wrong way (which contrariwise would be the right way for your foreign bank account holdings). But one big advantage is that your original investment can be relatively small, and another is that you cannot lose more than that original investment. Which is more than you can say for futures contracts. Foreign currency futures are traded on the Chicago Mercantile Exchange (30 S. Wacker Drive, Chicago, IL 60606). They involve much larger sums of money than options contracts do, and you can very easily lose much, much more than you originally put into them. The futures contracts traded in Chicago are for 100,000 Australian dollars, 25,000 British pounds, 100,000 Canadian dollars, 125,000 marks, 250,000 French francs, 12,500,000 Japanese yen, 125,000 Swiss francs, and 125,000 European Currency Units.

At the time of writing you would have to put up $2,000 margin to buy one Australian dollar futures contract. If the Aussie currency declined by 2 U.S. cents, this investment would be wiped out and your broker would require you to put up another $2,000, failing which he would sell you out, whether you liked it or not, for a total loss. The futures markets are for the big-time gamblers, the big bankrolls, and people who fancy themselves as financial high-wire artists. They are not for nervous insomniacs who bet $2,000 at a time.

There are other angles to the foreign-currency game. The latest wrinkle is the U.S. Currency Exchange Warrant, a new type of security that has been pioneered by General Electric Credit Corp., Ford Motor Credit Co., and the credit subsidiaries of American Telephone and Telegraph and Xerox Corp. These warrants are traded on the stock market. They give investors the right to sell a foreign currency (the Japanese yen and the German mark so far) at a set rate to the company issuing the warrants. By buying the Ford warrant, for example, you are betting that the Japanese yen will fall against the dollar over the next five years (when the warrant expires). If the yen rises you lose everything. These warrants seem to be a far better deal for the issuing companies, which hedge all their risks on the futures market, than they are for the individual small investor.

One doesn't have to be an innocent abroad to lose money. An innocent at home is just as readily plucked if he doesn't understand what is going on in his chicken coop.

# EPILOGUE

## LORDSHIPS OF THE MANOR, CZARIST BONDS, AND CASTLES IN SPAIN

"The time has come," the Walrus said, "to talk of many things:
Of shoes—and ships—and sealing wax—Of cabbages—and kings—
And why the sea is boiling hot—And whether pigs have wings."

"And (we might add to Lewis Carroll's list of conversational subjects from *Through the Looking Glass*) of czarist bonds and mad milords, of German luck, of Ernie and Laddie's, and castles in Spain."

For the fact is that a lifetime consumed entirely by the meticulous computation of yields to maturity to the last hundredth of a basis point, and by the judicious comparison of price earnings ratios between Peoria United Gas Works subordinated debentures and Dubuque Sewerage Sinking Fund Bonds, can become abominably boring to a chap who likes to get some fun out of life.

So in this last chapter let's take some time out for a number of wild and woolly investments, speculations, and pure gambles in which you don't really care one Dow Jone about such mundane matters as bond yields, incremental tax rates, or what your trusty stockbroker has to say about it all.

If you live in New York, New Jersey, or other states that run weekly lotteries, you may already be playing the numbers now and again in the forlorn hope of becoming an instant millionaire. There are two rather large drawbacks to this. First, the odds are so astronomically high that one never seems to win anything worth mentioning. And second, even if one did hit the $10 million jackpot, the prize would be doled out over twenty years and Uncle Sam would invite himself into the deal for a large share of the loot.

There are a number of alternatives available north of the border, where several Canadian provinces run lotteries. One of them is Lotto 6/49 (Canadian Overseas Marketing, P.O. Box 48120, 595 Burrard Street, Vancouver V7X 1S4, British Columbia) which has two draws a week and costs a minimum $45 for twenty drawings. The odds there are still astronomically high, but at least the prizes are tax-free in Canada. Lotto 6/49 has also attracted large numbers of non-Canadian gamblers with its promise that "your winnings will be converted into any currency you wish and confidentially forwarded to you anywhere in the world." However, Uncle Sam will still want his share of the loot if you try moving to Canada or some Caribbean island with your $13,890,588.80 (the biggest prize ever paid by Lotto 6/49). The United States is about the only country in the world that taxes its citizens who reside outside their homeland. The United States is in fact so sticky about foreign lotteries and taxes that Canadian lottery sellers are reluctant to market their tickets in the United States. You may have to buy them on a trip to Canada. There are intermediary firms that market Canadian lottery tickets through the mail, but the advice here is don't. These firms charge a markup, and some of them are not too scrupulous about actually buying your tickets, or handing over your prize if you win.

Lotteries in other countries too have learned that privacy applies not only to Swiss banks—bank secrecy becomes lottery secrecy. If you win, they swear they won't snitch on you to the IRS. West Germany has several government-run lotteries where prizes are exempt from German income tax and where the winners remain anonymous. One seller of these is Hans Herzog (Nordwestdeutsche Klassenlotterie, Alsterdorfr Strasse 326, 2000 Hamburg 60), which occasionally advertises in English-language publications and accepts payment for tickets in American dollars. One ticket costs 720 marks (about $400 at the time of writing this), but you can also buy half, quarter, or one-eighth tickets. The main prize is 1 million marks, and you get twenty-one shots at it because your ticket is kept in that number of drawings over a six-month period. Thanks to a large number of smaller prizes, thirty-eight out of 100 tickets get at least something back. Nevertheless, at the end of six months you are likely to end up considerably shy of your original 720-mark investment in the German lottery.

It is the British who have invented the ultimate in this business, a lottery where you never lose your money. This ingenious contrivance is not even called a lottery ticket; it is called a Premium Bond, and you buy it from the British government at any British post office and at most British banks. The Premium Bond was evidently devised to soak up the loose cash of people who were more inclined to put their money on the horses than into stocks and bonds. The British have poured billions of pounds into these bonds, which pay 155,000 prizes every month. Each bond costs 1 pound and you can buy any number of them from ten to a maximum 10,000—so that your investment could range from about $17 to $17,000 or so. Instead of paying interest on these bonds, the British government calculates the amount in interest that would have been payable at 7% a year and then distributes this sum in prizes. After an initial waiting period of three months your bonds become eligible for all prizes and are entered in the weekly and monthly drawings. The top prize is 250,000 pounds tax-free, with smaller prizes ranging down to 10 pounds. Each of your 1-pound bonds has a different number and could win any one of these prizes. The winning numbers are selected by a computer called Ernie (Electronic Random Number Indicating Equipment is his full name). Winners get their prizes free of British income and capital gains taxes and are notified by mail of their good luck.

Buy ten of these bonds and consider them a gamble. Buy 10,000 and they start to look more like an investment, because over a period of one year your chances of winning at least one prize are theoretically 1 in 1.1. In the long run you are likely to come out with an average yield of 7%, and you always have that extra chance of hitting the 250,000-pound jackpot every month. When you want your investment back you simply redeem your bonds and get back exactly the number of pounds you put in.

The Premium Bonds people in England face the same problem as the Canadian and other foreign lotteries: Title 18 United States Code (Criminal Provisions) makes it illegal to use the U.S. mails to transmit information on lotteries. A spokesman for Premium Bonds (Lytham St. Annes, Lancashire FY0 1YN, England) says, "We are therefore unable to sell bonds to American residents." If you live in some other country, however, "there are no restrictions" unless there happen to be similar local regulations there. The British bonds people, incidentally, are sticklers for respecting U.S. laws to the letter. They say, "It is possible for a resident outside the United Kingdom to register a bond care of a bank in this country. But as any transaction, including the payment of prizes, requires the bondholder's signature, the same local or national laws would need to be observed. If we are aware of any local or national laws being contravened we would inform the holder and ask for the bonds to be repaid."

Now, once you have struck it lucky with Ernie and have your first 250,000 pounds in the bank (we'll ignore Canadian and German and other lotteries on the grounds that you won't gamble 10,000 pounds on them and so don't have much chance of winning there), you have the means to set yourself up as an English lord. Indeed, you probably have the means for that anyway, whether Ernie smiles on you or not, because you can purchase a lordship of the manor for only a few thousand dollars.

You may perhaps aspire to be lord of the manor of Claydon, or of Tandridge, or of Cleckheaton, or of Walton-on-Thames. It is all within your reach. If the current lord is a bit low on funds and wants to sell his title to you, that is his noble privilege. It has been done for hundreds of years, and his ancestors probably bought the lordship from some previous broken-down nobleman. When he does decide to sell, it is then just a rather vulgar question of money. In November 1986, for example, the lordship of Claydon was sold for 7,500 pounds, Tandridge went for 19,000 pounds. In March 1987 the lordship of Cleckheaton fetched 9,000 pounds, Walton-on-Thames 16,500 pounds, and Shepperton 23,000 pounds.

All of this is quite legal and above board. There are British auctioneering firms that sell off lordships as though they were prize Hereford bulls. One firm is Strutt & Parker, Surveyors and Estate Agents (13 Hill Street, London W1). Another is Bernard Thorpe and Partners (1 Buckingham Palace Road, London SW1). You understand, of course, that what you are buying here is pure snobbery, legal possession of a title that may go back to William the Conqueror or even earlier. The lordship does not usually carry any land or property with it, although the lordship of Snodhill was sold by Strutt & Parker "including the ruined Castle of Snodhill and four acres of land."

"This important lordship was held by Hugh L'Asne at the time of the Domesday Survey in 1086. In the 16th Century Elizabeth I gave the Manor and Castle to her favourite, Robert Dudley, Earl of Leicester." One hesitates to add that some lordships do have mineral rights attached, and for this crass reason tend to sell at a premium.

Your lordship may carry some antique perks, such as the right to the first twelve plovers' eggs collected on the lordly acres, as well as some picturesque obligations, such as the duty to deliver six geese and one hen to the local bishop of Oglethorpe every Easter Sunday. Some of the rights might be rather hard to enforce, particularly those involving *droit de seigneur*. Others might really prove to be quite valuable, such as the Lordship of Little Holland, which includes "1,333 yards of foreshore and the valuable Royal Right of wreck of the sea." Really quite lucrative if the QE2 should sink there. In 1987 Little Holland was knocked down for 26,000 pounds, incidentally.

When William the Conqueror surveyed his new English possessions in Domesday Book in 1086, he counted 13,418 manors, so the market is larger than you might have supposed. None of them, unfortunately, entitle you to a seat in the House of Lords. But a lordship of the manor does enable you to join the The Manorial Society of Great Britain, an association of lords and ladies of the manor headed by the Earl of Onslow. The Society publishes an *Annual Bulletin* and holds regular meetings throughout the year, including a drinks party at the House of Lords.

Looked at from a plebeian and mercenary point of view the lord-of-the-manor market has been performing rather nicely. Mr. R. A. Knappet of Strutt & Parker recalls that the minimum price of a lordship has risen from a mere 250 pounds in 1950 to 7,000 pounds in 1987. It pains us to go into gross commercial details in a matter like this, but Thorpe the auctioneer charges a 10% sales commission plus value-added tax plus 300 pounds for marketing costs—all of which, you will be glad to hear, is paid by the outgoing lord.

The outlook for lordships of the manor looks quite decently bullish too. The *Financial Times* of London reported in April 1987 that "as lordships of the manor receive more and more attention and attract the interest of Americans and other foreigners, the price of them should rise." One last advantage, if you should ever wish to leave the ranks of the aristocracy, is that, in the opinion of the *Financial Times*, "it is debatable whether or not capital gains tax is payable when selling it, since most lordships do not possess land, and so all that is being sold is the title."

Titles may also be purchased outside the United Kingdom, but here you do have to be rather more careful. One former king of Serbia, who shall remain nameless here, was publicly reported in the *Wall Street Journal* in 1986 to be offering a select number of noble titles for a "suggested contribution" of $10,000 each. His kingdom being at present in the hands of the communist government of Yugoslavia, his majesty was in a bit of a financial bind, and the Royal Exchequer, located in a rather rundown Rome apartment building, was in urgent need of replenishing. Italian Mafia dons were reported to have made out blank checks, but the king had his principles and was not about to hand out ancient Serbian titles without rather strict character references. A spokesman for *Debrett's Peerage* considered the royal offer "absolutely disgraceful," which seems rather hard, considering that English lordships of the manor usually go to the highest bidder, whether they are Mafia dons or not. Nevertheless, we are not prepared at this time to give you the king's name or address, although for another reason. The king is either a Karageorgeovich or an Obrenovic—it matters little which—two dynasties that alternated, with considerable Balkan intrigue, violence, and general mayhem at the changeover points, on the Serbian throne for centuries. So any title you purchase from a Karageorgeovich will almost certainly be disputed with vigor by an Obrenovic. A rival claimant may even challenge you to a Balkan duel to the death. A pity really. If this book does well in the bookstores, Lord Smyth of Sarajevo would have a certain Domesday ring to go with the lordship of the manor of Hingham, Norfolk, ancestral home of the family of President Abraham Lincoln. The Lincolns, incidentally, were involved in a bit of a fracas at Hingham in 1605, when the lord of the manor, Sir Francis Lovell, appointed the Reverend Robert Peck as Parson of Hingham. This ecclesiastic, it appears, was "a man of a very violent schismatical spirit. He pulled down the rails and levelled the altar and the whole chancel a foot below the church. Being prosecuted for it by Bishop Wren, he fled the Kingdom, and went over into New England, with many of his parishioners," among whom were the Lincoln family.

Now, as Bertie Wooster might say, for a spot of serious business. As a lord of the manor you would be expected abroad to act like a mad *milord anglais*—*noblesse oblige*, as they say across the Channel—and some suitable business activity should be found for you in this capacity. You might tout yourself discreetly for a directorship of a British company. No British Public Liability Company feels itself complete without a lord on its board of directors. And while you are having Lord Bottitors in Kimberley, or Gurneys and Swathings, or Kettleburgh Ufford, or Newby-cum-Whitton, or East Hendred Framptons—or whatever your new title is—engraved on your business cards, you might consider some appropriate investments. Czarist bonds is what first comes to mind. They are sold by a chap called Karl Marx. Well, not actually THE Karl Marx. This man is a colonial financial wallah who spells his name Carl Marks and owns a business at 77 Water Street, New York, NY 10005. He sells czarist bonds, among other things. Has been selling them for years, and appears to do quite well at it.

In fact, if you ask Jeeves for the actual details you might find a rather fascinating proposition. These are two bond issues floated by the Imperial Czarist Russian Government in July and December 1916 for a total of $75 million to finance World War I against Kaiser Wilhelm's Germany. One is the Imperial Three Year Credit that paid 6½% interest until Lenin's Bolshevik government repudiated all czarist debts in 1918. The other is a similar issue that has been piling up unpaid interest at 5½% a year for the last seventy years. If they were ever paid off in full they would be worth more than $1 billion now. They will of course never be paid in full, but they do offer some interesting price fluctuations for the shrewd speculator. Consider these historical price oscillations as possible buying or selling points: Lenin repudiates the bonds in 1918—$7.50 per $1,000 bond. The United States grants diplomatic recognition to the Soviet Union—$85. World War II breaks out—$2.50. The Yalta Conference at the end of World War II—$210. The Cuban missile crisis of 1962—$10.

And then there is always the unexpected. The Soviets might actually pay up. In 1986 the Soviets did finally settle their czarist-era debts with the British, and agreed to pay off at about 10 pence on the pound on assorted debts including a 1908 City of Moscow municipal bond. The question is whether it is really good business to sell out at that sort of price. We Woosters are rather shrewd financial chaps with Jeeves at the elbow to offer a spot of advice, and we know that some of the czarist bonds are worth more as collector's items. One little old lady in Bournemouth who was upset at missing the Soviet deadline for filing claims in 1987 was told by an auctioneer that her 500-pound 1910 bond for the Latvian Wolmar Railway would probably fetch 3,000 pounds from a scripophilist, a collector of old financial paper.

Anyway if the Russians jolly well don't pay up, the chaps to talk to are the Foreign Bondholders Protective Council, who for years had an office in Manhattan and claimed to have settled defaulted bond disputes with dozens of countries such as Poland and Czechoslovakia. Unfortunately, its more recent settlements were rather sharply characterized by *Barron's* magazine as a sellout to the Commies, and the Council's last recorded address was a post office box in Brooklyn. We learned that the Council's Brooklyn telephone had been disconnected when we inquired. Anyway, if you run into any trouble with the Russians over czarist bonds, these are the fellows who should be able to give you a hand if you can find them.

Mad English milords in the eighteenth century founded the Hellfire Club, to be a member of which required mainly that you submit proof of having broken every single one of the Ten Commandments. Nobody would expect such a high standard of you nowadays, of course, but a predisposition to gambling has always been the hallmark of a true-blue lord. The fellows to deal with here are Ladbroke's (Ladbroke Group PLC, Chancel House, London NW10 2XE). Ladbroke Racing, the sporting member of the Group, claims to be "the world's largest commercial betting organization" and in its 1987 yearly report it says it considers itself "in an excellent position to take advantage of the opportunities for growth which exist nationally and internationally." Laddies will take your bet on just about anything, including the next president of the United States. (Having taken a flier on George Romney a few elections back, Bertie Wooster and I would now recommend a long shot on Harold Stassen.)

On a more businesslike level, I.G. Index Ltd. (9-11 Grosvenor Gardens, London SW1W OBD) will take your wagers on just about any commercial speculation from the level of the London Stock Exchange Index three months from now to the prices of zinc, aluminum, cocoa, potatoes, or gold a year hence. Stuart Wheeler, a former investment banker who founded I.G. Index in 1974, approaches his business with a refreshing candor. His deals are not investments or speculations, he says. They are bets. And he runs what he quite frankly calls a betting shop. Nothing could possibly be plainer. Nor, it seems, could it possibly be better business. "Betting with I.G.," says the firm, "is much more tax-efficient than conventional investment. If you win, there is no tax whatsoever to pay. I.G. is responsible for betting tax, but this is taken into account in its quotations—there is no separate charge for it." In Britain, gambling winnings are not subject to taxation.

If it amuses you to bet on political races, I.G. will accommodate you too. It runs a book on the British elections, among other things. You had better watch those bets, though. Some of the I.G. wagers appear to be something like Chicago futures contracts, open-ended risks on which you are liable to lose much more than you put in initially.

Betting against Ladbroke or I.G. Index may strike you as a rather addle-pated Berty Woosterish sort of game. A deal that might appeal more to the hardheaded instincts of the inimitable Jeeves would be an investment in Ladbroke itself, which is quoted on the London Stock Exchange and in fact is available in the United States in ADR form, or an option on Ladbroke stock, which is also available on the London Exchange.

You might also consider a partnership in Lloyds of London (Stafford House, King William Street, London EC4), the insurance brokers to the world against any conceivable mischance, from computer failure to earthquakes. These are the people who insured Marlene Dietrich's legs, who insure Texans against hurricanes, and who will insure anybody against just about anything else, from the sinking of the *Titanic* to the loss of satellites in outer space. All you have to do, if you have a net worth of several million dollars, is to sign up as a "name" in one of the Lloyds insurance syndicates. It has been lucrative for many people over the years, but you realize of course that as a "name" you are liable for everything you have in this world to pay off any losses your insurance syndicate may involve you in. Ladbroke is a limited liability company.

Since, in all probability, your lordship of the manor will not come with living quarters attached, there is another matter to be resolved: where to establish your lordly residence. The outstanding service in this field is Previews Inc. (230 Park Avenue, New York, NY 10169). These are the people to talk to when you are in the market for (to quote some items from a recent Previews catalogue): Marlon Brando's Tahitian atoll ($1.5 million), a villa in Florence that belonged to the Medici, a French manor house on the Riviera near Biarritz ($2.5 million), a Georgian mansion overlooking the Pacific near Sydney, Australia ($1.95 million), an old sugar mill converted into a luxury residence in Barbados ($495,000), a stone villa looking out on the Pitons volcanic peaks on St. Lucia in the Caribbean ($150,000), a 1,100-acre estate with your own copra plantation in Fiji ($350,000), a 144-acre private island in the Bahamas ($1.8 million), an 18,000-acre cattle ranch in Andalusia ($3.5 million), an old Moorish palace in Marbella, southern Spain, a Moorish villa in Morocco, formerly the residence of Baron Krupp of Germany ($750,000), and a 2,700-acre game ranch in the Transvaal.

Such dream residences are not really all that unattainable. The villa in St. Lucia cost only $150,000. For $295,000 you could buy Ballyhannan Castle, a fifteenth-century Irish stronghold, completely restored and modernized, with 3 acres of land overlooking the River Shannon. There are 100-year-old restored three-bedroom condominium apartments in Hoboken, New Jersey, that cost more than that.

The world is your oyster. And dream a little. There is more to life than Hoboken, New Jersey.

You may even get tired of your dream when you achieve it. So trade it in for another. Try the Vacation Exchange Club (12006 11th Avenue, Youngtown, AZ 85363) or the Inter-Service Home Exchange (Box 387, Glen Echo, MD 20812). Even if you do own that condominium in Hoboken, it is twenty minutes from New York by subway and you might be able to trade it as a temporary vacation home with the owner of that Moroccan villa, or even with the lord of Ballyhannan.